Water and society in early medieval Italy, AD 400–1000

This book offers an original discussion of an element – water – and its relationship with people. In particular it shows how early medieval Italian societies coped with the problems of having too much or too little water, and analyzes their use of it. Such treatment illuminates the workings both of postclassical societies and of the environments in which these societies lived. Domestic usage, bathing, irrigation and drainage, fishing, and milling all receive full coverage.

This is a groundbreaking, interdisciplinary study which proves that, even after the "fall" of Rome, people continued a dialectical relationship with the natural resources that shaped their experiences just as decisively as their efforts redesigned the waterscape. It will be of interest not only to Italianists; historians of technology, agrarian, social and cultural historians, and environmental historians will all find here much that is stimulating.

PAOLO SQUATRITI is Visiting Assistant Professor in the Department of History, University of Michigan, Ann Arbor.

Water and society in early medieval Italy, AD 400–1000

Paolo Squatriti

CAMBRIDGE
UNIVERSITY PRESS

PUBLISHED BY THE PRESS SYNDICATE OF THE UNIVERSITY OF CAMBRIDGE
The Pitt Building, Trumpington Street, Cambridge, United Kingdom

CAMBRIDGE UNIVERSITY PRESS
The Edinburgh Building, Cambridge CB2 2RU, UK
40 West 20th Street, New York NY 10011–4211, USA
477 Williamstown Road, Port Melbourne, VIC 3207, Australia
Ruiz de Alarcón 13, 28014 Madrid, Spain
Dock House, The Waterfront, Cape Town 8001, South Africa

http://www.cambridge.org

First published 1998
First paperback edition 2002

Typeface Monotype Plantin 10/12 pt.

A catalogue record for this book is available from the British Library

Library of Congress Cataloguing in Publication data
Squatriti, Paolo, 1963–
Water and society in early medieval Italy, AD 400–1000 / Paolo
Squatriti.
     p.   cm.
Includes bibliographical references and index.
ISBN 0 521 62192 5 (hardbound)
1. Water-supply – Italy – History. 2. Social history – Medieval,
500–1500. I. Title.
HD1697.I8S6 1998
306′.0945′0902–dc21 97-38745 CIP

ISBN 0 521 62192 5 hardback
ISBN 0 521 52206 4 paperback

For Alison and Sofia, who both like water

Contents

Acknowledgments

So many people accompanied me along the meandering course which led to the completion of this book that I have almost come to doubt the truism according to which scholarship is a solitary endeavor. I take this occasion to express my gratitude to all for solidarity and help in many forms, and to exculpate them from any responsibilities for the book's remaining faults, which are due solely to me.

Among those who merit special thanks, I must single out Tom Noble for his generous advice throughout and for his broad-mindedness when the project was first hatched, which enabled me to develop an eccentric interest into a dissertation. My other teachers at the University of Virginia, Elizabeth Meyer, Duane Osheim, and John Yiannias, were benign and insightful readers of early versions. Sam Miller and Bill Daly offered encouragement and wisdom whenever it was needed. Chris Wickham was a tolerant reader of drafts, and his criticisms have consistently improved my thinking and writing. Richard Hoffmann read chapters, encouraged my investigation of fishing, and offered useful criticism even when he would have preferred to be fishing himself. Paul Freedman and Giusto Traina commented intelligently on one section. Jim Scott and the acute, really interdisciplinary audience he gathers to discuss agrarian issues at Yale provided me with eye-opening new perspectives on things I thought I knew and showed me what investigations of rural societies might be. Patient audiences at the medieval and early modern reading group hosted by Tom Green in Ann Arbor, at Penn State University, and at a Medieval Academy of America meeting in Boston asked keen and thoughtful questions that sharpened my comprehension of milling. Wide-ranging conversations with Marvin Becker always put things in proper historical perspective, and I am grateful to him for his probing curiosity. Michael Allen faithfully pointed out faults and omissions, and was always able to turn up yet another accurate reference. Anonymous readers at CUP, as well as the far-from-anonymous copy-editor, Karen Anderson Howes, who weeded out numerous infelicities and errors, greatly improved the book. Finally, Jack Ullman, "fons et origo," provided the inspiration to study such things in the best of all history classes.

Institutions are made up of people, but I will follow convention and thank several institutions that facilitated my work. The University of Virginia was almost irresponsibly generous in supporting my doctoral studies, one (now far-removed) result of which this book is. The Program in Agrarian Studies at Yale University was also lavish in its aid to my cause, even in inauspicious circumstances (when Kay Mansfield showed her immense kindness at its best). The University of Michigan contributed above and beyond the call of duty to my research with travel grants, for which I am grateful. The libraries in all three of these universities were very useful, and their staffs helpful. Similarly solicitous staffs in the libraries of the American Academy and Ecole française in Rome, at the Apostolic Vatican Library, and at the Archivio Arcivescovile in Lucca eased my work.

Last, but definitely not least, I am grateful to my family. My parents, aunts, and sisters have observed the long course taken in making this book with bemusement, but have unfailingly proclaimed themselves enthusiastic about its potential and furnished me with every possible support. But it is to another branch of my family that I have dedicated the work, a small token of my devotion to them.

Abbreviations

"Gli archivi"	"Gli archivi come fonti della storia di Ravenna: regesto dei documenti," ed. B. Cavarra, G. Gardini, G.-B. Parente, and G. Vespignani, in A. Carile (ed.), *Storia di Ravenna* II.1, Venice, 1991, pp. 401–547
AM	*Archeologia medievale*
AS	*Acta Sanctorum*
CCARB	*Corsi di cultura sull'arte ravennate e bizantina*
CCSL	*Corpus Christianorum. Series Latina*
CDC I	*Codex Diplomaticus Cavensis* I, ed. M. Morcaldi, M. Schiani, and S. de Stefano, Naples, Florence, and Pisa, 1873
CDC II	*Codex Diplomaticus Cavensis* II, ed. M. Morcaldi, M. Schiani, and S. de Stefano, Naples, Milan, and Pisa, 1875
CDC V	*Codex Diplomaticus Cavensis* V, ed. M. Morcaldi, M. Schiani, and S. de Stefano, Naples, Milan, and Pisa, 1878
CDC VI	*Codex Diplomaticus Cavensis* VI, ed. M. Morcaldi, M. Schiani, and S. de Stefano, Naples, Milan, and Pisa, 1884
CDC VII	*Codex Diplomaticus Cavensis* VII, ed. M. Morcaldi, M. Schiani, and S. de Stefano, Naples, Milan, and Pisa, 1887
CDCajetanus	*Codex Diplomaticus Cajetanus* I, ed. Monachorum Montis Casini, Montecassino, 1887
CDL I–II	*Codice diplomatico longobardo* I and II, ed. L. Schiaparelli, *FSI* 62–3, Rome, 1929–33
CDL III–IV	*Codice diplomatico longobardo* III and IV, ed. C.-R. Brühl, *FSI* 64–5, Rome, 1973–81
CDL V	*Codice diplomatico longobardo* V, ed. H. Zielinski, *FSI* 66, Rome, 1986

CDLangobardiae	*Codex Diplomaticus Langobardiae*, ed. G. Porro Lambertenghi, Turin, 1878
CIL	*Corpus Inscriptionum Latinarum*
Codex Iustinianus	*Corpus Iuris Civilis: Codex Iustinianeus*, ed. P. Krueger, Berlin, 1892
Digest	*Corpus Iuris Civilis: Digesta Iustiniani Augusti*, ed. T. Mommsen, Berlin, 1868–70
FSI	*Fonti per la storia d'Italia*
Guerra Gotica I–III	Procopius of Caesarea, *La Guerra Gotica di Procopio di Cesarea*, ed. D. Comparetti, *FSI* 23–5, Rome, 1895–8
HL	Paulus Diaconus, *Historia Langobardorum*, ed. G. Waitz, *MGHSRL*, pp. 12–187
LP	*Le Liber Pontificalis: texte, introduction, et commentaire*, ed. L. Duchesne, Rome, 1886–92
LPR	Agnellus of Ravenna, *Liber Pontificalis Ecclesiae Ravennatis*, ed. O. Holder-Egger in *MGHSRL*, pp. 265–391
M&D IV	*Memorie e documenti per servire all'istoria del ducato di Lucca* IV, ed. D. Bertini, Lucca, 1818
M&D IV.2	*Memorie e documenti per servire all'istoria del ducato di Lucca* IV, part 2, ed. D. Bertini, Lucca, 1836
M&D V.2	*Memorie e documenti per servire all'istoria del ducato di Lucca* V, part 2, ed. D. Barsocchini, Lucca, 1837
M&D V.3	*Memorie e documenti per servire all'istoria del ducato di Lucca* V, part 3, ed. D. Barsocchini, Lucca, 1841
MEFR	*Mélanges de l'école française de Rome*
MGH	*Monumenta Germaniae Historica*
MGHAA	*Monumenta Germaniae Historica. Auctores Antiquissimi*
MGHSRL	*Monumenta Germaniae Historica. Scriptores Rerum Langobardicarum et Italicarum*, ed. G. Waitz, Hanover, 1878
Monumenti I–VI	*Monumenti ravennati de'secoli di mezzo* I–VI, ed. M. Fantuzzi, Venice 1801–4
Museo	*Il museo diplomatico dell'archivio di stato di Milano* 1, ed. A. Natale, Milan, n.d.
Papyri Italiens I–II	*Die nichtliterarischen Lateinischen Papyri Italiens aus der Zeit 445–700*, ed. J.-O. Tjäder, Lund, 1955; Stockholm, 1982

PBSR	*Papers of the British School at Rome*
PL	J. Migne (ed.), *Patrologiae Cursus Completus. Series Latina*
Settimane	*Settimane di studio del Centro italiano di studio sull'alto medioevo*, Spoleto, 1953–
Urkunden der Karolinger I	*Die Urkunden Pippins, Karlmans, und Karls des Grossen, MGHDiplomata Karolinorum* I, ed. F. Mühlbacher, Berlin, 1956
Urkunden der Karolinger III	*Die Urkunden Lothars I., MGHDiplomata Karolinorum* III, ed. T. Schieffer, Berlin, 1966
Urkunden der Karolinger IV	*Die Urkunden Ludwigs II., MGHDiplomata Karolinorum* IV, ed. K. Wanner, Munich, 1994
Urkunden Konrad I	*Die Urkunden Konrad I., Heinrich I., Otto I., MGHDiplomata Regum et Imperatorum Germaniae* I, ed. T. Sickel, Hanover, 1879–84
Vat. Lat. 4939	Vaticanus Latinus 4939, "Chronicon Sanctae Sophiae," Biblioteca Apostolica Vaticana, Rome

Introduction

"Paradoxically, one must begin with water," or so Fernand Braudel, the great historian of the early modern Mediterranean, once stated.[1] Taken out of the context of Braudel's justly famous study of material culture, the paradox is opaque. Braudel meant only that water played a very significant role in early modern nutrition, but his recommendation to begin with water may be usefully applied more generally to any sort of study of the economic, social, and cultural conditions of past societies. Braudel may not have intended it thus, but (paradox within the paradox) he was right.

Water, in fact, is an essential element for any community. Without it organized human life becomes difficult or downright impossible. All societies are therefore obliged to confront the many problems of organizing an adequate supply of water of different types for different purposes. From prehistoric times mankind has experimented with many systems to secure such a supply, and it is no coincidence that the earliest forms of "civilization" in Mesopotamia and Egypt occurred among people who had solved the problems of water management brilliantly. Indeed, the contemporaneous emergence of "civilization" and "hydraulic societies" in those places induced Karl Wittfogel to hypothesize that organized water supply was closely connected to state formation of the most bureaucratic and despotic kind.[2] Regardless of the accuracy of the Wittfogelian hypothesis, it was accurate in its proposition that procuring water sufficient in quantity and quality for the needs of its members has been one of the principal preoccupations of most societies.

Both the methods communities developed to control water in their environments and their attitudes to water generate historical documents which can shed light on how these communities organized themselves and functioned. Whether in the form of a spring where people filled their

[1] F. Braudel, *Civilisation matérielle et capitalisme (XVe–XVIIIe siècles)* I (Paris, 1967), p. 168: "Il faut paradoxalement commencer par l'eau."

[2] K. Wittfogel's intelligent but now disputed and slightly threadbare contentions are outlined in his *Oriental Despotism: A Comparative Study of Total Power* (New Haven, 1957).

1

urns, or in a bath hall, or in an irrigation channel, or even flowing, swiftly or sluggishly, in stream beds, water gave life its contours. It was biologically necessary to each individual, of course, but, because few took to the total solitude of the Christian desert ascetics of late antiquity, the management of water was equally relevant as a backbone of organized community life. Historians of the classical world have long known this and have investigated many aspects of water-provisioning in Greek and Roman societies. Roman historians have diligently studied the technological aspects of water management, and have built a sound understanding of aqueducts and urban water distribution. They have moreover delved into the impenetrable rural landscape of antiquity to investigate water allocation.[3]

In contrast, there are few studies of the history of water and its management in the European Middle Ages, and the historiography of early medieval Italy has concerned itself only tangentially with this issue.[4] Yet the study of water and of the systems societies adopt, as they inevitably must, to control it is profoundly revealing. From them technological levels can be assessed and, thanks to the fact that all societies must develop such systems, compared. From them social and economic relations emerge; an example is irrigation communities and their systems for sharing water, always an index of hierarchy (whoever has more right and access to the water is generally most powerful in the community). From the attitudes of a society toward the control of this natural resource its cultural presuppositions, how it locates culture in nature, can be reconstructed. In short, water-management schemes supply excellent vantage points from which to observe and understand people as they interact with each other and their environments.

Strategies of water management, moreover, change over time and thus

---

[3] There are scores of works about Rome's aqueducts. See, for example, H. Evans, *Water Distribution in Ancient Rome* (Ann Arbor, 1994). For rural work, see B. Shaw, "Lamasba," *Antiquités africaines* 18 (1982), pp. 61–103. For Ö. Wikander's fine research on water mills in antiquity, see the articles in *Opuscula Romana*: "Water Mills in Ancient Rome," 12 (1979), pp. 13–36; "The Use of Water Power in Classical Antiquity," 13 (1981), pp. 91–104; "Mill Channels, Weirs, and Ponds," 15 (1985), pp. 143–54.

[4] Happily there are exceptions. A. Guillerme, *Le temps de l'eau* (Seyssel, 1983), provided one model of aquatic history for the Middle Ages and later times. Iberian waters have been studied by T. Glick (see his *From Muslim Fortress to Christian Castle* [Manchester, 1995]). Two excellent series dealing with the history of water supply in past societies (mostly Europe) are being published: the Frontinus-Gesellschaft's *Geschichte der Wasserversorgung*, and *L'homme et l'eau en Mediterrannée et au proche orient* of the Maison de l'Orient, Lyons. The latter, which treats all periods in theory, omits in practice the Middle Ages. Encouraging signs that hydraulic factors are being considered historically significant can be found in the French regional studies of Italy, modeled on P. Toubert's classic, *Les structures du Latium médiéval* (Rome, 1973); see, for instance, J.-M. Martin, *La Pouille du VIe au XIe siècle* (Rome, 1993), pp. 70–87.

have a history. Certainly systems of water supply are "structures" in the sense Braudel gave to the term, fundamental, almost changeless geographical backdrops to human activity which strongly influence that activity. At the same time, such systems are not immobile, but evolve. Rome in 300 BC had no aqueducts, after all, while the city was famed as "queen of the waters" at the end of its imperial career. Even so structural a water-control system as the Mesopotamian irrigation network collapsed, more than once, and was replaced by less ambitious aqueous adaptations. A further example of change in strategies for the supply of water, and one which will concern us in what follows rather more closely than the Tigris–Euphrates plain, is postclassical Italy. There the shift from abundant public water supplies to overwhelmingly private ones as a result of the retreat of the state from this arena, especially after the 700s, was a decisive development for all involved. As it does everywhere else, the "aquatic history" of early medieval Italy illuminates oscillations in social relations, economic conditions, and cultural expectations in the peninsula. It does so in the best possible way, namely, by setting these variables against an environmental backdrop. Thus water's history in early medieval Italy offers a chance to "do" environmental history at its richest.[5]

The early medieval period is a particularly useful one in which to analyze changing systems of water procurement, allocation, and control. This period, stretching across fully six hundred years, allows for analysis of the structures of water over the *longue durée*. After Gibbon invented the notion of decline and fall, historians have been acutely aware of the deep transformations ancient society underwent in the centuries now called early medieval. A study of how societies coped with problems of hydraulics gains relevance precisely when it covers a crucial period of social, economic, political, and cultural transformation. Because between the fifth and the tenth centuries much changed, it is instructive to trace how water management changed, or did not, alongside social hierarchies, religious values, and economic networks. The examination of how postclassical societies dealt with water thus contributes to the ongoing debate on the transition from antiquity to the Middle Ages, or on the decline and fall of the Roman Empire, as Gibbon would have it.

Among postclassical societies, the Italian ones are especially suited to an "aqueous history" which attempts to gauge change from ancient

---

[5] As outlined, a bit categorically, by D. Worster, "Doing Environmental History," in Worster (ed.), *The Ends of the Earth* (Cambridge, 1988), pp. 289–307. Not all the components of environmental history as Worster and other Americanists conceive it are applicable to premodern European societies, but the tripartite model of such history (an ecological base, an economic structure within it, and cultural assumptions interacting with both) is useful.

conditions. In the peninsula Roman civilization had been born and had taken root most vigorously, and there it left the thickest sediment after its demise. Italy is thus a cultural sphere within which ancient norms and ways had developed fully and in which they retained relevance long after AD 476, when the last emperor was retired and the Roman Empire formally ended in the West. Italy is also a geographic zone of great hydrological interest. Between the Alps and the Ionian Sea exists an array of conditions determined by climate, relief, geology, and vegetation. This variety lends special usefulness to the study of human adaptations to the Italian environment. From the continental climate of the Po valley to the arid table of Apulia, passing over Apennine mountains, hills, and enclosed basins, the Italian peninsula offers a greater variety of geographical "structures" than any other Mediterranean region. The history of water management in the peninsula is therefore appropriate for comparisons with many other places, whether "continental" or "Mediterranean," where similar conditions exist.

An analysis of human adjustments to water in the evolving postclassical Italy is thus both an analysis of a sometimes neutral, almost inert thing, an element with stable characteristics such as chemical composition, boiling and freezing temperature, or susceptibility to gravity, and an analysis of people's imaginative reactions to it. This study demonstrates one thing above all others: water was indissolubly both matter and custom, both nature and culture in the diverse landscapes of Italy during the early Middle Ages. This duality shaped the modes of water procurement, distribution, and usage. Practical and biological necessities contributed to people's intake of water, to their settlement patterns, to their ability to exploit the resource. Alongside the necessities, the choices people exercised, their willingness to do some things with water but not others, their perseverance in seeking to modify the behavior of the waters so as to suit their cultural expectations, strongly affected water management. The interaction of natural and cultural components is a leitmotiv of Italy's early medieval "aqueous history."

Of course there were as many different types of water as there were things to do with it in early medieval Italy. Such variety has lent this study its structure. In the first place, physiological needs meant that people lived in close proximity to water for domestic uses, like drinking and cooking. As chapter 1 of this study reveals, early medieval systems to secure this "purest" type of water were numerous and flexible, designed to lessen the risk of shortfall in a most sensitive area of water supply. Such variety and flexibility represented a continuation of Roman traditions as in fact did the apparent early medieval reluctance to drink water neat. Sparing use of water in the domestic context has been linked to the purported mediocre quality of water available, but in the first chapter an alternative explanation is advanced which places the consumption of water in its proper cultural context rather than understanding it in exclusively biological terms.

Water was a vital substance necessary to life, but also had voluptuary, frivolous destinations. Among ancient societies, the Roman one was most noted for its willingness to allocate huge hydraulic resources to such unnecessary things as baths and bathing. Within the Roman Empire, the Italian peninsula was the region perhaps fondest of baths. Postclassical Italy's baths and their transformations provide an excellent microcosm in which to observe the end of antiquity and the beginning of the Middle Ages. Patronage of public baths by prominent citizens was replaced by episcopal patronage, and the charitable washings of the eighth century are a faint echo of the public establishments of Roman Italy. The shrinking state left bathing to ecclesiastical institutions and private water supplies. Technologies evolved, too, with fewer baths fed by aqueducts and more by cisterns. Subsequent discussions disclose that, as patronage and technologies associated with baths evolved after about 400, how people bathed changed as well, though the custom of communal bathing showed a surprising resilience. For in Roman times bathing was not merely a matter of hygiene or bodily relaxation, but a social event which combined both. In late antiquity and with gathering emphasis thereafter, the division of the cleansing bath from the recreational bath drove the history of the practice of bathing. As moral fulminations struck the recreational bath with increasing frequency, its cultural prominence faded. Thus, by the tenth century, few baths existed in Italy open to a socially diverse public eager to lounge naked in company. Several small, private baths fit for a solitary bather graced urban houses instead.

In rural areas water had still different uses. Agriculture in the broadest sense depended on the regulation of waters, whether in pampered vegetable gardens, arable fields, pastures, or even in the utilizable wilderness. How water functioned in a given landscape depended on precipitation, relief, soil composition, hydrology, and an array of other ecological factors; it was thus a Braudelian structure, but one which changed over a *durée* as *longue* as the early Middle Ages. Agricultural adaptations to these conditions could and did change correspondingly in that period. Irrigation and drainage took different forms in different places, and accordingly shaped the social relations that they evoked. For example, the drainage of long-uncultivated lands toward the end of the first millennium, particularly in northern Italy, was closely connected to the interests of large landlords and dependent on subaltern workers' hunger for land. The removal of water from the Po lowlands provided an opportunity for the construction of vast estates populated by subject tenants.[6] Thus the story of agricultural hydraulics can mirror the social and demographic history of early medieval Italy. The water in the fields likewise had a cultural history. Willingness to drain or irrigate, or willingness to use over-watered lands and their swamps, are as much mentalities as they are products of economic and natural constraints. Chapter 3 explores these issues.

Chapter 4 investigates a further type of water and a way of using it. Fish teemed in the water courses of the peninsula, something of which its human inhabitants were aware in the early Middle Ages. How they reacted to this abundance reveals far more than the technologies they had available. The preponderance of fresh-water fish on early medieval tables, or on those about which we know most, resulted from tastes and preferences and from legal patterns which made ownership of fresh-water courses possible. Water for fishing became a valuable commodity while fish became a viable substitute for meat among practicing Christians during the early Middle Ages. In this respect, too, the period was dynamic and its adaptations to available aqueous resources were subtle and varied.

Finally, water was a resource which, carefully guided and coaxed, generated energy. As there is virtually no sign in the early medieval Italian peninsula that flowing water powered machines which did anything but grind grain, chapter 5 of this study considers the use of water in milling. It considers the technologies and their dissemination but also how this form of water use shaped social relations, brought people together, affected the allocation of work, and served as a tool of surplus extraction from grain producers. Once again, water emerges as far more than a placid element; rather, it is a locus of social exchange and power relations whose history ties in with the decisive political, economic, and social trends of the times.

Throughout the postclassical centuries, from the Alps to the Mezzogiorno, the most prominent theme in aqueous history is probably the seizure of water resources by powerful landlords. Their attempt to monopolize this resource and turn it into private property depended on the unwillingness and incapacity of rulers to perpetuate the Roman imperial tradition of water as a public, common resource available to all.[7] Thus, from at least the eighth century onward, monasteries, churches, and then secular magnates won legal rights over rivers, streams, and other

---

[6] See F. Menant, *Campagnes lombardes du moyen âge* (Rome, 1993), pp. 42–5.

[7] Roman law contained numerous provisions to free up access to "public" (that is, perennially flowing) waters: an emphatic example is *Digest*, 39.2.24 (Ulpian), p. 389: "fluminum publicorum communis est usus." See also 43.12.1–2, pp. 578–80, 43.14.1, p. 581, and *Institutiones*, ed. P. Kreuger (Berlin, 1872), 2.1.2–5, p. 12. Not all waters were "public," naturally.

sources of water. They did not become the sole proprietors of all the waters, something to which they probably did not aspire anyway. But by the tenth century significant proportions of the waters in the most convenient locations and with the greatest use-value belonged to powerful people who could exclude others from access. This process of patrimonialization of water resources was an integral part of the redefinition of social and economic equilibria which characterized the last two centuries of the first millennium in Italy. Its exposure as the central theme in the history of water after the demise of imperial Rome has been a central object in this study.

Water, then, had almost endless applications and forms. This makes a *histoire totale* of it in early medieval Italy almost impossible. The use of water as a means of transporting people and goods in the Middle Ages is certainly one of the foremost usages of water, but it has been quite well served already and is not tackled here.[8] Magic water and water in ritual is another area overlooked, for this vast subject, which has also attracted some attention, would require a separate monograph rather different in scope from the present one, one more focused on ecclesiastical sources.[9]

Of course most sources preserved from the early Middle Ages are ecclesiastical in some sense, including most of those employed here. Even the charters recording agrarian contracts were preserved in ecclesiastical archives and defended ecclesiastical interests, though they are one of the best windows onto everyday use of water by ordinary folk in the areas where they were written. Together with legal texts and court cases, the contracts reveal much. For instance, they unveil what certainly appears as an appropriation of water resources by the powerful, which had already begun in the eighth century, the first century for which charter evidence survives in reasonable quantities. Charters are most communicative when integrated with narrative sources, letters, chronicles, and biographies. These exist for the entire period between AD 400 and 1000, and contain much information on the social contexts within which water was

---

[8] A sampling of relevant works is listed here, to which should be added the papers dealing with water transport in *Settimane* 40 (1993): A. Leighton, *Transport and Communication in Early Medieval Europe, AD 500–1100* (New York, 1972); L. Bellini, *Le saline dell'antico delta padano* (Ferrara, 1962); L.-M. Hartmann, *Zur Wirtschaftsgeschichte Italiens im frühen Mittelalter* (Gotha, 1904); M. Montanari, *Alimentazione e cultura nel medioevo* (Bari, 1988), pp. 147–63; G. Fasoli, "Navigazione fluviale," *Settimane* 25 (1978), pp. 565–607.

[9] Most subjects related to water in Christian ritual and belief (baptism, blessings, etc.) are clearly treated in Leclercq and Cabrol's *Dictionnaire d'archéologie chrétienne et de liturgie*. Ritual water is treated in G. Binding, "Quellen, Brunnen, und Reliquiengraber in Kirchen," *Zeitschrift für Archäologie des Mittelalters* 3 (1975), pp. 37–56; H. Reinitzer, "Wasser des Todes und Wasser des Lebens," in H. Bohme (ed.), *Kulturgeschichte des Wassers* (Frankfurt, 1988), pp. 99–144. A recent study of one aspect is J. Rattue, *The Living Stream* (Woodbridge, Suffolk, 1995).

employed, on the expectations about water of their authors and audiences. The latter subjects are also illuminated by normative writings such as synodical decrees and monastic rules. And, throughout, archeological data, which is now beginning to be fairly copious on postclassical Italy, helps. It indicates whether hydraulic cement lined cisterns in Tuscany about 1000 (it did), how eighth-century monasteries filtered their water in Brescia, the extent to which Apulians irrigated their gardens, and the patterns of bathing in Rome in the eleventh century. Perhaps because water is of so many types and so many uses the study of its history in early medieval Italy requires a certain interdisciplinary openness to different types of evidence.

The scarcity of such evidence even over the course of the six hundred years this study addresses is most striking. It is one inducement to approach the question of water procurement and water control over a *longue durée*. The rarity of postclassical sources is compounded by the difficulties of extracting information about water from texts which, with exceptions like the anonymous *Cosmographia* from seventh-century Ravenna, did not concern themselves explicitly with hydrology or water. An "aqueous history" requires ransacking texts and using them in ways their authors did not envision for them. The passing reference to water-sharing arrangements in a charter, a description of an encounter at the baths in a historical work, orders not to drink while engaged in the monastic day – these were not intended to form a coherent picture of how water was seen and used in early medieval Italy. Yet coherence, pattern, synthesis, and generalization, even about a place as geographically and culturally diverse as the Italian peninsula, are the aims of this study. For an understanding of the history of the structure of water within its shifting human contexts requires a synoptic view. This broad picture takes into account as much as possible the ecological and cultural idiosyncrasies of each situation, and particularly of the areas of Salerno, Lucca, Ravenna, and the Po valley whose documents are most numerous. Perhaps future work will add detail, precision, nuance, and corrections, but in the meantime the analysis offered in these pages can provide a model to critique and a guide to the cultural history of an environmental resource.

Writing in the early seventh century, the encyclopedist and orthodox bishop Isidore of Seville remarked that water is by nature diverse and has many properties.[10] Isidore went on to list some of them, drawing on the classical tradition of wondrous waters (water with unusual qualities) which the elder Pliny had known so well. Water could cure or sicken

[10] Isidore of Seville, *Etymologiarum sive Originum Libri XX*, ed. M. Lindsay (Oxford, 1911), 13.3.1: "aquarum naturae diversitas multa est." See also 13.2.3–4 – "aquarum elementum ceteris omnibus imperat" – and 13.3.2–4.

people, could make plants grow, wash dirt off, quench thirst, and even remove sins. The *Etymologies* were not the only text to consider the importance of water, even in the Dark Ages. Isidore's interest in water was shared by the likes of the anonymous seventh-century Ravennan cosmographer, who in fact cited the bishop of Seville's works.[11] The cosmographer's approach was different from Isidore's. For the Ravennan, water was first and foremost an element of nature whose behavior ought to be described and explained at every stage of the water cycle. Between the two of them, these seventh-century *érudits* provided a full, composite picture of what water was in the postclassical centuries. Water, in other words, was not only the element which ruled over all others, but was a resource upon which people relied heavily and which imbued their cultural values, Christian ones in this case. Water was a natural element but produced cultural reactions (ultimately Isidore's encyclopedic list was one of these). The pages which follow trace the history of water as an element in nature, but also as a resource and a commodity able to reflect the varying outlooks of people who dealt with it during the early Middle Ages in Italy.

[11] *Ravennatis Anonymi Cosmographia*, ed. M. Pinder and G. Parthey (Aalen, 1962), 1.6–10, 4.36, pp. 16–26, 288–290. Isidore is cited as an authority on sunsets: 1.5, p. 13.

1 Water for everyday use

Domestic water supply, or the obtaining of water reliable enough in quantity and tolerable enough in quality to satisfy the drinking, cooking, and washing needs of a household community, is always a pressing problem. Lugubrious Old Testament prophets knew the sense of hopelessness which gripped Mediterranean people, even privileged folk, when their customary sources of water ran dry.[1] In early medieval Italy those deprived of a supply of water for their domestic needs felt as disheartened as people always have in such circumstances.

Solutions to the problem of domestic water procurement were various. In a Virgilian mood, the Lombard historian Paul the Deacon presented the inhabitants of Italy's cities as the drinkers of various rivers: the riverine water people drank established their identity.[2] Certainly rivers, brooks, and other natural water courses provided many early medieval households with their water, perhaps more so in rural districts, where these resources were more accessible and "purer" than in cities. Yet mention of these water sources appears surprisingly little in the documents, and when natural sources do appear circumstances are exceptional. We may observe people turning to streams and similar natural sources primarily in emergencies, such as during wars, when normal supplies had been subverted.[3] In the surviving record even natural springs, whose "purity" was less questionable than rivers into which sewage flushed, are not often approached by people, though they presumably *were* frequented and used for specific purposes, like washing clothes.[4]

---

[1] Jeremiah, 14.1–3, is a good example.

[2] Paulus Diaconus, *Die Gedichte des Paulus Diaconus*, ed. K. Neff (Munich, 1908), p. 146, lines 35–7.

[3] *Guerra Gotica* I, 1.19, p. 146; 2.25, p. 166; Jordanes, *De Origine Actibusque Getarum*, ed. T. Mommsen (Berlin, 1882), 40, p. 111.

[4] See *Guerra Gotica* I, 1.19, p. 147, on sewage in the Tiber. (Early medieval rulers worried almost as much as later communal ones did about sewers: Cassiodorus, *Variarum Libri Duodecim*, ed. T. Mommsen [Berlin, 1894], 3.30, p. 94; 8.29–30, p. 258; *Capitularia Regum Francorum*, in *MGH Legum Sectio II*, vol. I, ed. A. Boretius [Hanover, 1883], 105.3, p. 216. Pavia's sewers were the stuff of literature: Liutprand of Cremona, *Antapodosis*, ed. J. Becker [Hanover, 1915], 1.35, p. 26; 3.3, pp. 75–6.) A rare instance of evidence of actual use of springs is *Vita S. Apiani*, *AS* March 1 (Antwerp, 1668), p. 326, where the saint is claimed to have been "modice de fontibus haustus."

The reason for the relative invisibility of these natural sources of water for domestic use is probably their banality. Nevertheless, they suffered from disadvantages which induced many early medieval people to turn to artificial sources. Rivers were not always "clean" and using them may not have been prestigious. They were also temperamental enough to discourage life too close to their ever-shifting banks.[5] Like water courses, springs too were not always where they were most useful and convenient, and not everyone could enjoy the miracle of having a spring gush forth in their backyard.[6] Therefore, throughout the peninsula considerable energy was lavished on man-made water-supply systems, and people relied heavily on them. Without seeking to minimize the role of the natural sources of water, this chapter will treat the artificial means of procuring water in early medieval Italy, and will consider the various ways in which households used water.

The supply: aqueducts and their water

In the ancient Mediterranean, from at least as early as Eupalinus of Megara, whom Polycrates employed to bore a tunnel-aqueduct through Mount Ampelos in Samos, aqueducts were part of the rhetoric of power. Rulers had them built as acts of munificence and as tangible statements of their solicitude for the ruled and for the public well-being. Roman emperors were of course particularly active in this branch of "evergetism," and they endowed numberless provincial towns, as well as the city itself, with famous water channels whose ruins are still impressive for length and skillful construction. In the Empire, provincial dignitaries also patronized aqueducts, for these structures combined utility, visibility, and longevity in a mixture alluring for people who wished grateful communities to remember them and their beneficent rule.[7] Though there is evidence that rich people appropriated part of these aqueducts' water for use within

---

[5] Examples of rivers leaving their bed can be found in Gregory the Great, *Dialogi*, ed. A. de Vogüé and P. Antin (Paris, 1978–80), 3.9–10, pp. 289–91; 3.18, p. 346; *HL* 3.23–4, p. 104; 4.45, p. 135; 6.36, p. 177. A royal charter from 744 (*CDL* III, 18:84) reveals that the Po was restless, and left its old bed. The authority on flooding is V. Fumagalli; see, for instance, his "Note per una storia agraria altomedioevale," *Studi medievali* 9 (1968), pp. 366–76. Also, see chapter 3 below.

[6] A hagiographic *topos*: Gregory the Great, *Dialogi* 2.5, p. 155; 3.16, p. 328; *Vita S. Venerii*, *AS* September 4 (Antwerp, 1763), p. 118.

[7] See N. Purcell, "Rome and the Management of Water," in G. Shipley and J. Salmon (eds.), *Human Landscapes in Classical Antiquity* (London, 1996), pp. 194–5, who stresses that aqueducts were the result of the Roman choice to reside on plains. M. Corbier, "De Volsinii à Sestinum," *Revue des études latines* 62 (1984), pp. 236–74, and her "L'évergétisme de l'eau en Afrique," *L'Africa romana* 3 (1986), pp. 275–85, are good introductions to the subject. See also W. MacDonald, *The Architecture of the Roman Empire* II (New Haven, 1986), p. 99. Herodotus (*Histories* 3.60) did not explicitly make Polycrates responsible for the Samian tunnel, but other Greek writers, including Aristotle, did.

their own domestic walls, the main function of Roman aqueducts, to make ample supplies of water readily available to entire communities, was generally achieved.[8] The Roman system of water supply through patronage worked smoothly because all parties involved benefited from it. While the patrons obtained glory, their fellow citizens obtained good water.

This sort of patronage and the resultant water supply dwindled in early medieval Europe. However, aqueducts and their fresh, controllable water delivered to public places did not vanish altogether. Indeed, early medieval people admired and sought after them, as is clear from a passage in the *Gesta* of the bishops of Le Mans, datable to the close of Louis the Pious' reign in Francia:

The aforementioned bishop [Aldric] in the very first year of his episcopacy also by his own effort and ingenuity saw fit to lead water through an aqueduct to Le Mans, which no one had seen happen before; and he arranged for all to have enough water, with the help of God, whereas before they sorely lacked it and not even with great tribulation could have it. Earlier no one was able to have one or two measures [*modia*] of water in the city unless they gave a *denarius* to those who brought it from the Sarthe or another spring, since no one had a well there and thus water was so expensive.[9]

The deeds of Bishop Aldric took place far from Italy and centuries after the imperial decurions had ceased to maintain the Empire's water-supply systems. Yet it is worth crossing the Alps and leap-frogging several centuries because the account is poignant and illustrates the point that evergetism, suitably transformed, lived on after the collapse of Roman civilization. The *Gesta* show the deep concern felt by early medieval people for their water supply and their admiration for aqueducts, understood to be the best means of making free, pure water widely accessible. Aldric's deeds illustrate the continued willingness of early medieval patrons to erect water channels for public use, too. Both patrons of aqueducts and appreciative communities of users existed in the ninth century, much as they had in the second.

---

[8] In the first century, Frontinus had complained of theft from aqueducts, as did Pliny (*Naturalis Historia*, ed. L. Ian and C. Mayhoff [Stuttgart, 1967], 31.23, p. 44). In late antiquity, *Codex Theodosianus*, ed. T. Mommsen and P. Krueger (Berlin, 1905), 15.2.2–7, pp. 815–16, and Cassiodorus, *Variarum* 3.31, p. 95, joined the chorus.

[9] *Gesta Aldrici Episcopi Cenomannensis*, ed. G. Waitz, *MGHScriptores* XV.1 (Hanover, 1887), 2, p. 310: "predictus quoque pontifex in primo pontificatus sui anno aquam per aqueductum in predictam civitatem Cenomannicam, quam nullus hominem ibi antea venire viderat, suo opere et bono ingenio adducere meruit omnibusque, qui antea valde aqua indigebant nec etiam nisi per magnum laborem eam habere poteant, sufficienter, auxiliante Domino, habere fecit. Unum siquidem vel duo modia aquae infra civitatem antea emere nemo valebat, nisi unum denarium afferentibus eam de Sarta vel de aliquo fonte dedisset, quoniam nec puteum inibi aliquem habebat; idea tam kara erat." A. Guillerme, "Puits, aqueducs, et fontaines," in *L'eau au moyen âge* (Marseille, 1985), p. 188, suggests that Aldric had been reading Vitruvius (while at Aachen as Charlemagne's chaplain).

They existed in Italy as well as Francia.[10] From the fourth century onward, in fact, water evergetism in the peninsula survived by assuming new forms. Much as was the case in ninth-century Le Mans, in late antique Italy bishops replaced secular builders of aqueducts. Indeed, by Aldric's day, Italy had developed a distinguished tradition of episcopal involvement in urban water supply. The atria of great church complexes like St. Peter's in Rome received plenty of water through aqueducts in late antiquity (and, as we shall see, in the eighth century). But thanks to Paulinus of Nola's eloquence the best-documented case of this sort was not Rome, where Pope Symmachus did, however, preoccupy himself with ecclesiastical water supply;[11] rather, it was St. Felix's shrine at Cimitille, on the fringes of the small provincial city of Nola in Campania. Bishop Paulinus' letters and poems from around AD 400 describe the building and operation of a conduit at St. Felix's basilica, in whose splendid court-yards fountains gurgled, available to all visitors.[12] Though the Nolans, whose consent was vital to the construction project, presumably because of an age-old entitlement, resented the monopoly of water by the Church, for Paulinus right order demanded that the six-mile aqueduct first replenish the saint's residence and only thereafter the city. The Nolans even rioted in an effort to keep the aqueous *status quo ante*; initially, they understood the new aqueduct as detrimental to their watery interests. They were not alone in their skepticism. Paulinus also chided the "dejected farmers" who were unpersuaded by his views on hydraulic justice; they should never have believed that St. Felix would fail to provide for them too.[13]

In Paulinus' case the Church became the pretext around which to organize a public work of great utility for a water-poor region. Paulinus listed the unintended beneficiaries of the improved waterworks: thanks to this channel, villagers in the hills above Nola, landlords with big estates, and the inhabitants of Nola itself, as well, of course, as the religious commu-

---

[10] Guillerme, "Puits," pp. 187–8, paints an overly catastrophic picture of the Gaulish situation. A similar stereotypical view of the "agony" of Rome's aqueducts after Vitiges "cut" them in 537 is offered by A. Malissard, *Les Romains et l'eau* (Paris, 1994), pp. 267–9.

[11] *LP* I, p. 262. Symmachus was not concerned for the city's general aqueous welfare. He helped only churches, unlike Bishop Aemilianus (Cassiodorus, *Variarum* 4.31, p. 128) who sought to slake his whole flock's thirst.

[12] Paulinus of Nola, *Carmina*, ed. G. de Hartel (Vienna, 1894), 27.399, p. 279, 27.466–76, p. 283, and 28.33–43, pp. 292–3, describes the fountains prior to the conduit's completion. See also B. Ward-Perkins, *From Classical Antiquity to the Middle Ages* (Oxford, 1984), p. 142.

[13] Paulinus of Nola, *Carmina* 21.650–67, pp. 179–80: "videbantur maestis orare colonis." Paulinus sought to compensate Nola for appropriating so much water from the refurbished aqueduct by inciting the villagers of Abella, who had provided the labor for the project "tamquam ludo," to work for free once more and restore another aqueduct to lead water into Nola (21.788–821).

nity gathered around St. Felix's tomb were better bathed, refreshed, and even fed (the aqueduct also irrigated crops). The poetically inclined bishop further remarked upon the aesthetic delight procured for everyone by the fountains the aqueduct fed.

The scale of this project, like our information about it, is unequaled in late antique Italy, where several Roman aqueducts were adjusted but no comparable channels are known to have been constructed.[14] The Nolan bishop's evergetism of water, at a time when the Roman state was still able to manage aqueducts, marked the emergence of a new style of aqueduct patronage which was destined to prevail in the following centuries. Late antique and early medieval bishops in Italy willingly tackled the problems of water supply and aqueducts but generally subordinated the requirements of their communities to those of their churches. St. Felix's aqueduct was built specially for a suburban church, to solve the domestic water-supply problems of a small elite and add to its prestige. However many pilgrims gaped at the bubbling fountains or bathed in the sanctuary's baths, the aqueduct was not conceived as a public benefaction in the Roman sense. The aqueduct, resented by many local people (Paulinus claimed they came to recognize their error), was a success in spite of its nature. Only its side effects, bringing water to several other communities, not its principal purpose, bringing water to St. Felix, made its laborious construction palatable to the Campanians.

Still, the fact that, in the end, Paulinus' aqueduct did bring water to many outside the church compound is important. These "episcopal" aqueducts of late antiquity and the early Middle Ages distinguished themselves from the conduits many Italian monasteries built, especially in the 700s, in that they made water available to households outside the church compound. For the aqueduct of Paulinus had much in common with those Pope Hadrian I repaired. At Rome in the 770s Pope Hadrian restored four ancient aqueducts, which gushed with water once more after decades of imperfect spouting or of total silence. Such restoration was almost as complex and costly as construction *ex nihilo*. It was also vital to the quality of water aqueducts delivered.[15] While the *Gesta* of Le

---

[14] Cassiodorus, *Variarum* 8.29–30, p. 258, claimed that his grandfather built an aqueduct at Parma. Theodoric was active in this field too: see n. 21 below.

[15] Early in the sixth century, Cassiodorus (*Variarum* 7.6, pp. 205–6) noted the difficulty of maintaining Rome's aqueducts and the dismal quality of water from decrepit channels (5.38, p. 164). Justinian's Pragmatic Sanction seemed unaware of the troubles, and depicted the magistracy responsible for "care of the waters" as fully effective (Belisarius did make some repairs: T. Ashby, *The Aqueducts of Ancient Rome* [Oxford, 1935], p. 15). Pope Honorius repaired the Trajanic channel from Bracciano, vital to St. Peter's, around 630, but he ignored the other aqueducts: B. Ward-Perkins, *From Classical Antiquity*, p. 48. For Hadrian, see *LP* I, 94.59, p. 503, and 94.81, p. 510; 94.61, p. 504; 94.62, p. 504

Mans ignore the technicalities implicit in Aldric's munificence, the *Liber Pontificalis* is almost as forthright about the difficulty of organizing such work as Paulinus had been. Materials, skilled workmen, and unskilled laborers had to be found, brought to Rome, possibly even recompensed (for the sake of comparison it is important to recall the gigantic aqueduct-restoration project undertaken in 767 at Constantinople, when 6,900 craftsmen were imported into that city, including two hundred potters to shape the piping[16]). Hadrian gathered together "a multitude of people from the districts of the Campagna," according to his biographer, and this cannot have been an easy task. Nevertheless, for the good and clever early medieval patron such an effort was worthwhile. This pope renewed the ancient, typically urban glory of aqueduct-borne pure water for "almost the whole city" as well as for the ecclesiastical complexes at St. Peter's and the Lateran. The famous pine-cone fountain in the atrium in front of St. Peter's made water available to Romans and pilgrims in much the same way terminal fountains of ancient aqueducts had.[17] Thus the meritorious goals of providing water and winning honor allowed a happy fusion of public water supply and ecclesiastical interests.

The writer of the *Liber Pontificalis* entry clearly approved of Hadrian's project. This Lateran insider's approbation of the pope's evergetism suggests that by the eighth century episcopal patronage of aqueducts, inaugurated by Paulinus, had deep roots. But in the papal account old-fashioned notions of the proper relations between town and country coexisted with acceptance of the new evergetism. The pope's campaign of reconstruction was admirable also because it ensured the city's preeminence over the country. Rural labor had been rightfully turned to solving Rome's problems of domestic provisioning and display, as had been the ancient

("modica aqua" still traversed the Claudian aqueduct, but the project required "aggregans multitudinem populi partibus Campanie"); 94.65, p. 505 ("vix modica aqua" still flowed in the Virgo aqueduct, but afterwards so much flowed that it "poene totam civitatem satiavit"). Duchesne dates these repairs to 776. See also L. Pani Ermini, "'Renovatio murorum' tra programma urbanistico e restauro conservativo," *Settimane* 39 (1992), pp. 500–2; B. Ward-Perkins, *From Classical Antiquity*, pp. 48, 142–4; R. Vielliard, *Recherches sur les origines de la Rome chrétienne* (Macôn, 1941), pp. 123–5; and the vague M. Greenhalgh, *The Survival of Roman Antiquities in the Middle Ages* (London, 1989), p. 110.

[16] Theophanes, *The Chronicle of Theophanes*, tr. H. Turtledove (Philadelphia, 1982), AM 6258, p. 128, was impressed; C. Mango, "The Water Supply of Constantinople," in C. Mango and G. Dagron (eds.), *Constantinople and Its Hinterland* (Aldershot, 1995), p. 17. The tough work of building aqueducts is well described in an unlikely source: *La Vita S. Marini*, ed. P. Aebischer (San Marino, 1974), 8, p. 65, probably of the tenth century.

[17] See MacDonald, *Architecture* II, pp. 99–103; B. Ward-Perkins, *From Classical Antiquity*, pp. 142–4, insists on St. Peter's uniqueness. See also C. Kosch, "Wasserbaueinrichtungen in hochmittelalterlichen Konventanlagen Mitteleuropas," in *Geschichte der Wasserversorgung* IV (Mainz, 1991), p. 103.

custom.[18] The restoration of Rome's aqueducts in the 770s thus reflects the continuation of classical ideals of urban splendor in water supply as well as the transformation of the methods employed to maintain such splendor. These ideals still inspired some ninth-century popes, who repaired and caused water to flow through some of the ancient conduits. Mostly it was the Lateran complex which benefited, but ordinary Romans could also use this water. Certainly the "comfort" of ordinary people could determine some papal hydraulic projects. When Leo IV rebuilt Centumcellae in a Saracen-proof location, he first discarded one possible location as unsuitable on account of its water supply. Divine inspiration led the worthy pope to the best site "suitable for building a city," one that "provided a supply of water to comfort the people."[19] This type of modified classical evergetism, however, became rare in the 800s. It had been utterly transformed by the time the bishop of Verona won "the right to lead an aqueduct to the episcopal residence over the public bridge or through any other place he requires, without anyone's contradiction" in 873. There is no sign here that the *episcopium* shared the water with anyone else.[20]

For Italy's aqueducts the eighth century was a remarkable period. Among urban communities, Rome, Benevento, and Milan enjoyed aqueducts' bounty, whereas before the 700s few urban aqueducts are known to have functioned, though until the middle of the seventh century the lucky inhabitants of Byzantine outposts like Ravenna or Naples consumed aqueduct water, and archeological traces of a stone aqueduct in

---

[18] Aqueducts were an assertion of urban dominance over the rural hinterland in antiquity: B. Shaw, "Water and Society in the Ancient Maghrib," *Antiquités africaines* 20 (1984), pp. 132–4. Ancient public aqueducts had uncontested right of passage (*Ancient Roman Statutes* II, ed. A. Johnson and P. Coleman [Austin, TX, 1961], 114:101; 136:114), and imperial law codified this right (*Codex Theodosianus* 15.2.2, p. 814). The obligation to maintain the area around aqueducts fell on the local landowners (*Ancient Roman Statutes* II, 319:253; *Codex Theodosianus* 15.2.1, p. 814; 15.1.23, p. 806), and was unpopular, as Cassiodorus attests (*Variarum* 3.31, p. 95). This may be the context within which to understand Pope Hadrian's corvées.

[19] In the 830s, 840s, and again in the 860s Rome's aqueducts required attention: *LP* II, p. 77, makes the connection between the "priscis … temporibus" and Gregory IV's restoration of the Trajanic aqueduct clear; see also pp. 91, 154, for repairs of the "demolished" and "broken" *forma Iovia*. Writers of Sergius II's biography repeated segments from Hadrian's life, applying them to *their* aqueduct hero. The *Itinerarium* of Einsiedeln (in *Codice topografico della città di Roma* I, ed. R. Valentini and G. Zucchetti [Rome, 1940], pp. 186, 187, 192) noted only the Lateran aqueduct's working; other channels may have broken down like the "forma Virginis fracta." *LP* I, 105.99–100, records the construction of Centumcellae. The discussion of *incastellamento* in Italy would benefit from consideration of water supply, very obviously important for fortification builders like Leo. See T. Glick, *From Muslim Fortress to Christian Castle* (Manchester, 1995), p. 87, for comments on Iberian *incastellamento* and water supplies.

[20] *Urkunden der Karolinger* IV, 61:187: "potestatem habeant aqueductum per pontem publicum vel per quemcumque locum previderit, ad episcopium absque ullius contradictione." "Contradiction" is a technical term for efforts to deny rights of passage. The charter was tampered with in the eleventh century.

Brescia, built in the seventh century, suggest that Lombard towns too could support such structures.[21]

Almost contemporary with Pope Hadrian's industrious campaign of restoration was the construction of another extraordinary *fistola publica*, in Salerno. The local duke (and later prince) Arechis II was probably responsible for this conduit, perhaps the last in Italy to be built from scratch for several centuries. Although it is first attested to in charters from the 850s, it was an accepted landmark by then. It supplied the new residence and the capital city of Arechis' southern Lombard state. For Arechis, as for his princely successors, aqueducts conveyed more than their liquid contents: this one led water from the De Palmula spring through the new settlement to the ducal palace, and it simultaneously delivered a patent ideological message. It signaled to all that its patron fit the Roman rulers' mold perfectly, living in splendor but mindful of his subjects' needs. For while the aqueduct was called "public" because it was under the ruler's control, the adjective also suggests that the conduit's waters were available to Salerno's inhabitants, perhaps through a fountain such as those that adorned classical aqueducts' *termini*. In 959, after two centuries of service, it was rightly called "ancient" by Arechis' successors, for whom it was still the "aqueduct of our republic." Throughout its early medieval history this aqueduct was therefore associated both with rulers' power and with the welfare of the ruled.[22] Salerno's aqueduct was excep-

---

21 Trajan built Ravenna's aqueduct, much restored in the 500s: Cassiodorus, *Variarum* 5.38, p. 164; Anonymus Valesianus, *Chronica*, ed. R. Cessi (Città di Castello, 1913), 22, p. 18; *CIL* 11.1, ed. E. Borman (Berlin, 1888), insc. 11, p. 8. Lead pipes with Theodoric's name on them prove his preoccupation with Ravennan hydraulics: G. Bermond Montanari, "Topografia di Ravenna e di Classe," in her *Ravenna e il porto di Classe* (Bologna, 1983), p. 124; M. Giuliani, "Ravenna, ricerche di geografia urbana," *Annali di ricerche e studi di geografia* 14 (1958), p. 124. For Milan, see: *Versus de Verona*, ed. G. Pighi (Bologna, 1960), 18, p. 146; G. Fantoni, *L'acqua a Milano* (Bologna, 1990), pp. 97–100. B. Ward-Perkins, *From Classical Antiquity*, p. 129, dismisses the poem's evidence (unlike M. Cagiano de Azevedo, "Milano da sant'Ambrogio a Desiderio," in *Casa città e campagna nel tardoantico e nell'alto medioevo* [Galatina, 1986], p. 160). For Naples, see Gregory the Great, *Registrum Epistularum*, ed. D. Norberg (Turnhout, 1982), 9.77, p. 632, who implies that the powerful struggled over control of the aqueduct, perhaps a source of income (Cassiodorus, *Variarum* 7.6, p. 206, imagined such sources to be "venality"). For Benevento in 723, see Vat. Lat. 4939, 70v, "aque ducto publico." These sources employ diverse terms to describe open and closed conduits bearing water for domestic use. Not all "aqueducts" were for this purpose, though; some were for milling or irrigation (see K. Elmshäuser, "Kanalbau und technische Wasserführung im frühen Mittelalter," *Technikgeschichte* 59 (1992), pp. 2–5). For the Brescian aqueduct, see "Schede 1991," *AM* 19 (1992), p. 597.

22 Arechis' classicism is evident in his palace: P. Peduto, et al., "Un accesso alla storia di Salerno," *Rassegna storica salernitana* 10 (1988), pp. 12–13, fig. 1. See also H. Taviani-Carozzi, *La principauté lombarde de Salerne, IXe–XIe siècle* I (Rome, 1991), pp. 188–91. *Fistolam publicam* appears in *CDC* I, 36:43 (853), and is referred to again, 61:76; 64:79. Prince Gisulf called it "aquario antiquo nostrae reipublicae pertinente": M. Schipa, "Storia del principato longobardo di Salerno," *Archivio storico per le provincie napoletane* 12 (1887), p. 255. For public fountains at aqueducts' terminal points in Roman times,

tional, therefore, in lacking episcopal associations. However, princely evergetism in the early Middle Ages was not unlike the episcopal form. Salerno's aqueduct existed primarily for the benefit of the ruler's residence, though less exclusively than contemporary aqueducts for Carolingian palaces on the Rhine. The Salernitans benefited from it only incidentally.

The trends in aqueduct construction between late antiquity and the millennium were thus mixed and slightly contradictory. Some aqueducts conveyed water to a prestigious central place, where builders' interests were focused, but appear also to have furnished water for everyday use to wider communities. Other aqueducts were built by patrons for whom evergetism was less important than the prestige and comfort private piped water supplies conferred. Regardless of how open to public use they were, many aqueducts shared a technical similarity: they were restored Roman structures, originally designed for public use. The presence of a Roman skeleton was important to the continuation of water supply by this means; without Roman ruins even the munificent episcopal and princely patrons of the 700s could not perpetuate ancient water evergetism.[23]

The functioning of these aqueducts affected the history of their communities. Aqueduct water rendered life easier, or indeed possible, for many people. The layout of neighborhoods and the very shape of the inhabited portions of cities could depend on aqueducts. In Rome, during the ninth and tenth centuries, the distribution of population within the walls was determined to a large extent by the routes followed by those aqueducts which still bore water. The urban topography of Salerno was equally affected by the history of the aqueducts in the same period.[24]

see T. Potter, *Roman Italy* (Berkeley, 1986), p. 143; G. Garbrecht, "Die Wasserversorgung des antiken Pergamon," in *Geschichte der Wasserversorgung* II (Mainz, 1987), p. 34. On Arechis' building at Salerno, see P. Delogu, *Mito di una città meridionale* (Naples, 1977), pp. 13–69. See A. Amarotta, "Dinamica urbanistica nell'età longobarda," in A. Leone and E. Vitolo (eds.), *Guida alla storia di Salerno* I (Salerno, 1982), pp. 69–86, and Amarotta, *Salerno romana e medievale* (Salerno, 1989), pp. 246–67, on aqueducts. The "Via Arce Aqueduct" in Salerno, adventuresomely dated to the ninth century (Amarotta, "Dinamica," p. 77; Amarotta, "L'ampliamento longobardo in *plaium montis* a Salerno," *Atti dell'Accademia Pontaniana* 28 [1979], p. 307), was probably a princely creation too: Carolingian residences made use of the power-laden ideology of aqueducts, Ingelheim's four-kilometer aqueduct being an example (K. Randsborg, *The First Millennium AD in Europe and the Mediterranean* [Cambridge, 1991], p. 70 and fig. 39).

[23] *Urkunden der Karolinger* IV, 67:198–9 (Piacenza, 874), shows how ninth-century builders piggy-backed on the glorious past: "antiquos aquedutus in eodem comitatu Placentino, quos, si voluerit [the new monastery] in pristinum statum reformet aut certe in alteram partem transmutet vel certe novellos instituendi."

[24] E. Hubert, *Espace urbain et habitat à Rome du Xe siècle à la fin du XIIIe siècle* (Rome, 1990), pp. 75–9; R. Krautheimer, *Rome: Profile of a City, 312–1308* (Princeton, 1980), pp. 111,

These topographical circumstances confirm that aqueducts' water was accessible to common people and that, in special circumstances at least, patrons supported this type of water supply five centuries after the end of the Empire.

Aqueducts, which the *Gesta* of Le Mans and the *Liber Pontificalis* and many other postclassical sources depict as the natural solution to problems of supplying water for the daily use of households, were actually best adapted to urban situations. No early medieval aqueduct arose where there was no agglomeration of appreciative water consumers. Aqueducts, indeed, made economic and cultural sense only in the presence of relatively high demographic densities, though this density level was relative and variable and could be affected by outside factors (primarily the number and quality of alternative sources, but also the presence of willing patrons and technical know-how).[25] In rural areas the number of people required to sustain aqueduct repairs, or to create the admiring audience for this exploit by patrons, did not exist. Still, the early medieval countryside was not wholly devoid of aqueducts designed to deliver it water. In the rural areas where monasteries or, more rarely, palaces provided the required concentration of consumers some aqueducts did arise.[26]

Monasteries, many in rural areas, were particularly prone to build water channels and thus invert the ancient norm that cities were places of water consumption while rural areas were only places of water "production." The monks of Farfa, for example, built themselves a conduit in the 760s and 770s, more or less when the papacy brought water through the Roman aqueducts again. Thus monks and nuns of the early Middle Ages, unable to replicate the miraculous solutions for water supply of Benedict's first community at Subiaco, nevertheless confronted the issue with energy. Private and monastic water channels, indeed, became a distinguishing trait of the opulent and self-confident monasteries of the eighth century and beyond. Along with Farfa, urban and suburban houses like S. Giulia in Brescia and S. Sophia Outside-the-Walls at Benevento overcame local hydrological impediments with aqueducts in

232, 250–2. For Salerno, see Amarotta, "Dinamica"; M. Dell'Acqua, "Morfologia urbana e tipologia edilizia," in Leone and Vitolo, *Guida alla storia di Salerno* I, pp. 55–67. While medieval people lived where aqueducts led them, in Roman times aqueducts went where populous neighborhoods had arisen: H. Evans, "Water Distribution," in A. Hodge (ed.), *Future Currents in Aqueduct Studies* (Leeds, 1991), p. 23.

[25] For early medieval hydraulic technology, best represented in baptisteries (e.g., Ennodius, *Carmen*, in *Opera*, ed. F. Vogel [Berlin, 1885], 2.149, p. 271), see K. Grewe, "Wasserversorgung und -entsorgung im Mittelalter," in *Geschichte der Wasserversorgung* IV, pp. 18–26.

[26] Grewe, "Wasserversorgung," pp. 27–8, describes Carolingian palaces at Ingelheim and Heidesheim with new, status-enhancing conduits. Italian rulers habitually lived in cities.

the 700s. In the following two centuries other monasteries, even in well-watered cities like Salerno, equipped themselves with comparable structures.[27]

Water, delivered in the most conspicuous and convenient way to the monastic enclosure, raised the standards of living of the nuns and monks within to levels few outside could equal. At Brescia, Abbess Ansilperga was able to indulge the nuns of S. Giulia in the greatest and most "imperial" of luxuries, lead tubes to distribute their aqueduct's water within the convent.[28] S. Giulia, like other important houses, used its elaborate system of water provisioning to enhance its status and living standards while also fulfilling the monastic vocation. With aqueducts monastic communities became more self-sufficient and inward-looking, and the need to leave the cloister in search of necessary water evaporated. Eighth-, ninth-, and tenth-century monasteries' propensity for aqueducts developed from their desire to limit contacts with the "world" at a time when their mastery of its resources reached new heights. As monastic houses expected to exist in the same place for generations and hence to benefit from the effort of construction and maintenance for centuries, the construction of aqueducts was worthwhile.[29] Stability of place and the expectation of permanence fostered the willingness of the abbeys to construct their own water channels.

As we have seen, when the eighth-century monasteries adopted aqueducts as the best solution to their double need for water and honor, they

---

[27] For Farfa, see *Il regesto di Farfa*, ed. I. Giorgi and U. Balzani (Rome, 1879), II, 66:66 (766); 99–101:91–2 (777). Entry lxxxvi in Gregory of Catino's late eleventh-century *Regesto* describes abbot Probatus' building: "cooperuit os fontis aquae manantis ab aevo et traxit aquam a pristino cursu suo ab hoc loco miliarios tres. Porro hanc fabricari iussit formam per montis huius latera haesam, sub terram decurrens constricta, opitulante christi gratia, hoc loco honeste fluit aqua [in 779]." The *Destructio* of Farfa (c. 1030) records that two baths were fed by this conduit (*Il Chronicon Farfense di Gregorio di Catino* I, ed. U. Balzani [Rome, 1903], p. 30). For Brescia, see *CDL* I, 151:66–7; 152:69–70; 153:71–2 (all from early 761); and *CDL* III, 39:234 (767); see also G. Brogiolo, "Trasformazioni urbanistiche nella Brescia longobarda," in C. Stella and G. Brentenghi (eds.), *S. Giulia di Brescia* (Brescia, 1992), pp. 202–6. For Benevento, see Vat. Lat. 4939, 70v–71r, where the abbot of S. Sophia won the right to draw water to the monastery from the "public aqueduct." For Piacenza, see *Urkunden der Karolinger* IV, 67:198 (874). For Salerno, see *CDC* III, 469:27 (994); *CDC* VI, 1000:199 (1042). Gregory the Great, *Dialogi* 2.5, pp. 154–5, illustrates the monastic preference for in-house water supply very effectively.   [28] Brogiolo, "Trasformazioni," p. 206.
[29] I find the notion that the superior intellectual level in monastic communities was responsible for aqueduct construction (Grewe, "Wasserversorgung," pp. 40–1) doubtful. Kosch, "Wasserbaueinrichtungen," p. 89, indicates the importance of the desire for a cloistered life. On the importance of monasteries' longevity, see C. Bond, "Water Management in the Rural Monastery," in R. Gilchrist and H. Mynum (eds.), *The Archaeology of Rural Monasteries* (Oxford, 1989), pp. 84–5. It was also relevant to several houses (S. Giulia, Farfa, Piacenza) that they had royal patronage.

did not invent anything new. Long before the monks and nuns became interested in such commodious supplies, other ecclesiastical complexes had built or rebuilt aqueducts. In the great monastic houses, however, conduits transferred water for the sole gratification of the cloistered communities. These more private water channels were akin to ancient conduits which led water to Roman houses and villas, privatizing the resource. But while such conduits were perceived as illegitimate by Roman imperial authorities, no one in eighth-century Italy thought the monastic aqueducts illicit. Indeed, Abbot Zacharias of S. Sophia, whose derivation channel sapped the Beneventan aqueduct, received ducal approval for his deed in 723.[30] The monastic aqueducts of the eighth and following centuries, therefore, represent a shift toward private means of obtaining water for domestic use which is also visible in the history of wells and cisterns.

The supply: wells, cisterns, and springs

Around AD 700, when the Frankish bishop Rigobert built new facilities for the canons of Rheims, he made piped water available, but "wells also within the monastery were not absent."[31] This description from a transalpine context illuminates the relationship between piped "live" water from conduits and "still" well or cistern water throughout the post-classical era. Having noted the surprising resilience of aqueducts in post-classical Italy, we know that they remained a viable solution to the problems of domestic supply. As aqueducts and people willing to support them for the common good grew rare, other methods of water provisionment became more common, without altogether replacing aqueducts or "wild" sources. Just as aqueducts coexisted with simple reservoirs in the early medieval world, in ancient times wells, cisterns, and springs were never absent, though aqueduct-builders abounded. Among the pampered, aqueduct-riddled cities of the ancient world, Rome – the "queen of the waters" whose aqueducts Frontinus compared favorably to the pyramids of Egypt and the temples of Greece, and which Rutilius Namatianus four centuries later still considered one of the world's

---

[30] Vat. Lat. 4939, 70v. Ansilperga worried, though, and "bought off" possible resistance to her channel: *CDL* I, 151–3:66–72. *Codex Theodosianus* 15.2.2, pp. 815–16, and 15.2.7, p. 816, expressed imperial disapproval for builders of derivation channels. For an example of such "usurping," already known to Frontinus, in the fourth century, see M. Fouet, "Exemples d'exploitation des eaux par des grands proprietaires terriens dans le sud-ouest au IVe siècle," *Caesarodunum 10. Actes* (Tours, 1975), pp. 130–1.

[31] *Vita Rigoberti* 5, *AS* January 1 (Brussels, 1863), p. 175: "puteis quoque intra septa monasterii non deesse."

wonders – never plugged its numerous springs and was full of wells and cisterns.[32]

In Italy's lesser cities, for example Florence or the much-studied Pompeii, the Roman aqueduct supplied baths but never supplanted wells either.[33] In fact, the relationship between aqueduct-borne water supplies and humbler systems for the procurement and storage of water was as close in imperial Italy as it was in Merovingian Francia. Aqueducts complemented and did not replace springs, cisterns, and wells. Thus the ruin of Roman aqueducts could be faced without panic by most late antique communities, for much of their water went to non-essential uses, and domestic supply depended on older systems. Consequently, during the Gothic wars, when populous cities like Naples or Rome saw besiegers cut off their conduits, life continued with minimal discomfort. Procopius, the Byzantine historian who witnessed much of the war first hand, noted that the Neapolitans' wells were sufficient to replace the aqueduct when Belisarius interrupted it, and that the failure of Rome's aqueducts deprived the citizens of baths and mills, but not of water for domestic uses: "even those who lived far from the river got water from wells."[34]

The emergence of wells, cisterns, and springs as the main providers of

---

[32] D. Crouch, *Water Management in Ancient Greek Cities* (Oxford, 1993), p. 22, wisely observes that "the basic principle of water supply" was "to use as many different sources of water as were available." See also Frontinus, *The Stratagems and Aqueducts of Ancient Rome*, ed. C. Bennet (London, 1925), 1.16, pp. 356–8, who noted some springs' excellent reputation (1.7, p. 338); Rutilius Namatianus, *De Reditu Suo*, ed. E. Doblhofer (Heidelberg, 1972), 1.96–106, p. 94. On springs and wells in imperial Rome, see R. Lanciani, *I commentarii di Frontino* (Rome, 1880), pp. 6–31; Evans, *Water Distribution in Ancient Rome* (Ann Arbor, 1994), pp. 135–6. See also Cassiodorus, *Variarum* 3.53, p. 109.

[33] G. Fanelli, *Firenze* (Bari, 1980), pp. 1–2, 5; see the plan of Pompeii's water-supply systems, revealing the integration of diverse sources, in Crouch, *Water Management*, p. 177. Aqueducts could break, could shut for repairs, and did not bring water to the best location (i.e., to everyone's house), so they never replaced archaic water systems resilient to these inconveniences. On the integration of public (aqueduct) and private (cistern) water supplies, see H. Schwartz, "Patterns of Public and Private Water Supply in North Africa," in J. Humphrey (ed.), *Excavations at Carthage 1977* VI (Ann Arbor, 1981), pp. 50–2; A. Hodge, *Roman Aqueducts and Water Supply* (London, 1992), pp. 5–11, 48–9; and R. Thomas and A. Wilson, "Water Supply for Roman Farms in Latium and South Etruria," *PBSR* 64 (1994), pp. 139–96, for discussion of cisterns and aqueducts in rural contexts.

[34] *Guerra Gotica* I, 1.8, p. 64; 1.19–20, pp. 140–8. Malissard, *Les Romains*, p. 154, implies, wrongly, that aqueducts replaced cisterns. Because of a similar misconception of the relation between water-supply methods, the excavators at the Ligurian port of Luni erroneously ascribed the late antique wells there to the collapse of the aqueduct, despite the stratigraphy; see A. Frova (ed.), *Scavi di Luni* I (Rome, 1973), p. 101; and Frova (ed.), *Scavi di Luni* II (Rome, 1977), pp. 638, 671. For a Rhenish comparison (Cologne's aqueduct broke in the third century and was never replaced, in spite of several urban revivals), see Grewe, "Wasserversorgung," pp. 14–15; M. Gechter, "Wasserversorgung und -entsorgung in Köln," *Kölner Jahrbuch für Vor- und Frühgeschichte* 20 (1987), pp. 219–21.

domestic water was no abrupt development in late antiquity. Italian and indeed most Roman cities had long been endowed with these sources of water and never depended on aqueducts exclusively. This cautious strategy of combining as many water sources as possible lasted throughout the Middle Ages. Indeed, only modern Western communities rely on a single source for water; all other human societies hedge their bets and simultaneously draw on numerous sources and types of water for domestic use.

Like aqueducts, cisterns and wells were man-made systems of water provisionment, but unlike aqueducts neither cisterns nor wells were usually designed to provide water to large numbers of people. Cisterns and wells were alike in that both were small-scale, privately managed reservoirs of water generally directed at household use. They differed in that wells made groundwater available to those who lived above, while cisterns were tanks into which rainwater, gathered on roofs and pavements, was channeled by gutters for storage.[35] This meant that cisterns were associated with more built-up, humanized landscapes, whereas wells could be found amidst fields, as long as the water table was not too deep below the earth's surface. On hilltops, where the water table was difficult to reach, or in marshy places like Ravenna, where the groundwater was tainted by salt, cisterns were especially preferred. In Italy they were probably more widespread than wells.

The charters, however, refer far more often to *putei* than to *cisternae*. This paradox is a product of early medieval nomenclature. In most documents it is far from clear that the term "well" was not used to describe a "cistern," an underground tank storing rainwater.[36] In the Lombard laws, for instance, the water-raising mechanism connected to the well was the counterbalanced lever called a "swipe." The swipe is not suited to lifting water from deep cavities like those wells required to reach the water table. The swipe instead works perfectly with shallow reservoirs such as cis-

[35] Vitruvius, *De Architectura*, ed. L. Callebat (Paris, 1973), 8.6.14, pp. 31–2, explained how to build them, though he considered them a last resort (see also Palladius, *Opus Agriculturae*, ed. R. Rodgers [Leipzig, 1975], 9.9.1–2, pp. 181–2). Early medieval charters revealing gutter-fed reservoirs can be found in *Breviarium Ecclesiae Ravennatis (Codice Bavaro)*, ed. G. Rabotti (Rome, 1985), 64:31 (about 700); 65:32 (about 750); 69:34 (about 840), all from Rimini; *CDL* I, 23:90 (720, Pisa).

[36] However, careful linguists knew the difference: Sidonius Apollinaris, *Carmina: Epistulae*, ed. W. Anderson (London, 1936), 1.5.6, p. 356; *HL* 5.2, p. 143; 5.41, p. 160; and, even in the same area, both *cisterna* and *puteo* existed as distinct entities at least in notaries' minds (see, e.g., *CDCajetanus* I, 21:39 [909] and 23:42 [914]). Hubert, *Espace urbain*, p. 161, suggests that most Roman "wells" *were* wells and cisterns were very rare until 1300. Not all *putei* or *cisternae* need have stored water: treasure (*HL* 3.2, p. 99) and grain (D. Andrews, "Underground Grain Storage in Central Italy," in D. Andrews, J. Osbourne, and D. Whitehouse [eds.], *Medieval Lazio* [Oxford, 1982], pp. 123–31; *Guerra Gotica* I, 2.1, p. 6) also filled some.

terns. This implies that despite the use of the term "well" the Lombard
laws envisioned cisterns, and indeed this usage appears to have been
almost universal in Italy. In Ravenna, where reservoirs drawing on
groundwater were not practical, a water tank was generally called *puteus*,
again suggesting that not all reservoirs called by this name were wells.[37]
Since Isidore of Seville succinctly defined *puteus* as "a dug-out place from
which water is extracted, called thus from potation," and blithely ignored
the source of the water, he implied that technical distinctions were not as
important as the reservoir's function.[38] Early medieval Italian writers
were equally casual about distinctions between cisterns and wells, applying the same word to both because both furnished water to households.

Whether cistern or well, almost every reservoir replenished a single
household; the underground tanks often lay in the central courtyard of
the house, a position which made clear who had free access to the water.[39]
The seclusion of these private systems of water supply facilitated their
defense while also rendering the water handy for the household. Unlike
aqueducts, vulnerable in insecure and warlike times and orphaned by
generous patrons, wells and cisterns were an excellent system of water
supply for uneasy societies. Indeed, they were an antidote to insecurity
and sustained the viability of the household even in the face of monstrous
calamities. Thus, the abandonment of an imposing rural house near
Chieti in the late 600s arose not from Lombard or Byzantine rampages,
but from the obstruction of its life-giving cistern.[40] Unsurprisingly, such
private reservoirs were common in fortified settlements, such as those

---

[37] See *Leges Liutprandi*, ed. F. Bluhme (Hanover, 1869), 136, p. 167, on swipes and wells.
Tenth-century Ravenna had an exceptional number of reservoirs called wells (e.g.,
Monumenti I, 29:143; V, 27:248; "Gli archivi," 206:468), and in one instance in 975 the
notary, like Sidonius, distinguished between well and cistern (*Monumenti* I, 51:190) but,
as F. Deichmann, *Ravenna* II.3 (Wiesbaden, 1969), pp. 25, 232, pointed out, the groundwater was saline. See also T. Lipparini, "Geomorfologia del territorio di Ravenna e di
Classe," in *Atti del convegno internazionale di studi sulle antichità di Classe* (Ravenna, 1968),
pp. 67–8.

[38] Isidore of Seville, *Etymologiarum sive Originum Libri XX*, ed. M. Lindsay (Oxford, 1911),
13.21.5: "Puteus est locus defossus ex quo hauritur aqua, a potatione dictus."

[39] Wells in courtyards are standard in charters. For examples from Tuscany, see *CDL* I,
30:109 (722); 65:204 (738); 91:264 (747); *CDL* II, 175:139 (764); 178:146 (764);
229:283 (769); 276:391 (772). Ravennan documents linking courtyards to reservoirs are
found in *Papyri Italiens* I, 24:374 (about 650); 2, 38:134 (616–19); 44:176 (about 650);
Monumenti I, 34:150 (960); 56:198 (978); 58:202 (978); 62:210 (982); 66:27 (987). For
Rimini, see *Breviarium Ecclesiae Ravennatis* 64:31 (about 700); 65:32 (about 750); 69:34
(about 840); 71:35 (about 750); 72:36 (about 815); 73:36 (about 800). On Rome, see
Hubert, *Espace urbain*, p. 161; on Piacenza, see P. Galetti, *Una campagna e la sua città*
(Bologna, 1994), p. 60. This spatial arrangement replicated Greek and Roman patterns.
In early medieval Bavaria, on the other hand, wells were in public areas, available to entire
communities: B. Engelhardt et al., "Early Medieval Wells from Pettfach, Bavaria," in
Environment and Subsistence in Medieval Europe, ed. G. De Boe and F. Verhaeghe (Bruges,
1997).   [40] "Schede 1991," *AM* 19 (1992), p. 593.

which redesigned the Italian landscape in the tenth century and which often were responses to raids. For instance, the selection of the site of Centumcellae, the fortified papal settlement on the Tyrrhenian coast north of Rome, depended heavily on water supplies. Similarly, the early residents of Caputaquis (today Capaccio), inland from Paestum, built themselves cisterns on the hilltop where they gathered to elude coastal piracy (the low water table discouraged the excavation of wells). By the twelfth century few houses there lacked one, their builders having learned from the tenth-century settlers who first sought refuge on the site. Even when enemies overran the hinterland, Capaccio's houses had water.[41]

While providing security, domestic reservoirs also affected the domestic economy and the allocation of work. Going to and, what was more burdensome, returning from a spring or fountain or other remote water source on a regular basis were hard work even if the interlude at the source itself was pleasant. In Gregory the Great's words, "it was very laborious" and could induce dedicated ascetics to consider abandoning their "desert": this reaction was very human, for transporting enough water to satisfy a group of five people could mean carrying one hundred liters per day in freezing or scorching weather.[42] These tasks drained labor even if they were delegated to the least prestigious members of the monastic (or domestic) group and assigned to times like dawn or dusk when little else was going on. They also added costs in equipment, for transportation and storage vessels were needed. Gregory's saints contented themselves with a wooden bucket, but others were less austere. In 570 a Ravennan house without a private supply of water held a host of basins, barrels, and tanks for these tasks, as did a Tuscan dwelling of the middle of the eighth century and a Reatine one in 778.[43] Costs in labor

[41] P. Delogu, "Storia del sito," p. 26; and his "La cisterna dell'Orto del Granato," in *Caputaquis medioevale* I (Salerno, 1976), pp. 79–80; P. Natella, "Il *castellum caputaquis* fra documentazione e storia," in *Caputaquis medioevale* II (Naples, 1984), pp. 40–2. On water supply and military insecurity, see Grewe "Wasserversorgung," pp. 48–51. Cosa's castle used a cistern after 1000, though the locals may have been using the Roman ones on the site too: M. Hobart, "Cosa-Ansedonia (Orbetello) in età medievale," *AM* 22 (1995), pp. 572–82. In central Tuscany, the Guidi castle also had a cistern in the central tower (tenth century?): "Schede 1985," *AM* 13 (1985), p. 477. The question of water supply in fortification is touched upon by D. Balestracci, "I materiali da costruzione del castello medievale," *AM* 16 (1989), p. 242.

[42] Gregory the Great, *Dialogi* 2.5, p. 154: "et erat fratrum valde laboriosum semper ad lacum descendere ut aquam haurire debuissent." There were spiritual dangers too, as devils waylaid monks en route to the well: 2.7, p. 221. The least prominent members of the community would be delegated to fetch water: 2.7, p. 159. Guillerme, "Puits," p. 187, makes the calculation, to my mind excessive even for climates hotter than northern France's, that twenty liters per person per day were needed.

[43] Gregory the Great, *Dialogi* 1.1, p. 13. For Ravenna, see *Papyri Italiens* I, 8:240–2; for Tuscany, *CDL* I, 50:169; for Rieti, *CDL* V, 82:273. See also C. Laganara Fabriano, "L'acqua: i suoi contenitori nel medioevo," *MEFR. Moyen âge* 104 (1992), pp. 373–4.

and equipment such as these might be curtailed in households controlling a well, which might turn out to be an excellent and cost-effective method of provisioning the house in the long run.[44]

After the glummest Dark Ages, Italian charters show that wells and cisterns usually were attached to the plushest houses, controlled by rich and powerful people.[45] This is understandable, given the elevated costs of construction and maintenance associated with water reservoirs. In the eighth century the remuneration levels for masons who built wells were high, compared to other types of construction: a well one hundred feet deep cost thirty gold *solidi* to build; and since, as Paul the Deacon informs us, Lombards used wells as a metaphor for enormity, we can assume large wells were common, though some medieval wells excavated by archeologists are stark and small. A tenth-century well discovered near Brescia was only six and a half meters deep, though it was solidly built with cut stone and brick.[46]

Reservoirs' size was not the only factor which could influence their cost and thus ownership patterns. The cistern which operated throughout the seventh century at Classe, outside Ravenna, had ceramic filters and was carefully built, as was S. Giulia's cistern in Brescia, whose filtration systems, datable to the middle of the eighth century, resembled a labyrinth.[47] On Lombard wells the counterweighted mechanism for

---

[44] Once built, they did not need much restoration, and excavated examples are in good shape: Hobart, "Cosa-Ansedonia," pp. 572–4. Crouch, *Water Management*, p. 155, discusses the economic rationality of cisterns.

[45] There are regional and chronological variations, but the generalization is valid: examples from Milan can be found in *Museo* 44 (812); 137 (879); 138 (879); from Gaeta, in *CDCajetanus* 7:13 (841); 19:36 (906); from Pavia, in *Urkunden der Karolinger* III, 97:236 (846); from Salerno, in *CDC* I, 131:168 (912). Status and well-owning were linked in medieval Rome (Hubert, *Espace urbain*, p. 161) and in medieval France, as well (D. Alexandre-Bidon, "Archéo-iconographie du puits au moyen âge," *MEFR. Moyen âge* 104 [1992], p. 523). The same is true for the Roman Mediterranean; see Malissard, *Les Romains*, pp. 138–43.

[46] For bare excavated wells, see O. Mazzucato, "Relazione sui pozzi medievali rinvenuti sotto il Teatro Argentina," *Bullettino della commissione archeologica comunale di Roma* 81 (1968–9), pp. 102, 111–12; B. Ward-Perkins, "Sepolture e pozzi d'acqua," in Frova, *Scavi di Luni* II, p. 671. For the tenth-century well near Brescia, see M. Perini, "Fiesse (Brescia): pozzo medievale," *Soprintendenze archeologiche lombarde. Notiziario* (1983), p. 65. On ancient techniques, see K. White, *Greek and Roman Technology* (Ithaca, 1984), pp. 157–8; and Vitruvius, *De Architectura* 8.6.12–14, pp. 32–2. On the pay rates of the *magistri commacini*, see *Memoratorium de Mercedibus Commacinorum*, ed. F. Bluhme, *MGHSRL*, p. 180. Pay rates may have reflected danger, which even Palladius, *Opus Agriculturae* 9.9.1, p. 181, acknowledged. On size, see *HL* 5.41, p. 160; 3.12, p. 99. Construction of early medieval wells is seldom recorded, but *Museo* 138 has an 879 "puteum illo . . . quod ego noviter edificare feci, cum accessis sua."

[47] For Classe, see M. Maioli, "Classe, podere Chiavichetta," in Bermond Montanari, *Ravenna e il porto di Classe*, pp. 71, 84. S. Giulia, when built after 753, had a fine cistern at the center of the cloister; Brogiolo, "Trasformazioni," p. 202, suggests that it dates from several decades earlier.

raising water also added to the expense of construction, as did pulleys and rope.[48] In addition to these more functional elements, the materials required to build a well could include ornamentation which added to prestige but also to costs. Both wells and cisterns could be elaborate and decorated. Surviving examples of early medieval well-heads are exceptional pieces, associated with richly appointed churches; illustrations of various Biblical scenes in which wells appear also depict more splendid reservoirs than those most houses relied upon.[49] Still, marble well-heads or portions of wells embellished some domestic spaces: in Ravenna in the ninth and tenth century marble, presumably spoliated, was a popular construction material for water reservoirs.[50]

Nor was this all. Both wells and cisterns required periodic emptying for cleaning and occasional repairs. These maintenance costs were neither negligible nor altogether avoidable, though, at the cost of lowering the quality of water supply, they could be delayed. Only very deep (and hence very expensive) reservoirs maintained the temperatures which guaranteed that no plant or insect life would sprout in the water. If the tale incorporated in an account of relic translation from about 900 is a good guide, Italy's inhabitants abhorred reservoir water which had taken on extraneous, dank smells or tastes through stagnation and improper maintenance.[51] The desire for solidity, functionality, water purity, and probably also the desire to impress, which guided the builders of early medieval reservoirs, raised their costs.

Maintenance and repair costs summed with construction costs go a long way to explaining why few Italian settlements matched the one-well-per-house density of early medieval Kootwijk, in the Netherlands – why, in other words, such an overwhelming proportion of these reservoirs whose memory early medieval charters preserve belonged to powerful people.[52]

---

[48] For "swipes," see *Leges Liutprandi* 136, p. 167. Their mechanisms are explicated by White, *Greek and Roman Technology*, p. 158.

[49] See, for example, the ivory *cathedra* of Maximian in Ravenna for the image of a pulley-equipped well. The wear-marks on the inside of many early medieval Italian marble wells (like the one in S. Marco in Rome or the one from Murano in the Victoria and Albert Museum) indicate that even these luxurious pieces lacked both pulleys and swipes.

[50] For a marble well in Ravenna, see "Gli archivi," 255:485; for wells with marble components, 227:476; 405:535. For seventh-century evidence, see *Papyri Italiens* II, 44:17: "puteo et puteales atque libellos [labellos?] et arca saxea."

[51] A supernatural punishment struck the Lucchesi who stole the relics; their water rotted in their wells according to the *Translatio Iuvenalis et Cassii Episcoporum Narniensium Lucam*, ed. A. Hofmeister (Leipzig, 1934), 11, p. 982. Water which remains colder than 8 °C runs few risks of infestation: Malissard, *Les Romains*, p. 152. However, to obtain this effect one might need to dig so deep that the rope to haul water out became too heavy to lift.

[52] Kootwijk was a homogeneous community of small farmers until about 1000: W. Groenman-van Waateringe and L. van Wijngaarden-Bakker (eds.), *Farm Life in a Carolingian Village* (Assen, 1987). On wells there, see J. Chapelot and R. Fossier, *Le village et la maison au moyen âge* (Paris, 1980), p. 91.

Environmental factors clearly played a part in shaping the social distribution of wells in Italy, since wells too close together tend to empty each other out and lower the water table. Moreover, settlements on hilltops or in especially arid regions were driven by circumstances to rely more on cisterns, which had the additional complication of requiring feeding systems. But even in places with copious aquifers like Salerno or Pavia, the ownership of wells was restricted and many households lacked wells altogether, while cisterns, less affected by the drawbacks of deep excavation, also tended to belong to the mighty. Taken together, technological difficulties, economic costs, and ecological constraints produced a situation which gave control of these water-supply systems to elites.

As King Liutprand knew, in a situation of scarcity the well became a nexus of relations between the powerful, who owned wells, and "the rest who are poor" and who required well water to live (or at least to avoid exhausting excursions to acceptable alternative sources). In places where options were few, the well-owners held the key to prestige and authority. They could administer access to their water so as to build grateful, even dependent clientèles. Although owners are never observed actually denying water to others in the early medieval documents, rulers like Liutprand considered this possible. Ninth-century diplomats also imagined that those in vulnerable positions, far from their bases, might suffer from not being allowed to use local water sources, implying that the right to deny water both existed in theory and could be exercised in practice. Renters of houses in tenth-century Ravenna secured *accessu* to nearby reservoirs in writing, another sign that early medieval people envisioned suffering want of water when other users denied them use of a well.[53] Yet the potential to exclude people from the private waters in reservoirs did not induce many early medieval well-owners actually to exclude users or impose intolerable conditions for use; the well's political and social utility ended when the "aqueous community" (the circle of people who drew on its water) it evoked shrank or disappeared, which was always possible since no one was obliged to use a particular well.

As their location in the courtyard of houses made explicit, wells and cisterns were private property over which the domestic group exercised full dominion. In the sixth-century codification of Roman law the right of the owner to dispose of the well's contents was total, and access to the water

---

[53] *Sicardi Principis Pactio cum Neapolitanis*, ed. F. Bluhme, 45, p. 218; *Radelgisi et Siginulfi Divisio Ducati Beneventani*, ed. F. Bluhme, 3, p. 221. In 1102, beyond this study's chronological scope, the cathedral chapter of Lucca deprived a church at Tassignano of the faculty of using a well as it had been doing: *Regesto del capitolo di Lucca* I, ed. P. Guidi and O. Parenti, *Regesta Chartarum Italiae* VI (Rome, 1910), 623:261–2 (I know of no similar early medieval exchange). *Accessu* to wells were a commodity in Milan, too: *Museo* 44 (812). For Ravenna, see "Gli archivi," 206:468; *Monumenti* V, 27:248.

was only at the owner's discretion. Lombard legislators accepted this situation though the kings, in what represented a last gasp of state involvement in public water supply, attempted to encourage owners to open their reservoirs up to everyone. Following in the footsteps of the wise Solon, who tried to create incentives for well-building and foster the Athenians' aqueous generosity at the same time, both Rothari and Liutprand limited the liability of owners for accidents which occurred around their well.[54] In Lombard law, despite royal efforts, wells were exclusive, private property from which owners could banish others (the poor, according to Liutprand) who lacked both water and the resources required to build and maintain a well.

According to the *Gesta*, the situation at Le Mans, where no water was available inside the city, led to a desperate situation: water was bought and sold. In early medieval Italy few communities were so penuriously provided with water as Le Mans, which may explain why there are so few signs of water being sold in the peninsula before AD 1000. Yet the abundance of water was not always associated with its free availability. Despite the magnificence of the systems of supply in Roman Italy and the resulting abundance of water, the occasional sale of water did occur.[55] The instances of sales of Roman water appear to have been exceptional, and the expectation that water be paid for as a commodity, rather than being a free resource, never took root. Thus Rutilius Namatianus, who traveled in western Italy in 416, inveighed in scandalized tones at the fact that he was compelled to pay for drinking from a spring near Populonia.[56] The spring was in a marshy place, and likely a unique resource in those peculiar

---

[54] *Digest* 43.22.1, p. 600, allows private control of cisterns. *Edictus Rothari*, ed. F. Bluhme (Hanover, 1869), 306, p. 71, seeks to establish that private wells be open to all ("communis omnium utilitatis"). *Leges Liutprandi* 136, pp. 166–7, built on this but was more exact in its respect for private rights. Liutprand's interest seems to have been sparked by a specific case in which a clumsy user mishandled the water-raising mechanism attached to a well, and was killed by it, awakening the vengeful wrath of relatives. Men, not women, seem to work the well concerning which "adnuntiatum est nobis" (Liutprand), perhaps because they led herds there to drink (the deaths Liutprand imagined as the outcome of private, secluded wells may have come from hunger, the result of the *pauperes* not finding water for their animals).

[55] W. Eck, "Die Wasserversorgung in römischen Reich," in *Geschichte der Wasserversorgung* II, p. 80, gives examples of water for domestic consumption sold in Roman Italy. See Evans, *Water Distribution*, p. 141, on sales in Rome itself. Augustus' edict for Venafro (*CIL* 10.4842) is instructive: rich people paid to have water piped to their houses. Martial, who hoped to sell a cistern's water in Ravenna, was probably joking (*Epigrammaton Libri*, ed. I. Borowskij [Leipzig, 1982], 3.56, p. 71). Ancient sanctuaries sometimes sold water: G. Panessa, "Le risorse idriche dei santuari greci," *Annali della Scuola normale superiore di Pisa* 13 (1983), p. 364. Vitruvius, *De Architectura* 8.3 (Praef.), p. 3, thought that water was by nature *gratuita*. Gregory the Great, *Registrum Epistularum*, 9.29, p. 808, thought it valueless. See n. 21 above for evidence that late antique aqueduct administrators could seek profit from their office.

[56] *De Reditu Suo* 1.383–6, p. 116, where the author's antisemitism surfaces.

environmental conditions (which rendered potable water valuable enough to be sold), but the weary traveler of late antiquity still did not expect to pay for water.

These expectations had not changed much four centuries later. A marvelous ninth-century marble well-head, recently moved from the narthex to within the church of S. Marco in Rome, displays an inscription laying a curse upon those who dare to sell its water after the original patron erected it.[57] The church of S. Marco was not in an especially dry region of Rome, a city whose bishops were diligent with aqueduct repairs in the ninth century. Nevertheless, even there penury of water could turn the resource into a commodity, tempting those with control over water to sell it. In this case the priest and patron John sought to prevent any such temptation; his inscription is important evidence for the reality of the sale of water in the city as well as for moral disapproval of such sale. But to find further evidence of water sale in Italy, we must follow another testy traveler, Liutprand of Cremona, all the way to Constantinople. The bishop of Cremona complained acidly of his accommodations in the Byzantine capital and, in doing so, suggested that purchasing water for domestic use was accepted behavior where he came from.[58]

Occasional glimpses of water transactions certainly reveal that, in special circumstances, in both urban and rural environments, water could become an economic commodity, but it seems that water was seldom sold.[59] Wells and springs or brooks remained a resource for whose use formal payments were not levied.

Even if they did not become economic assets, domestic reservoirs and their use did bring about complex social relations. As we have seen, Liutprand imagined these relations to be unequal, vertical. But the relationship of dependence between the water's haves and have-nots was not the only relationship wells created. Groups of part-owners or owners of access rights, more or less equal in status terms, existed. An interesting example of this comes from Milan, where one Brunigo, "negotians de

[57] "De donis Dei et Sancti Marci Johannes presbiter fieri rogabit. Omnes sitientes venite ad aquas et si quis de ista aqua pretio tulerit anathema sit." The inscription vaguely echoes several scriptural passages (Proverbs 25.25, Canticle 4.15), but is original. C. Russo Mailler, "L'acqua dall'antichità al medioevo," *Quaderni medievali* 26 (1988), p. 83, interprets the well as non-liturgical and refers to canonical texts carved on well-heads; see R. Goldschmidt, *Paulinus' Churches At Nola* (Amsterdam, 1940), p. 115, for other examples.
[58] Liutprand of Cremona, *Relatio de Legatione Constantinopolitana*, ed. J. Becker (Hanover, 1915), 1–2, pp. 175–6, was satirical. Liutprand found the *inaquosa* house in which he lodged surprising, but was even more surprised not to be able to buy water to quench his thirst.
[59] The payments "in denaro o in natura" which, according to P. Racine, "Poteri medievali e percorsi fluviali nell'Italia padana," *Quaderni storici* 61 (1986), p. 10, early medieval kings exacted for use of the rivers, were tolls on goods transported and not sales of water.

Mediolano," exchanged land "and access to the well to which other similar access rights are held by the heirs of Odo" with Hernost, "vassus domini regi" in 812. Here a merchant, a military man with royal connections, and a group of other figures were all bound together by a well.[60] Networks of co-users existed at market places in tenth-century Lombardy too: the well was at the center of the selling tables and was also at the center of everyone's concern.[61] Moreover, alongside these horizontal well-centered groupings, there are some interesting assortments among the people whom the charters show us thrust together in legally defined alliances by shared use of wells. Inheritance customs and the partibility of aqueous property gave rise to these formations in which powerful landlords mingled with less powerful folk, like shoemakers, on a technically equal footing, each having, for example, "a third of the well." The tenth-century documentation from Ravenna shows how people (the shoemaker again) controlled portions of several different wells at the same time, thereby becoming members of several different well-centered communities.[62]

The social consequences of all these formations can be imagined. Shared control of wells enforced cooperation and sociability among people, among business associates, among neighbors, among relatives. Even though there is no early medieval Italian evidence of the remarkable late medieval German formal alliances of well-sharers, some level of interaction had to subsist.[63] "Use of the well" for one partial proprietor was abuse for another, especially in the hotter and drier months, so part-owners had to reach agreements on what was fair use, and what constituted a third of a well, and how to organize maintenance and repairs. In cities particularly, where shared ownership was more common, partible control of wells enforced, as water management often does, social ties

---

[60] Examples of fragmented ownership of wells where the owners' social status appears roughly equal can be found in: *Papyri Italiens* I, 24:374; 2, 44:176; *CDL* I, 91;264; *CDL* II, 130:15 (rural *usum potei* near Piacenza); *CDL* II, 148:60 (761); *M&D* IV.1, 107:60. On Salernitan shared ownership, see Delogu, *Mito*, p. 139. See *Museo* 44: "et accessis ad podeo unde ad ipso podeo alias accessis habere vetetur heredes ipsius quondam Odoni."

[61] *Urkunden Konrad I.*, 145:226 (952) at Milan; *CDLangobardiae* XIII, 393:658–9, in Pavia.

[62] The bishop of Lucca was a part-owner in 769: *CDL* II, 229:282–3; 276:391 (a Pavese church received two portions of a well); for a shared well in Bobbio, see *CDL* III, 1–2:6–11; powerful women shared "use" at Lodi: *CDL* II, 155:79; for shared use in Ravenna in the tenth century: *Monumenti* I, 25:142 ("usum potei qui modo clausum esse videtur"); 30:148; 34:150; 51:190; 62:210; "Gli archivi," 88:428; 206:468 (the *calligarius*); 340:514 (another *callicario*); 389:529; 405:535; 407:536; 425:542.

[63] *Brunnengemeinschaften* are discussed by Grewe, "Wasserversorgung," p. 66; W. Wijntjes, "The Water Supply of a Medieval Town," *Rotterdam Papers* IV (Rotterdam, 1982), p. 200. The *comuni* also formed associations of citizens by making those who lived close to a given well responsible for its upkeep: *Statuti urbanistici medievali di Lucca*, ed. D. Corsi (Venice, 1960), 122 (of 1371), p. 68.

and collaboration among people whose theoretical entitlement was equal.[64]

While wells and cisterns were, by their nature, linked to private and domestic water supply, a handful of reservoirs appear to have served the public at large. In this regard, some of Italy's prominent subjects did more than the rulers themselves for public water supply. Following the example set at Cimitille by Paulinus of Nola, at Pavia, in the fifth century, Ennodius sponsored a decorative lion-headed fountain outside the suburban cathedral, refreshing and delighting all comers with water provided by a cistern. At S. Apollinare in Classe, from the sixth century into the twelfth, according to archeologists, a large cistern served the needs of all who wanted its water.[65] An inscription carved at Vicenza on a water basin fashioned from a Roman sarcophagus suggests that some gastalds (Lombard officials) fretted about water and access to it for the inhabitants of their districts.[66] This tradition of the powerful providing access to well water did not die in the eighth century, for in 879 the archbishop of Milan had dedicated a well to charitable ends "for my soul."[67] Even in the 950s Otto I administered a "well of the king" in Milan, used by non-royal people.[68] Evergetism had many incarnations. Adapting themselves to this most private of water sources, some patrons threw open their reservoirs to all who needed their water.

Fountains fed by springs were almost as rare as monumental fountains and cisterns maintained as a public service in early medieval Italian communities. Among these, a fountain in Salerno, reserved for the residents of its immediate environs in 975, remains unique, a far cry from the numerous public fountains to be found in the *opulenta Salerno* of the eleventh and twelfth centuries.[69] Simple fountains, whose water was not reserved to any particular person's use, may have been more common in the countryside, along roads, and close to pastures, though the surviving documents do not brim over with information on them; on the contrary, rural fountains pop up infrequently in charters and they were seldom used as border markers in agricultural contracts. Indeed, *fontes* in the countryside appear mostly as private property within sizable estates, under the control of the greater landlords whose transactions the charters

[64] Rural wells could be divided too: *CDL* II, 130:15 (758); 289:423 (773).

[65] For Pavia, see Ennodius, *Carmen* 2.19, p. 134; for Ravenna: Maioli, "Classe," p. 71.

[66] *Le iscrizioni dei secoli VI–VII–VIII esistenti in Italia*, ed. P. Rugo (Cittadella, 1975), 2, p. 13. A well on a road outside Lucca may have been public too: *CDL* I, 28:102 (720).

[67] *Museo* 138.

[68] *Urkunden Konrad I.*, 145:226, whose *puteus regis* was in Milan's market place.

[69] For Salerno, see *CDC* II, 286:93, *fontana*; on later fountains there, see C. Carucci, *La provincia di Salerno dai tempi più remoti al tramonto della fortuna normanna* (Salerno, 1922), p. 192. The *fontanella* at Palmenta in southern Tuscany may also have supplied several houses: *M&D* V.3, 1092:35 (905).

record. Their acquisition of these resources was probably ancient, but even in the eighth century aggressive grandees could "happen upon" fountains and appropriate them.[70]

The demand: domestic water usage

Three systems supplied the water for domestic use in early medieval Italy. In cities and quasi-urban rural monasteries, aqueducts could do the job. Many households, even in the urban centers which could rely on aqueducts and other fairly pure sources of water, had a private well or cistern, an independent source of water which did not place them in a position of obligation to a patron, or force them to support the establishment and maintenance of consensus and toleration on which the proper functioning of aqueducts depended. Rural communities did not enjoy the luxury of piped water, but if the quality of the constructions for the transfer of water was inferior, in the country the quality of the water itself was probably superior, being exposed to fewer opportunities for pollution in cisterns and wells. In addition to these man-made sources of water for domestic consumption, but not necessarily substituting for them, springs, lakes, streams, and similar "wild" or non-man-made sources of water were also exploited for domestic purposes. The usage of these water-supply systems was shaped by physiological needs, but also by the cultural needs which a household's water satisfied.

Once the water from any of these sources had reached the household, it was employed variously in domestic operations, from washing to cooking to drinking. Several objects in daily use required washing to ensure they were functional. Among these were pots, dishes, and clothing items. Such washing was a humble operation almost invisible in the documentation. The best evidence on the washing of items in daily use comes from monastic *Regulae*, which are early, mostly from the sixth

---

[70] For a rural fountain near Subiaco, see Gregory the Great, *Dialogi* 2.13, p. 179; and 1.1, p. 19, for one in the Apennines. For a spring trickling into a cistern near Osimo, see *Guerra Gotica* II, 2.27, p. 175. For Calabrian spring used to water cattle, see Cassiodorus, *Variarum* 8.32, p. 261. For a rural fountain in Lombardy, see *CDL* III, 11:48 (714). For a *fonte* of a stream's water, see *Chronicon Vulturnense*, ed. V. Federici (Rome, 1925), 37: 254 (817). For a "funtana que dicitur a Stalsi," see *M&D* V.2, 934:573 (884). For "fontana Brocoli" near Parma, see *I diplomi di Guido e di Lamberto*, ed. L. Schiaparelli (Rome, 1906), 2:7 (890). The rarity of rural fountains which did not belong to a farm is odd. For some *fontes* on rural property, see *CDL* I, 84:249 (c. 744, near Volterra); 124:368 (757, Collina); *CDL* V, 80:268 (778, near Farfa); *Urkunden der Karolinger* III, 41:129 (840); *Monumenti* I, 15:114 (918); 26:136 (955); II, 14:33 (970); V, 32:258 (982); "Gli archivi," 91:429 (908); 95:430 (909); 260:487 (970). *Vita S. Walfredi*, ed. H. Mierau (Tübingen, 1991), 3, p. 44, explains how Walfred "repperit" a spring which already had a local name and was therefore well known, and built his monastery on it (he already owned the land).

century.[71] The rules were often normative long after their composition, and can help in establishing a standard, but their evidence must be treated cautiously for they can distort our understanding of domestic washing. For in the *Regulae* men, monks, do the washing, whereas in secular domestic situations such water-related, unprestigious tasks would have been a female preserve.[72] Secular legislation like Charlemagne's capitulary of 789, which claimed to reiterate his father's injunction and was itself oft repeated in the ninth century, forbade *women* from washing clothes on Sundays; thus eighth- and ninth-century rulers expected females to do the laundry.[73] Though they did little more than spill water over the dishes and pans of the monastery in preparation for their next use, the monks who took week-long turns at this task were in effect mortifying themselves by carrying out subordinate, specifically "womanish" duties, and must have been conscious of it.

The clerical texts can further mislead because the rules suggest that the washing was done every day, while, in the smaller community of the family, discipline was more lax and there was not the same sense that "all utensils, both earthenware and iron and all others, are sanctified" and hence deserved the most reverent treatment.[74] Moreover, in the monastic rules water is lavishly used, for monasteries had more lavish supplies, but elsewhere washing might be done with other substances. As Gregory the Great attests, scouring pots with soil was customary and efficacious.[75] This parsimonious washing style would have called for water only in the last stages, to rinse out the muck of soil and scoured material from the container.

[71] *Regula S. Patris*, ed. A. de Vogüé (Paris, 1982), 2, p. 594; *Regula Eugippii*, ed. A. de Vogüé and F. Villegas (Vienna, 1976), 2–3, pp. 17–19; *Regula Magistri*, ed. A. de Vogüé (Paris, 1964), 19, p. 96. Benedictine provisions that monks "vestimenta sua oportuno tempore lavent" were reiterated in later times: *Capitularia Regum Francorum*, in *MGHLegum Sectio II*, vol. I, p. 344, and, in the same volume, Ansegis' *Capitularium Collectio* 75, p. 404. After 900, Regino of Prüm, *De Synodalibus Causis*, ed. F. Wasserschleben (Leipzig, 1840), 1.80, p. 60 (repeated in 1.274, p. 128), required priests to wash vestments and altar cloths in special basins.
[72] On watery domestic chores as womanish, see P. Ariès and G. Duby (eds.), *Histoire de la vie privée* II (Paris, 1985), p. 518; D. Herlihy, *Opera Muliebra* (Philadelphia, 1990), pp. 28, 34; F. Robins, *The Story of Water Supply* (Oxford, 1946), p. 177.
[73] *Capitularia Regum Francorum* I, p. 61; see also *Die Konzilien der Karolingischen Teilreiche*, ed. W. Hartmann, *MGHConcilia* III (Hanover, 1984), p. 250; Ansegis, *Capitularium Collectio* 75, p. 404; Regino, *De Synodalibus Causis* 1.385, p. 176.
[74] *Regula S. Patris*, p. 594: "oportet quoniam quidquid tractaverint in monasterio in omnibus utensilibus, tam vasis quam etiam ferramentis sive cetera omnia esse sanctificata." Ritualization of what today would be considered mundane chores was not a monastic prerogative: Hincmar of Rheims, *De Divortio Lotharii Regis*, ed. L. Böhringer, *MGHConcilia* IV.1 (Hanover, 1992), responsio 6, p. 159.
[75] Gregory the Great, *Registrum Epistularum* 5.43, p. 328, in a complicated metaphor: "Nam sordida vascula, ut inquinatione terrae careant, cum terra mundari solent." Macrobius (*Saturnalia*, ed. F. Eyssenhardt [Leipzig, 1893], 7.13.22, p. 459) knew this technique in the fourth century.

Even viewed through the unfocused lens of the ecclesiastical texts, domestic chores are difficult to trace. Most obscure is the washing of clothes. Nevertheless, two sample references in Lombard sources show how wearing unclean clothes was shameful to upright Lombards. In the *Historia Langobardorum* an incident occurs involving a deacon who proudly defended his integrity and honor by maintaining that his leggings were freshly washed, not soiled as was being insinuated.[76] And in the laws issued by Aistulf we perceive the horror felt by those whose clothes were insultingly sullied with "impure water" as an attempt to demean them and cast the rightfulness of their marriage into doubt.[77] Dirty vestments were also thought shameful for priests, whom numerous synods enjoined to do the laundry often. Thus even if the domestic cleansing tasks are too lowly to emerge in written sources, they were important tasks related to social status and image.

How water was allotted to the task of the cleaning of dishes and clothes is never explained. We might suppose that, especially in dry areas or seasons, the water reserved for these purposes had been previously used for other ones, such as corporeal ablutions.[78] The evidence from seventh- and tenth-century Ravenna, however, suggests that houses with a well in the courtyard could use a stone basin installed next to the well, presumably for just such domestic washing.[79] In Ravenna, then, pure well water may have been used to wash dishes and clothes. The allocation of water for domestic chores is also hinted at in monastic sources, which suggest that clothes and bedding would be washed within the monasteries of central and southern Italy in late antiquity.[80] Since these were privileged situations, to judge from the dimensions and fixtures of the Ravennan houses, more normal arrangements, especially in other regions of Italy, may have differed. In-house scrubbing may not have been the pattern for

[76] *HL* 5.38, p. 158.
[77] *Leges Aistulfi*, ed. F. Bluhme, 15, p. 201, with an exorbitant fine of 900 *solidi*, partly because the act was expected to cause rioting and violence.
[78] Liutprand of Cremona, *Relatio* 63, p. 211, 65, p. 212, is revealing. His satire depended on knowledge of the proper order of water use, foolishly inverted by the Byzantine prelates who sipped water previously bathed in.
[79] *Papyri Italiens* II, 44:176 (mid-600s); "Gli archivi," 227:476 (965); 405:535 (994); 407:536 (995).
[80] See *Regula Benedicti*, ed. A. de Vogüé (Paris, 1972), 35, p. 566, on napkins of the monks, to be washed on Saturday as the last act of the week-long kitchen service; *Regula Magistri* 19, p. 96, on napkins, table cloths, and the *res sordidas* of the monks; *Regula S. Pauli et Stephani*, ed. J. Migne (Paris, 1866), 28, p. 956, "vestimenta vel lectuaria nullus sibi lavare audeat, absque oratione et permissu prioris" (if necessary, late antique laymen could do their own washing: Macrobius, *Saturnalia* 7.13.18, p. 458). As noted above (n. 71), the *Capitulare Monasticum* of 817, 4 (in Ansegis' *Capitularium Collectio*, p. 344), also urged monks to wash their clothes. Benedictine commentators of the ninth century (*Vita et Regula SS. P. Benedicti*, ed. R. Mittermüller [Regensburg, 1880], pp. 398–9, 519–20; *Smaragdi Abbatis Expositio in Regulam S. Benedicti*, ed. A. Spannagel and P. Engelbert [Siegburg, 1974], p. 247) added little to the original *Rule*.

most secular households, for whom the banks of streams may not have seemed awash in the moral dangers that preoccupied monks. Moreover, unlike the monks who were bound to ask the permission of the prior before they washed their clothes at strictly regulated times, secular people probably adopted a less regimented approach to laundry.

Considerations of purity were paramount in water destined for domestic use, but particularly for the water people consumed. "Purity," however, was an elastic term. It was defined differently at different moments and according to the function the water was expected to have (water pure enough to wash dishes with was not necessarily pure enough to ingest). But the central point is that during the early Middle Ages purity was gauged by criteria no longer in wide use in the industrialized West.[81] Thus nobody worried about bacteria, but many Europeans *did* preoccupy themselves with the limpidity and odor of their water. There are several indications of early medieval sensitivity to water quality understood in this sense. Fetid water disgusted Isidore of Seville, who was a good enough classicist to have known the many Roman authorities who had made pronouncements on this subject. Wells excavated at Pettfach, in Bavaria, datable to eighth- and ninth-century contexts, were repeatedly re-lined with wood when the local clayey soil infiltrated them, a sure sign that "optical purity," at least, mattered to the villagers. Then, in the middle of the ninth century, in one of his letters, Lupus, abbot of Ferrières, claimed that he drank water only in emergencies, when neither wine nor other alcoholic beverages were available, but also specified that his was clear water, drawn from a well or sparkling stream, not murky water from a cistern.[82] The discernment of purity in water for domestic consumption during the early Middle Ages must be understood in these terms. Before ingesting water, early medieval people satisfied themselves, if it was at all possible, that it was clear and did not smell.

Examples from different times and places prove that throughout the postclassical peninsula water purity was an urgent concern. Discussing the contents of Ravenna's aqueduct around AD 500, Cassiodorus distinguished between sweet-tasting water and tainted water which robbed

---

[81] The modern history of definitions of water purity is treated by J.-P. Goubert, *La conquête de l'eau* (Paris, 1988), p. 171. Cassiodorus, *Variarum* 5.38, p. 164, illustrates how water quality was assessed in the sixth century – it should not stain, it should taste sweet, and it should not cause indigestion.

[82] Lupus further said water was a natural drink, healthy for souls and bodies: *Epistolae*, ed. E. Dümmler, *MGHEpistulae* V.1 (Berlin, 1902), 109, p. 94. Isidore's *Etymologiarum* 20.3.1, advised "freshness" in water lest it "foetescit." Colorless, odorless water was praised by Roman writers like Palladius, *Opus Agriculturae* 1.4.1, p. 4. This was also the water writers of the high Middle Ages praised as "subtle": G. Sodigné-Costes and B. Ribémont, "'Aqua domestica,'" in D. Hue (ed.), *Sciences, techniques, et encyclopédies* (Caen, 1993), pp. 310–12. For Pettfach, see Engelhardt et al., "Early Medieval Wells."

the drinker of all appetite. He believed that clear water was pure and likely to make bodies limber, while opaque water was of lesser quality and was likely to congest the body and make its consumers sluggish. A decade or two later, Procopius relates that, at the siege of Urbino during the Gothic wars, when springs grew muddy from overuse, the population despaired. Their surrender was a reaction not to absolute dearth but to intolerable water quality.[83] Dank and verminous water from wells horrified Tuscans at the turn of the tenth century, and "brackish" water appalled tenth-century diplomats during their travels as much as it does modern tourists.[84] Clearly water quality was important to early medieval writers and, presumably, drinkers in Italy.

The roots of the early medieval system for the classification of pure and impure waters extend into antiquity. Rome's imperial writers had enunciated a hierarchy of waters, with the potable sort at the top. The details of the ranking were not settled, but the belief that certain waters were more pure and healthful to ingest than others was radicated firmly. For the senior Pliny no water was better than that drawn up from a well; but Columella observed that spring water was best, well water second, and cistern water least acceptable. According to Macrobius the problems were greatest for those who drank melted snow, for this type of water had lost its health-giving vapor and contained a predominance of solid, earthy elements.[85] The Roman literary tradition therefore allowed water to be drunk if its origins and purity were carefully checked. Though there was divergence about which types exactly, certain types of water, those with the best pedigree, were known to be preferable to others long before the fall of Rome. Like many other things, the waters' reputations survived, transformed, into the Middle Ages. When Lupus of Ferrières confidently asserted that, though water was not his usual drink, he considered cistern water most noisome, his connoisseurship echoed Columella's.

Early medieval people evaluated their water by appearance, feeling,

---

[83] Cassiodorus, *Variarum* 15.3, p. 372 (the point was that populations where air and water are pure are physically and intellectually superior); *Guerra Gotica* I, 2.19, p. 125.

[84] For Tuscan wells, see *Translatio Iuvenalis* 11, p. 982; Liutprand of Cremona, *Relatio* 13, p. 183; 63, p. 211; 65, p. 212. Similar medical opinions on safe water were expressed in the thirteenth century: M.-T. Lorcin, "Humeurs, bains, et tisanes," in *L'eau au moyen âge* (Marseille, 1985), pp. 262–3. Procopius, discussing a near-mutiny of the Byzantine navy in Sicily, reveals that water purity mattered on shipboard, that the sun was considered the agent of water spoilage, and that cool and shady storage was an especially canny innovation in the 500s: *History of the Wars*, ed. H. Dewing (Cambridge, MA, 1916), 3.13.22–4, pp. 124–5.

[85] Pliny, *Naturales Quaestiones*, ed. G. Serbat (Paris, 1972), 31.23, p. 42; Columella, *Res Rustica*, ed. H. Boyd Ash and E. Foster (London, 1941), 1.5.1–2, p. 58; and Macrobius, *Saturnalia* 7.12.25–6, pp. 452–3, who cited Aristotle as his authority. It is significant that a contrary learned opinion (favoring rainwater, hence cisterns) also existed: Y. Tuan, *The Hydrological Cycle and the Wisdom of God* (Toronto, 1968), pp. 58–60.

taste, and smell. Once they had ascertained that it was pure (clear, without odor, and cold), people in postclassical Italy did, in the end, drink water.[86] Willingness to drink water, particularly cool water, was expressed in late antiquity by writers as dissimilar as Paulinus of Nola, Sidonius Apollinaris, and Peter Chrysologus, who all extolled the cup of water.[87] For Paulinus to drink cold water when he was thirsty was the perfect image of satisfaction, and for Sidonius the water of his special spring, so cold that on warm days it clouded with condensation the glass that held it, was unsurpassed delight, while for the sainted bishop of Ravenna the thirsty ought always to be refreshed with this precious liquid. Procopius claimed that Belisarius and his table companions enjoyed drinking water on board ship, though this may have been only because the high quality of their water set them apart from the enlisted men, whose water was rancid. Five hundred years later, around the middle of the tenth century, Liutprand of Cremona wrote with some admiration of the boiled-and-frozen water Byzantine emperors drank, a much-manipulated and hence more cultural than natural substance. Liutprand was probably not aware that this was a specifically imperial affectation, though he did understand it as a mark of refinement: this was the proper lordly way to drink water. For Liutprand, furthermore, nothing conveyed the sense of deep longing better than the human desire for a drink of cold water, a desire not everyone could fulfill.[88]

In spite of such acute awareness of water's qualities and of the willingness to drink it, water was not a popular beverage in early medieval Italy. A search for people lustily drinking water in early medieval Italian sources results, as we have seen, in rather a meager catch. Few of the powerful about whom the sources reveal the most seem to have imbibed water. Even the sermons of St. Peter Chrysologus, when they call on the charitable Christian to offer the cool cup of water freely, could envision only poor people and vulnerable ones like wayfarers drinking it. Other water-bibbers, like the Franks Procopius described, suffered massive reverses on account of their barbarous consumption of the liquid. In Paul the Deacon's *History of the Lombards*, the act of drinking water was clearly out of the ordinary, designed to ward off attempts to poison the drinker, who was expected to drink wine. The elaborate drinking horns often found in Lombard grave sites were vessels designed to hold more luxurious drinks

---

[86] X. de Planhol, *L'eau de neige* (Paris, 1995), provides a long, sometimes stimulating discussion of the Mediterranean zeal for cold drinks, marks of luxury and power.

[87] Sidonius Apollinaris, *Carmina: Epistulae* 2.2.12, p. 426; Peter Chrysologus, *Collectio Sermonum*, ed. A. Olivar (Turnhout, 1982), 41.4, p. 235; 112.1, p. 685; Paulinus of Nola, *Epistulae*, ed. G. de Hartel (Vienna, 1894), 37.1, p. 316.

[88] Procopius, *History of the Wars* 3.13.23, p. 124; Liutprand of Cremona, *Antapodosis* 5.23, p. 144 (a citation of Juvenal), and 2.3, p. 37.

than simple water. Military elites could even be punished for unmartial drunkenness by being condemned to the humiliation of drinking water, as Carolingian capitularies prescribed.[89] Indeed, the manipulations to which Byzantine rulers submitted the harmless liquid were probably supposed to turn water into not-water, to transform a declassé thing into a special one worthy of imperial (and other aristocratic) goblets. Cold water was acceptable, and ordinary room-temperature water was not, because cold water was the product of work and ingenuity, an expression of control over manpower (the people involved in procuring the ice or hurrying the freshly drawn bottle to the place of consumption) and nature. Icy water was unlike normal water and conveyed appropriate messages about the status of its drinkers.

Just as happened in the secular world, so too in the monasteries of late antiquity water was not an appreciated drink. With a rueful literary shrug of the shoulders St. Benedict remarked that monks thought little of water as a drink although it was more suited to their ascetic vocation than was wine. The Master, his model, was less tolerant toward water. Indeed, the Master condemned water drinking and advised monks to stay away from the liquid, liable as it was to excite wild dreams and cause fits.[90] Other Italian monastic legislators stressed that water ought to be drunk with moderation, and only at fixed times.[91] The monks, especially the Master, appear to have thought that water would arouse the senses and stir the ideal *apatheia* of the brethren, just as wine was thought to do in the early times of monachism, before it began its climb to respectability, aided by eucharistic associations, a climb which reached an early summit in the *Rule of St. Benedict*. For the ascetics, whose minimal intake of liquids was much praised, dehydration may have been preferred because it actually promoted listlessness. Perhaps the Master was influenced by late antique

[89] *Guerra Gotica* I, 2.25, p. 166; *HL* 5.2, p. 143. On Germanic drinking vessels, see V. Evison, "Germanic Glass Drinking Horns," *Journal of Glass Studies* 17 (1975), pp. 74–87. A capitulary issued at Boulogne in 811 (*Capitularia Regum Francorum*, in *MGHLegum Sectio II*, vol. I, p. 164), makes water-drinking a punishment for drunkenness (ch. 6). Pliny, *Naturalis Historia* 19.19.55, noted that people ascribe class connotations to water, in itself a neutral liquid, by consuming "improved" or unusual waters for which they have paid.

[90] *Regula Benedicti* 40, p. 580, which does not mention water explicitly; *Regula Magistri* 27, p. 144, "potest et nimia aqua deebriare sensum in phantasiis somniorum et corpus necessitatibus occupare." A rush in the veins, vertigo, sleepiness, cold in the marrow, headaches, and sneezing assail the water drinker.

[91] *Regula S. Pauli et Stephani* 17, p. 954; 21, p. 955; *Regula Eugippii* 22, p. 40. The Master (*Regula Magistri* 27, p. 144) also warns the monk who drinks water between nones and the tenth hour not to drink more than one cup since "quod extra mensuram est, hoc est nimium et inustum." Cassian, instead, thought moderate intake of water was preferable to wine, to control lust by regulating the humors: A. Rousselle, "Abstinence et continence dans le monastères de Gaule méridionale," in *Homage à André Dupont* (Montpellier, 1974), p. 250.

medical notions, which tied the consumption of "wet" substances with the arousal of the senses and consumption of water with the production of sperm.[92]

Some influence from medical sources is very likely for the early seventh-century polymath Isidore of Seville, who listed a host of terrible aftereffects from drinking certain waters.[93] It is slightly less likely for St. Marinus, whose tenth-century *Vita* ascribes to him heroic abilities to drink only a few droplets of water trickling from the roof of his cave. Marinus was simply following the standards other famous ascetics had set.[94] Likewise, for Carolingian monks less familiar with ancient medicine, water was suspect not so much because of its supposed physiological effects (Lupus called it salubrious for soul and body) as for its class associations.

The Master and other writers of rules allowed water to be consumed in moderation as part of a regimen. This mitigated the dangers from water as aphrodisiac and inducer to excess. Along with frugal use, there was another way to render water a more acceptable drink. Water became less fearsome to both clerics and lay people if mixed with other substances.[95] Spiced or otherwise adulterated water was not conceived as an improvement at the bacteriological level, nor were the mixtures a half-hearted attempt to muffle a foul flavor. Rather, ice, wine, parsley seed, or vinegar were added to the water to elevate its status and make it a less low-class drink. Plain water was the drink of commoners, of boors, and of poor folk, and to drink it implied too little separation from them. Improved, altered water, water which had been boiled, or chilled, or came from an extraordinary place, was far better. The elites who populate the narrative sources and who produced them therefore appear in them consuming water to which some cultural process has been applied. Drinking scenes depicted in early medieval sources are not normal moments, but ritual or celebratory ones, where the need to improve the drink socially was felt even more acutely. Hence the Master mixed wine with the scanty water he allowed,

---

[92] On late antique notions of "wet" or "warm" nutrition, see M. Montanari, *Alimentazione e cultura nel medioevo* (Bari, 1988), pp. 66–7, who also traces the rise toward respectability of wine (p. 88). Rousselle, "Abstinence et continence," is very insightful on the alimentary fears of late antique Gaulish monks. See also de Planhol, *L'eau*, pp. 215–23.

[93] Isidore of Seville, *Etymologiarum* 13.13.1–4; similarly Vitruvius, *De Architectura* 8.3.1–28, pp. 11–24. Both authors list abnormal, wondrous water sources.

[94] *Vita S. Marini* 8, p. 69: "parum aquae de petra rupis ad extinguendum sitis ardorem sumebat." Written in the late 900s, this text is akin to much earlier texts in its insistence that its protagonist drank little water; see Gregory the Great, *Dialogi* 3.16, pp. 328, 334, or *Vita S. Apiani*, p. 326.

[95] Wine for communion was thinned with water in the late Carolingian world, something Regino of Prüm explained symbolically and by appeals to sobriety: *De Synodalibus Causis* 1.348, p. 163.

or parsley seed, or vinegar.[96] Hence, too, the drinking done at both southern and northern noble Lombard tables was of wine with water, for mere water was not gentlemanly enough on such occasions.[97] And hence, as we have noted, the proper emperor only drank boiled-and-frozen water. As the affluent societies of the late second millennium increasingly place icy bottled "mineral" water on their tables, it should become easier to understand the need to drink unusual water even among people whose usual water is perfectly potable.

This suggests that the reason usually advanced for the early medieval hesitation before water, the supposed poor quality of the ordinary drinking water available, is invalid.[98] It is not demonstrable either that the water drunk in early medieval communities was in fact polluted and unhealthy (bacteriologically "impure"), that this was anyone's concern, or that the quality of available ordinary water affects the desire to ingest other types of water. No one proposes that the Roman elite had bad water to drink, but still this elite did all it could to avoid consuming simple water in public; on such occasions they preferred water whose temperature had been modified or to which they added honey, salt, fruit, or an assortment of other substances.[99] In sum, the association between the quality of water and appreciation for it is tenuous. Other explanations for early medieval peoples' disdain for water must be found.

The search for "origins" is not always fruitful, but the most plausible explanation for postclassical hostility to water as a beverage is the influence of classical culture. Rather than in any hypothetical lack of purity in the water available, it is in Roman views of water as a dangerous liquid – the characteristic drink of the subaltern classes, the cheapest and most easily available drink, fit for children, slaves, and the women who had been forbidden from drinking wine very early in the Republic – that we find the best explanations for early medieval writers' disregard for water. In other words, early medieval hydrophobia was an inheritance

---

[96] *Regula Magistri* 27, p. 242: salt, cumin, and parsley seed are the additives mentioned. See also Montanari, *Alimentazione e cultura*, pp. 89–90, on later times.

[97] *HL* 5.2, p. 143, and *Chronicon Salernitanum*, ed. U. Westerbergh (Stockholm, 1956), 79, p. 77 – both of which are party scenes where the drinks are likely to have been better than ordinary.

[98] M. Montanari, *L'alimentazione contadina nell'alto medioevo* (Naples, 1979), p. 387; Montanari, *Alimentazione e cultura*, p. 89, expresses a negative view on the quality of the drinking water available to premodern societies (shared by F. Braudel, *Civilisation matérielle et capitalisme (XVe–XVIIIe siècles)* I [Paris, 1967], pp. 168–72).

[99] On Roman mixtures, see A. Gottschalk, *Histoire de l'alimentation* (Paris, 1948), pp. 108, 117; M. Turcan, "L'eau dans l'alimentation et la cuisine à l'époque romaine," in P. Louis (ed.), *L'homme et l'eau en Méditerranée* III (Lyons, 1986), pp. 23–4, lists honey, salt, vinegar, fermented grain or fruit, and wine as the favorite additives for water. On the preference for tepid water, see Malissard, *Les Romains*, pp. 39–41; on cold water, see de Planhol, *L'eau*, pp. 158–62.

from ancient high culture. In the fifth century BC the Hippocratic treatise *On Airs, Waters, Places* had expressed the opinion that the very finest water was undrinkable unless a little wine was added, and this was only the beginning of a classical literary convention.[100] Thus stigmatized, the humble liquid entered the early medieval period, and it is no surprise that the literate people of whom we know most perpetuated the biases of their literate Roman forefathers.

Early medieval monks and hermits may indeed have actually ingested little water, and perhaps no water jugs graced the tables at magnates' feasts. Yet hydrophobia was principally a cultural affectation. It was probably reserved for learned monastic regulators who took the scientific authority of the doctors very seriously, for the pages of literature, and for sumptuous banquets where guests needed impressing. Since early medieval texts hide the humdrum everyday routines, and especially the habits of ordinary people, it is natural enough that water sparkles so seldom in the cups our authors described, or appears only in pre-prandial ablutions.[101] Most of the writers who dismissed simple water probably also drank it regularly. If we knew more about the "low" meals or the drinking patterns of subalterns it might be more difficult to pronounce water an unpopular drink, always mixed with something else.

Thus, even if burdened with social stigma, water was probably an important drink. It was certainly a vital ingredient in cookery and much water was consumed in preparing food in early medieval households. Most cooking operations required water of good quality at some stage (again, "good" for medieval people and "good" enough for cooking, which is not always the same as "good" enough to drink). Boiling, an elaborate cooking technique compared to roasting, which requires fewer utensils and preparation, was the normal cookery style in the early Middle Ages. Virile characters like the emperor Charlemagne did not like boiled food (the model warrior-king preferred roasted meat, probably because the flame touched the flesh directly[102]) and fresh meat was not

[100] Hippocrates, *Airs, Waters, Places*, tr. G. Lloyd, in *Hippocratic Writings* (Harmondsworth, 1978), p. 152, recognized that "water plays a most important part in health," but went on to reckon the quality of water in terms of how much wine needed to be mixed in to make a palatable drink. Highly interesting is Vitruvius' opinion (*De Architectura* 8.3.9, p. 18): "Ita proprietas liquoris cum init in corpus proseminat intinctam sui cuiusque generis qualitatem." On Roman dislike for water as a drink, see Turcan, "L'eau dans l'alimentation," pp. 21–4.

[101] Charitable meals dispensed by early medieval hostels omit water, but probably because it was not worth mentioning rather than because it was absent. Liutprand of Cremona, *Antapodosis* 3.45, p. 97, describes hand washing in basins before formal meals in pornocratic Rome. In monasteries hands and sometimes feet were also washed before meals.

[102] And avoided the humiliation of contact with humble water? Einhard, *Vita Karoli Magni*, ed. G. Pertz, *MGH Scriptores Rerum Germanicarum I. U.S.* (Hanover, 1911), 24, p. 29.

often boiled. But fresh meat was not a staple for subalterns, or even for the Charlemagnes, who did not eat only at banquets. Thus boiling, a water-intensive method of preparing food, was widespread. Porridges and gruels, which began to compete with bread on medieval tables as they were better suited to some medieval grain varieties, also called for water. So did soups, great favorites on postclassical tables, for whose confection water is essential. Likewise, preserved foods such as dried legumes or salted fish or meat became edible only after soaking in water and boiling, the style most adapted to preserved foods.[103] In their progress from the *horti* to the table, fresh fruits and vegetables also had to pass through water, even if not everyone had to clean them perfectly so as to "eat in the cleanliness required by the Law," as did Rabbi Sephatiah of Oria late in the ninth century.[104] Hence early medieval cooking was very water-dependent, both because of the reliance on preserved foods and because of the predilection for boiled dishes.[105] Eating properly was difficult for early medieval households not provided with water, which is why water supply for domestic use was a crucial matter for all, a problem which had to be solved somehow.

In summary, then, cooking and food preparation created an inelastic demand for water of variable but generally high quality, in terms of color and odor, in the domestic setting. Probably more water went into cuisine than was drunk plain by the members of a given household. But cooking and quenching thirst were not the only domestic operations which called for water. Several other frequent and important activities like cleaning clothes and washing dishes (and, as we will see, corporeal washing) required water. Much of the need was satisfied by water obtained within the domestic walls in storage tanks for rain water or in wells. Some water was brought into the house from artificial fountains and aqueducts, or from natural springs and streams. A few household chores were done by "meeting" the water at a point outside the house with the objects to be cleaned or soaked, though this practice had some practical drawbacks, since many operations requiring water were thought to be private, suited to the intimacy of the house, whose walls could protect the household supply. Therefore, as Bishop Aldric of Le Mans in 840, King Liutprand of Pavia a century earlier, and Bishop Liutprand of Cremona a century later all recognized, existence without reliable, comfortable, and pure sources of water for the needs of the domestic group could be very bitter.

103 On boiling, see Turcan, "L'eau dans l'alimentation," pp. 25–7. On soups, see F. Ruf, "Die Suppe in der Geschichte der Ernährung," in I. Bitsch (ed.), *Essen und Trinken im Mittelalter und Neuzeit* (Sigmaringen, 1987), p. 171.
104 *The Chronicle of Ahimaaz*, tr. M. Salzman (New York, 1924), p. 71.
105 Montanari, *Alimentazione e cultura*, pp. 45–7.

2   Water, baths, and corporeal washing

In the first five hundred of the "thousand years without a bath," people invested considerable effort, ingenuity, and resources in securing water supplies for their various bathing complexes. Though this "frivolous" use of water cannot compare to vital functions like irrigation or quenching thirst, still water for bathing was important to early medieval Italians. Naturally enough, it was important in different ways at different times during the early Middle Ages, for the history of water supply is never static, being molded instead by shifts in the outlooks and requirements of users. This chapter delineates some of these differences in a panoramic sketch of the history of bathing, which highlights the gradual move away from large, easily accessible baths, the increasing reliance on private sources of water for an always more private, intimate bath, and the surprising endurance of very Roman notions on the purpose and function of baths in urban societies. As will emerge, the most relevant innovation in bathing customs in postclassical Italy was the gradual separation of the cleansing bath from the recreational bath (both types of bath existed in antiquity, but they went together[1]). Such an innovation had repercussions on how people bathed. As customs of communal bathing lost their allure (this is another theme in the history of early medieval bathing), the patronage of public baths by rulers did too: by the ninth century subsidized baths were rather rare, for rulers did not include provision of public baths among their duties. This development, closely related to the increasing private control of all water resources, links the history of bathing to the general trend toward private water supply in the early medieval peninsula.

The perpetuation of public baths

To the thriving urban world of the Roman Empire at its apogee, the baths and the bath houses had been a fundamental institution. Whether state-

---

[1] The introduction to A. Guillerme, *Le temps de l'eau* (Seyssel, 1983), ably makes this point.

sponsored or privately managed, the bathing complex was an indispensable structure for ambitious provincial towns, and no self-respecting center was without one. The city of Rome, which had some one thousand such establishments, both privately and state-funded, remained an exception, but baths were common in the most peripheral zones, too.[2] The public bath house was a useful, popular, and prestigious focus for the investments of patrons, and even when admission charges were levied it was also a pillar in the social relations of Roman communities.[3] Among all types of public buildings in Roman towns, baths persisted longest as the beneficiaries of patrons' generosity, far outstripping other amenities like theaters, few of which were erected or maintained in Italy after the third century.[4]

Given the reputation for uncleanliness of medieval people, it is well to begin by establishing that baths actually existed in postclassical Italy. Though certainly not on the scale of classical times, baths open to a fairly wide public *did* nonetheless continue to operate. In early medieval cities they played roles similar to ancient baths. Secular builders, restorers, and admirers of baths existed in Lucca in the eighth century and in Tyrrhenian cities like Salerno and Gaeta. Arechis II sponsored elaborate water-supply systems and baths in his capital cities as part of an effort to behave as rulers ought, especially admirable late antique rulers like Theodoric (who so impressed Charlemagne). The *forma mentis* of Gaeta's ambitious dukes (or *hypatoi*, as they styled themselves) likewise called for baths in their "official" residence during the 800s.[5] Thus, south Italian

[2] This is thoroughly researched ground: F. Yegül, *Baths and Bathing in Classical Antiquity* (New York, 1992), pp. 4, 32–3; and his "The Small City Bath in Classical Antiquity," *Archeologia classica* 31 (1979), p. 109; W. Heinz, *Römische Thermen* (Munich, 1983), pp. 142–9; I. Nielsen, *Thermae et Balnea* (Aarhus, 1990); W. MacDonald, *The Architecture of the Roman Empire* II (New Haven, 1986), pp. 111–17, 210–20; M. Corbier, "De Volsinii à Sestinum," *Revue des études latines* 62 (1984), p. 274; O. Robinson, "Baths, an Aspect of Roman Local Government Law," in *Sodalitas: scritti in onore di A. Guarino* (Naples, 1984), pp. 1065–8; J. Zellinger, *Bad und Bäder in der altchristlichen Kirche* (Munich, 1928), p. 4; P. Ariès and G. Duby (eds.), *Histoire de la vie privée* I (Paris, 1985), pp. 193–4; W. Eck, "Die Wasserversorgung in römischen Reich," in *Geschichte der Wasserversorgung* II (Mainz, 1987), pp. 57, 81.

[3] S. Dyson, *Community and Society in Roman Italy* (Baltimore, 1992), p. 174; Eck, "Wasserversorgung," pp. 71–3; Ariès and Duby, *Histoire* I, p. 115; B. Ward-Perkins, *From Classical Antiquity to the Middle Ages* (Oxford, 1984), pp. 4, 41.

[4] See the graph in K. Randsborg, *The First Millennium AD in Europe and the Mediterranean* (Cambridge, 1991), p. 85.

[5] P. Peduto, et al., "Un accesso alla storia di Salerno," *Rassegna storica salernitana* 10 (1988), p. 13 and fig. 1 on Arechis' classicizing; H. Taviani-Carozzi, *La principauté lombarde de Salerne, IXe–XIe siècle* I (Rome, 1991), pp. 31, 221–6, on Justinianic overtones. For Gaeta, see *CDCajetanus* 1, 19:33: "domum cum ipsum balneum et turrem ubi manere visus est." This bath was probably private, and reflects the switch from open baths to private ones in the ninth century. Carolingian residences also often had baths: A. Guillerme, "Puits, aqueducs, et fontaines," in *L'eau au moyen âge* (Marseille, 1985), p. 188.

rulers kept baths as status symbols for themselves and their cities, presumably because of their desirable classical associations as well as their actual pleasantness. Their subjects must also have ascribed value to them, perhaps on account of the baths' link with rulers' legitimacy, but perhaps also because in some instances the baths welcomed all in their warm embrace. The unusual "public bath" in tenth-century Nocera, between Naples and Salerno, might lead to this conclusion, though how it was supported, and by whom, is not clear.[6] In any event, both the postclassical rulers' patronage and some citizens' frequentation of baths mirror, however dimly, the social patterns of bathing in antiquity. In the baths, pragmatism, privilege, and obligation merged.

At Salerno, as in much of southern Italy, as patron of the waters the secular ruler had little competition from the Church, for the episcopacy carried little weight. In consequence the ducal–princely baths at Salerno did not have an episcopal counterpart. But in the rest of Italy bishops were among the most ardent fans of the baths. At Ravenna after the Gothic wars, the bishops, both Arian and orthodox, had furnished bathing facilities and through them acquired glory and gratitude in much the same way Arechis expected to. The episcopal baths of Pavia, a later construction (AD 711 according to the inscription), had provided a rival to the royal baths annexed to the palace. And though it may not come as a surprise to find baths in Rome, *regina aquarum* throughout the early Middle Ages, the efficacity of the famous *diaconiae* – a sort of community center run by the popes in the seventh, eighth, and ninth centuries – in providing baths on Thursdays, among many other services for the citizens, is truly impressive. The baths of Caracalla, most monumental of bathing complexes left by the pagan emperors, were themselves used as a *diaconia*, though not, it seems, for bathing. Of course the popes also had more secluded baths for their own use and for other ecclesiastical officials in the Lateran palace and nearby. As late as the 840s popes restored baths close to Rome's cathedral.[7] There was also the sizable (still enigmatic) tenth- and eleventh-century hypocaust-heated bath

---

[6] *CDC* I, 187:242: *balneum publicum*, attached to a *diaconia*.
[7] On the *diaconia*-baths, see O. Bertolini, "Per la storia delle *diaconiae* romane nell'alto medioevo sino alla fine del secolo VIII," *Archivio della Società romana di storia patria* 70 (1947), pp. 30, 50–2, 115; J. Lestcocquoy, "Administration de Rome et diaconies du VII au IX siècle," *Rivista di archeologia cristiana* 6 (1929), p. 291; R. Krautheimer, *Rome: Profile of a City* (Princeton, 1980), p. 111; E. Cattalini, "Aqua Antoniniana," in *Il trionfo dell'acqua* (Rome, 1986), p. 57 (on Caracalla); B. Ward-Perkins, *From Classical Antiquity*, p. 138, and for the Lateran, p. 146; P. Fevrier, "Permanence et héritages de l'antiquité dans la topographie des villes de l'occident durant le haut moyen âge," *Settimane* 21 (1974), pp. 110–12. L. Saguì, "'Balnea' medievali," in her *L'esedra della Crypta Balbi nel medioevo (XI–XV secolo)* (Florence, 1990), pp. 98–100, provides an overview of bathing in Rome. See also L. Pani Ermini, "'Renovatio murorum' tra programma urbanistico e restauro conservativo," *Settimane* 39 (1992), p. 501. See also *LP* I, 103.37, on papal efforts c. 840.

complex at the foot of the Palatine, whose excavation is providing surprising data to archeologists.[8]

These episcopally sponsored baths, open to a diverse lay and ecclesiastical public, are to be expected in Rome and perhaps even in Naples, for
the clergy was virtually obliged by pastoral duty to provide the under-
privileged in its flock with baths. The same was not true for the lay
patrons who likewise maintained baths for the poor. Such "charitable"
baths were one of the innovations of postclassical Italy which found a surprising diffusion and wide support from laypeople, particularly in the
eighth century. A Lucchese charter of 720 records laymen endowing a
xenodochium with baths for the "welcoming of pilgrims and consolation of
poor people, widows, orphans."[9] Kings Liutprand, Hildeprand, and
Ratchis also worked to widen the ranks of those who had access to collective baths by funding a supply of "soap for the bathing of the poor"; and,
although they delegated the responsibility of actually bathing the poor to
specialists (the bishops of Piacenza), the kings felt they should occupy
themselves with the proper cleansing of subjects whose status, poverty,
and distance from Pavia precluded their admittance to the palace baths of
the capital.[10] Into the ninth century, both secular and ecclesiastical
patrons, in several different combinations, continued to provide baths for
the urban elites and, at least at predetermined moments in the year, for
the subaltern classes.[11] Special cases worth mentioning in this context are
the Jewish population's baths in Apulia in the ninth and tenth centuries.
These structures were presumably maintained by the privileged within
the Jewish communities to facilitate ritual observances. Just like Christian
patrons, Jewish ones kept more or less public baths open.[12] Evidently this
type of patronage was still considered meritorious and was esteemed, in
Christian and Jewish communities, at the end of the first millennium.

The influential men who built and maintained baths open (in varying
degrees) to the public, were driven by their desire to be charitable toward
the poor, and to appear grand to people of high status. But this "supply-
side" explanation for the survival of so many baths in urban Italy in the
postclassical centuries is limited. Baths existed not merely because
patrons wanted to invest in them. There was also a "demand side," and

[8] Saguì, "L'esedra e il complesso dei bagni nel medioevo," in her *L'esedra*, pp. 95–7.
[9] *CDL* I, 24:93–5, for "peregrinis recipiendum, pauperis, viduis, et orphanis consolandum"
with the assurance of the donors "nunquam in ipso balneum invasionem faciendum."
[10] *CDL* III, 18:84: "pensionem illam de sapone . . . ad pauperes lavandum" (much like patterns of Roman patronage of soap for those who could not afford it: Eck,
"Wasserversorgung," pp. 72–6).
[11] And beyond the ninth century: in some sense, the bath Berengar I granted to a hapless
prisoner in Verona (Liutprand of Cremona, *Antapodosis*, ed. J. Becker [Hanover, 1915],
2.63, p. 66) was a "charitable bath" too.
[12] *The Chronicle of Ahimaaz*, tr. M. Salzman (New York, 1924), pp. 75–6.

the weight of the expectation of early medieval people of various social levels that baths be available to them should not be underestimated. If any of the bath-patrons had imagined that their expensive creations might go deserted, unnoticed, they would never have bothered themselves. Collective bathing at central, public places was instead ingrained in the social fabric. Going to the king's, duke's, or even to the bishop's baths was one of the expectations of the elite which supported these leaders, at least into the ninth century. The wise leader did not evade his responsibility to give what was expected of him as long as collective bathing in public remained acceptable, and the bath remained the standard place of gathering and intermingling among peers. The responsibility toward weaker people, whose expectations were far less menacing, was ineluctable too. This was true for Christians living in the expectation of the imminent Last Judgment, mindful of the exalted role the poor played in the celestial hierarchy, and for Jews who strengthened communal solidarity by maintaining baths. Water patronage, then, aimed at furnishing public baths because bathing was a social custom for urban dwellers in Italy, at least until the 800s.

The social world of the baths

Relevant and interesting as it would be to know the bathing customs of the subaltern classes, much more can be learned of the bathing of the privileged classes from early medieval sources, whose aristocratic and ecclesiastical slant is pronounced. The blacksmith imagined on his way to the baths in an account of miracles from tenth-century Naples is quite alone in early medieval literature from Italy.[13] Other bathers are represented as being of exalted status. In literary confections like the *Chronicon Salernitanum* or the *Historia Langobardorum* the bathing of nobles and high officials is in the forefront. For Lombards of high rank baths were an important meeting place, a vehicle of social interaction. Gothic nobles and Byzantinizing clergymen held similar views on the function of bathing complexes.

At Pavia, a Lombard elite of secular officials and warriors could meet at the bath to resolve crucial, sensitive matters, even the succession to the throne. When Aripert wanted to meet his rival, another pretender, he headed for Pavia's baths, probably those attached to the palace, secure in the knowledge that he would meet his foe there.[14] The public baths imposed the one more or less obligatory routine outing; the habit of frequenting them was so much a part of the Pavian nobility's routine that no

[13] *Libellus Miraculorum Sancti Agnelli (sec. X)*, ed. A. Vuolo, in his *Una testimonianza agiografica napoletana* (Naples, 1987), ch. 11, p. 172.   [14] *HL* 6.20, p. 171.

better place existed to be sure of encountering another noble. The same happened at Salerno in the early ninth century, where postulants who needed to see the prince awaited him along his usual route to the baths, as it was almost certain he would pass there.[15] Another tale in the *Chronicon Salernitanum* reveals how the crafty behaved when they wanted to find the duke of Benevento without delay, preferably in a vulnerable position; the devious Rofrit went to the baths.[16] In both the northern and the southern Lombard worlds, noble males went to the baths to meet their peers. The baths were a primary place of social encounter in Lombard life.

But the social encounters were arranged on a strictly segregated basis, at least according to the literary sources. Perhaps the aristocraticizing narratives minimize the amount of inter-class mingling at the baths, but this seems improbable. Though the Saxon princess Adeltruda may well have mingled with lesser women in a *xenodochium* at Lucca during her Roman pilgrimage in the 780s, her case was exceptional.[17] At the baths, sociability was horizontal, and it is consistently peers who are shown together in literary reconstructions of life in the baths.[18] If social segregation is probable, segregation by sex is virtually certain. Almost nowhere are men and women shown bathing together. At the very most members of the opposite sex could wait outside the bath, as did the famous Rosamund in Ravenna, when the time came to poison her erstwhile lover, the executioner of her terrible husband Alboin.[19] Only outside the rigid atmosphere of the cities, in springs and natural pools, was mixed bathing sometimes attempted; but even then the very waters were liable to heat up and froth with rage to repulse the shameless attempt, as Cassiodorus related.[20] Normal baths were separated for men and women, each having a turn and each meeting their equals.

Women could frequent the secular, semi-public baths in several cities.[21] Gothic women bathed collectively in establishments open to those of high

---

[15] *Chronicon Salernitanum*, ed. U. Westerbergh (Stockholm, 1956), 110, p. 123.

[16] *Ibid.* 148, p. 149.

[17] *M&D* V.2, 186:108. W. Moore, *The Saxon Pilgrims to Rome and the Schola Saxonum* (Fribourg, 1937), pp. 70–82, provides context.

[18] E. Merten, *Bäder und Badegepflogenheiten in der Darstellung der Historia Augusta* (Bonn, 1983), p. 130, notes that for Roman emperors to wash trustingly with commoners was meritorious.

[19] *HL* 2.29, p. 89 (he accepted her cup of poison because it was customary to drink after the bath to counter dehydration, I believe). Interestingly, Justinian's *Novels* 22.16.1 (ed. R. Schoell and W. Kroll [Zürich, 1957], p. 157) gave husbands the right to disown wives who bathed in the presence of other men.

[20] Cassiodorus, *Variarum Libri Duodecim*, ed. T. Mommsen (Berlin, 1894), 2.38, p. 68. On mixed bathing, see A. Berger, *Das Bad in der byzantinischen Zeit* (Munich, 1982), p. 42; Zellinger, *Bad und Bäder*, p. 36.

[21] Robinson, "Baths," p. 1076, makes subtle observations on the different bathing needs of Roman women (long hair, menstruation). Medieval sources do not allow investigation of this matter.

social extraction in sixth-century north Italy.[22] The eighth-century *xenodochium*'s bath at Lucca was open to "widows," one of the standard categories of unfortunate people this charitable foundation was intended to help. True enough, there is no evidence of women being admitted to the episcopal baths at Ravenna, nor are there references to women gaining admittance in episcopal baths at Rome and Naples. Yet at Pavia, Paul's *Historia Langobardorum* describes noble women, Lombard and not, bathing together in the later seventh century, apparently in the palace baths, happy to flaunt their undressed limbs before their equals.[23] Furthermore, Arechis had to chastise the effrontery of women who thronged to the baths too prettily attired, thereby arousing lust and causing disorder in his duchy.[24] These too were women of some means.

For all these women the visit to the baths was an unusual moment, one of the times when they could be in the company of their peers while not under the vigilant eye of male relatives and guardians. Even the most mastiff-like of guardians, our sources suggest, did not deprive the family's women of the right to frequent the baths. The baths, with their attendant suspension of some social strictures and simultaneous creation of naked camaraderie, thus acquired importance in the women's routine wherever they were available. (The excursion to the baths had a similar empowering effect for women in northern Greece at the height of the Roman Empire. In an anecdote reflected by an Italian hagiographic source of the ninth century, Apuleius described the adultery of a virtuous woman, made possible by her daily outing to the baths, the only moment in the day when she was at all approachable.[25]) If for the men of the early Middle Ages the bath and the attendant excursion from the domestic space into a public arena was important, it was equally so for women whose more secluded lives offered fewer such opportunities.

Because baths were the meeting place *par excellence* they also became the main site for flaunting one's status and – it follows almost directly – beauty. Baths afforded a fine opportunity to externalize one's importance in public, so whenever possible the Lombard nobles went to the baths with an entourage designed to advertise their power and status. Thus in the early ninth century we find the prince of Salerno on his way back from the baths surrounded by a retinue. In nearby Amalfi in 976, Lupino, the son of

[22] *Guerra Gotica* II, 3.1, p. 218. These rich matrons behaved unlike the poor women described by P. Brown, *The Body and Society* (New York, 1988), p. 316, whose public nakedness was a mark of their poverty; the valence of nudity depended on class. See also Robinson, "Baths," p. 1074.   [23] *HL* 5.37, p. 157.
[24] *Capitula Domini Aregis Principis*, ed. H. Pertz, 12, p. 209.
[25] Apuleius, *Metamorphoses*, ed. D. Robertson (Paris, 1945), 9.17; the *Miraculum S. Anastasii Martyris*, in *Analecta Bollandiana* 11 (1892), p. 236, also shows the promenade to the bath as insidious for virtuous women. On reluctance to let wives go to the baths, see Ariès and Duby, *Histoire* I, p. 439.

the count, also preferred to wash alongside his men in a bath house close to a walnut tree.[26] His behavior was not innovative. In a similar throng the wife of the Gothic king proceeded to the baths around 530. But her retinue was smaller than that of the nobleman Uraia's wife, who had the lack of tact to remark on this loudly, and later tasted the bitter wrath of the king for so public and painful a jolt to his queen's prestige.[27] Though the times and places were dramatically different, such incidents show that a long and splendid peacock tail of followers was the best means of underlining one's social standing at the most public of moments, at the baths. Consciously or not, these aristocrats mimicked late antique Romans, who, as Ammianus noted a bit peevishly, preferred to proceed to the baths with some fifty helpers, just to let everyone know who was who.[28] Such behavior was already offending the conventionally minded in Trimalchio's day, the first century, and was thought to be particularly crass when the powerful indulged in it.[29] But understatement found little place in the public baths, crowded with retinues in antiquity as in the early Middle Ages.

Of course there were other ways to show off status at the baths. The women whom Arechis dryly reprimanded, for instance, took great pains to be flashily elegant and visible on their way to the baths. Uraia's wife went similarly attired, and her poor taste led her to comment on the parsimonious queen's lackluster jewelry, as well as on the meager size of her entourage. Women seized the chance the baths afforded to inform others, even in less than subtle ways, of their wealth. Inside the bath house, the beauty of one's physique was also a measure of one's standing and could procure prestige. Women, and probably men too, had few other occasions to exhibit their undressed (not necessarily naked, though) bodies to their peers.[30] Especially in a society like the Lombard one, which gave much weight to physical appearance, the bath was a precious occasion.[31] Under King Cunimund (688–700), the youthful Theodote had created a stir in Pavia's bath when she unveiled her long hair. She lived among people who appreciated an eye-catching coif (they buried the

---

[26] *Chronicon Salernitanum* 110, p. 123 (but also 89, p. 78). Lupino (*CDC* II, 292:102) retained the right "quando ipsum valneum ab ipsa nuce facere volueritis at lavandum vos et hominis vestros, iterum licentiam haveatis" when he sold it. See also *CDC* IV, 627:157.

[27] *Guerra Gotica* II, 3.1, p. 218.

[28] Ammianus Marcellinus, *Res Gestae*, ed. M. Mariè (Paris, 1984), 28.4.9, vol. V, p. 173.

[29] Merten, *Bäder*, p. 123; Nielsen, *Thermae*, p. 131. See also Clement of Alexandria, *Pedagogue*, ed. E. Mondesert and C. Matray (Paris, 1970), 3.9.47.3, p. 102, for a Christian view.

[30] With the passage of time complete nudity grew rarer; by Carolingian times even at baptism people were clad. (Ariès and Duby, *Histoire* I, p. 439). A similar aversion to nude bathing existed in early modern France: G. Vigarello, *Le propre et le sale* (Paris, 1985), p. 185.

[31] P. Squatriti, "Physiognomics and Personal Appearance in Early Medieval Italy," *Journal of Medieval History* 14 (1988), pp. 191–202.

dead with their combs), so her dramatic unveiling was a conscious gesture. Theodote was using the bath as it was supposed to be used, to enhance her status and display her beauty.[32]

Habits of the bath

For ideological but also aesthetic reasons, the popularity of communal baths survived Rome's demise. Baths furnished an outlet to patrons who needed to propagate their glory, and provided a convenient public arena for various forms of interaction among their frequenters. At the same time the bathing complex had very concrete, down-to-earth ends. Certainly one went to indulge in ostentatious behavior, but one also went to scrub one's limbs, for bodily "cleanliness" was valued, at least in the higher echelons of society. "Bright and delicate limbs," polished hands and face, free of the "impure water" one was liable to be splashed with in Lombard city streets, were marks of distinction. Olfactory advantages of washing were also appreciated.[33] The goals were attained by lathering the body with soap brought to the bath by all bathers who could afford it, or donated to bathers who could not be expected to furnish it themselves.[34] The oils and unguents so fashionable in antiquity do not play a role in the early medieval documents, and seem not to have been employed. An eighth-century gentleman like Aethicus Ister was actually horrified that people should rub oils into their hair. The gradual disappearance of these cosmetics made bathing more austere and more economical.[35] Their dis-

---

[32] For skeptical commentary on this episode, see B. Ward-Perkins, *From Classical Antiquity*, p. 129. For late antique parallels of people showing off their physique, see P. Brown, *Body and Society*, pp. 315–16. Note, though, that *Codex Theodosianus*, ed. T. Mommsen and P. Krueger (Berlin, 1905), 7.1.13, p. 312, prudishly forbade soldiers from bathing nude and offending "the public eyes," presumably those of their comrades.

[33] Ambrosius Auctpert, *Vita Paldonis, Tatonis, et Tasonis*, ed. G. Waitz, *MGHSRL*, p. 549, refers to "delicata ac candida membra" as a sign of distinction. *Leges Aistulfi*, ed. F. Bluhme, 15, p. 201, mentions polluted water being thrown at a wedding party. *Capitula Domini Aregis Principis* 12, p. 209, refers to polished hands and face. *Die Kosmographie des Aethicus*, ed. O. Prinz (Munich, 1993), 2, p. 115, disapproves of stinking bodies.

[34] Lombard kings (*CDL* III, 18:84) and Neapolitan bishops (*Gesta Episcoporum Neapolitanorum*, ed. G. Waitz, *MGHSRL*, p. 418) donated soap. Soap makers were active in Naples (in 599), Ravenna (in 541), Cremona (eighth century), and Pavia (tenth century). See Berger, *Das Bad*, p. 116, and Nielsen, *Thermae*, pp. 142–3, on the need to bring soap. In Roman baths soap could be acquired *in situ*. Unguents were supplied more rarely by benefactors.

[35] Merten, *Bäder*, p. 120, records moral disapproval of these popular effeminacies in the *Historia Augusta*. The feeling that they were decadent may have contributed to their elimination from bathing rituals, though they were known in the 800s in the south: *Chronicon Salernitanum* 65, p. 63. *Die Kosmographie des Aethicus* 2, p. 115 marvels at the "Cannaneos" who "crines nutriunt oleo aut adipe fetore nimium reddentes, spurcissimam vitam ducentes" (they ate moles and mice). However, see *Vita et Regula SS. P. Benedicti, Una cum Expositione Regulae ab Hildemaro Tradita*, ed. R. Mittermüller (Regensburg, 1880), 3, p. 520, for contrary evidence.

appearance also signaled the demise of the patronage of an ephemeral but, to many Roman bathers, essential commodity.

Bathers seem to have washed themselves, unattended by bath-workers or servants. From the sixth century at least, monks had avoided washing others, a danger for their *apatheia*.[36] Their rigor appears to have been contagious and to have permeated the secular world, where people washed themselves, even when they bathed together. Such, at least is the image drawn in the literary accounts of early medieval bathing, like the *Chronicon Salernitanum*.[37] In the ninth century, when the duke of Benevento went to the baths he washed himself, although he was clumsy at it and allowed so much soap into his eyes that he was practically helpless. His shock when, in his blinded state, someone began to rinse his back was great. He could imagine only a conspirator approaching a bather in this way. The Liutprandean tale of how Alberic lost his cool in the Rome of the 920s confirms several of these details. Compelled to pour water in a basin for his mother's ally Hugh, Alberic did so "immoderately and indiscreetly," and received a mortifying slap for bungling the job.[38] His ineptitude may have been genuinely subversive, a response to the request to perform a gendered job, but splashing water on his quasi-father-in-law also indicates Alberic's unfamiliarity with the task. The daughter of Rabbi Sephatiah of Oria, almost a contemporary of Alberic's, was far more adroit at washing men's hands. This was presumably a consequence of her being used to the role. Yet her helping her pious father hardly amounts to communal washing (he washed ritually before praying, at home).[39] Though these literary scenes are exaggerated for effect, taken together they suggest solitary washing techniques were normal. Customs varied over time and context, but the actual washing of the body seems not to have been a social enterprise after 600. Thus, the most expensive luxury in Roman baths, servants to wash and massage the bather, vanished from early medieval bath houses. Whereas in a Roman public bath various patrons absorbed the burden of paying for this amenity for those unable to bring servants from home, in early medieval Italy the individual bather had to care for him- or herself.[40]

Beyond cleansing, baths were understood to have another practical

[36] A. Rousselle, *Porneia* (Paris, 1983), pp. 199–200. Monks washed other monks' hands and feet ritually, as a humble statement of submission, in early medieval monasteries, though they were enjoined to never wash others in everyday circumstances: *Smaragdi Abbatis Expositio in Regulam S. Benedicti*, ed. A. Spannagel and P. Engelbert (Siegburg, 1974), p. 247; *Vita et Regula*, ed. Mittermüller, pp. 519–20.

[37] *Chronicon Salernitanum* 48, p. 149.

[38] Liutprand, *Antapodosis* 3.45, p. 97: "non moderate et pudenter."

[39] *Chronicle of Ahimaaz*, p. 83. Another rabbi overawed a Byzantine visitor with the number of washing basins he owned (p. 91).

[40] On the Roman situation, see Robinson, "Baths," pp. 1068, 1070–3; Eck, "Wasserversorgung," pp. 70–7.

goal, namely the maintenance or reestablishment of health. After the seventh century few writers emphasized this aspect, but baths were normally considered therapeutic until the days of Gregory the Great, who understood virtuous bathing to be bathing "on account of the needs of the body," as opposed to idle bathing for recreation.[41] Paulinus of Nola described people immersed in a pool near St. Felix's great church, hoping to heal themselves.[42] Nor were late antique monks indifferent to the healthful appeal of baths. The *Rule* of Eugippius, in warning the monks never to go to the baths alone, required the most recalcitrant to go obediently if the prior ordered it on account of their infirmities. St. Benedict likewise linked baths with cures, giving the sick monk the right to bathe as often as expedient. Both these Italian rules echo that of the desert father Pachomius, whose work St. Jerome translated into Latin.[43] But the echoes had lost some of the original message's sonority and asperity, for Pachomius required visible illness before he allowed any monk to bathe, while Eugippius and St. Benedict could envision occasional baths for healthy monks, too.

The ties between water, baths, and health were strongest at determined sites. At these special places springs were tapped and bathed in. These waters were reputed to be unlike others and to be particularly salubrious, as they had been in classical times. Their popularity declined after the seventh century, when the view of baths as medicinal also suffered a partial eclipse.[44] Cassiodorus had been one of the last wholehearted admirers of these spring-baths and, during his spell as minister,

[41] On therapeutic bathing in antiquity, see K. Dunbabin, "'Baiarum grata voluptas,'" *PBSR* 57 (1989), pp. 12–14; R. Tölle-Kastenbein, *Antike Wasserkultur* (Munich, 1990), pp. 16–17; P. Aupert, "Les thermes comme lieux de culte," in *Actes de la table ronde organisée par l'Ecole française de Rome, nov. 1988* (Rome, 1991), p. 185 (contradicted in the same volume by J. Scheid, "Sanctuaires et thermes sous l'empire," pp. 208–9); M.-T. Fontanille, "Les bains dans la médicine gréco-romaine," in A. Pelletier (ed.), *La médicine en Gaule* (Paris, 1985), pp. 15–20. In a discussion over appropriate days for bathing (he said any day was acceptable), Gregory the Great separated bathing "pro luxu animi atque voluptate" from that "pro necessitate corporis" (*Registrum Epistularum*, ed. D. Norberg [Tournhout, 1982], 13.1, pp. 991–2). Cassiodorus (*Variarum* 9.6, p. 272) was far more classical: he harmonized the two in a single beneficial experience, as did earlier authors (e.g. Palladius, *Opus Agriculturae*, ed. R. Rodgers [Leipzig, 1975], 1.39.1, p. 45).
[42] Paulinus of Nola, *Epistulae*, ed. G. de Hartel (Vienna, 1894), 32.25, p. 300.
[43] *Regula Eugippii*, ed. A. de Vogüé and F. Villegas (Vienna, 1976), 1.119, pp. 12–13; *Regula Benedicti*, ed. A. de Vogüé (Paris, 1972), 36, p. 570 (see also *Vita et Regula*, ed. Mittermüller, p. 408). Both are inspired by *Praecepta Patris Nostri Pachomii*, in *Pachomiana Latina*, ed. A. Boon (Louvain, 1932), 92–3, p. 39.
[44] On ancient spring-baths, see Berger, *Das Bad*, pp. 72, 78–9; Zellinger, *Bad und Bäder*, pp. 122–6. Isidore of Seville, *Etymologiarum sive Originum Libri XX*, ed. M. Lindsay (Oxford, 1911), 13.13.5–6, lists some of the most salutary spas for bathing. Even savage Goths delighted in Anchialos' thermal waters (Jordanes, *De Origine Actibusque Getarum*, ed. T. Mommsen [Berlin, 1882], 20.109, p. 86) which they knew were "inter reliqua totius mundi thermarum innumerabilium loca omnino praecipua et ad sanitatem infirmorum efficacissima."

Theodoric had funded the restoration of the bathing complex over the springs of "Apona." After the king's death, Cassiodorus praised the spring of Arethusa, an amenable place near Vivarium, and the gout-curing powers of the waters of Bormio. Half a century later, St. Gregory related the story of the bishop of Capua Germanus, whom "the doctors instructed for the health of the body to bathe in the springs called Angulas," where apparently there was a bathing complex; and of a priest near Rome who also took curative baths.[45] Contemporaries like Isidore of Seville reiterated the belief that baths relaxed and cured the depressed, and, though the vogue for such sites had faded by the eighth century, a learned man like Paul the Deacon was still aware of the therapeutic powers once attributed to the waters of Aqui in Piedmont.[46] (More than two centuries later Liutprand struck a similar nostalgic note in describing the bath complex, but knew nothing of the local waters' restorative powers.[47]) The famous visit to the therapeutic baths of Pozzuoli, north of Naples, by Louis II, accompanied by his wife, was remarkable to Montecassino's chroniclers, and appears to have been exceptional.[48] During the postclassical era the links between water, bathing, and cures wore away. They were reforged only later in the Middle Ages.[49]

Whether baths were considered from a practical standpoint as places to clean dirty people and, more rarely, cure ailing ones, or whether they were considered as places of encounter and recreation, the visit to the baths was thought to be a pleasure. The collective bath at Vivarium was recreational, used by the monks to relax their tired bodies;[50] and the Italian monastic rules all imply that monks *liked* to bathe, for the experience was pleasant. The monastic legislators had to remind the brethren not to bathe for idle pleasure, just as the pope had to warn his Roman flock that bathing was good when not undertaken "for the pleasure of the spirit and

---

[45] Cassiodorus, *Variarum* 2.38, p. 69; 8.32, p. 261; 10.29, p. 316; Gregory the Great, *Dialogi*, ed. A. de Vogüé and P. Antin (Paris, 1978–80), 4.42, p. 152; 4.56, p. 184–6.

[46] Isidore, *Etymologiarum* 15.2.40; *HL* 2.16, p. 82 (a literary reminiscence). Like all good Benedictines, Paul could have absorbed from his reading of the *Rule* something of the old notion that baths were intended to cure illness.

[47] Liutprand of Cremona, *Antapodosis* 2.43, p. 56.

[48] *Chronicon Casinense*, ed. G. Pertz, *MGH Scriptores* III (Hanover, 1839), 7, p. 224 (see also *Translatio S. Sosii*, ed. G. Waitz, *MGHSRL*, 29, p. 462). The implication is that they bathed together, and indeed the local baths were notorious places for sexual encounters in antiquity, which the chronicler may have known.

[49] P. Braunstein, "Dal bagno pubblico alla cura corporale privata," *Ricerche storiche* 16 (1986), pp. 525–9; M.-T. Lorcin, "Humeurs, bains, et tisanes," in *L'eau au moyen âge* (Marseille, 1985), pp. 261–73. An example comes from Viterbo: A. Lanconelli, "I mulini di Viterbo (secoli XII–XIV)," in Lanconelli and R. de Palma, *Terra, acque, e lavoro nella Viterbo medievale* (Rome, 1992), p. 5.

[50] Cassiodorus, *Institutiones*, ed. R. Mynors (Oxford, 1961), 1.29, p. 73: "pro aegris corporis." Vigarello, *Le propre*, pp. 32–3, 40, 243, makes acute comments on the function of medieval baths, though he wrongly discounts hygienic functions.

for voluptuousness."[51] Yet manifestly it was just such pleasure which people sought in warm water, from Aachen to Calabria. The point could be driven home from the opposite side too. Whenever there was reason for sadness, people abstained from frequenting the baths. Thus no one went to the baths in seventh-century Ravenna when the city was mourning those killed when a riot erupted between citizens; and thus a Salernitan woman manifested her grief and shame over having been raped by interrupting her routine visits to the baths.[52] In normal circumstances, self-imposed avoidance of the baths was a heroic ascetic measure worthy of asocial holy men, imitators of St. Antony like Epiphanius of Pavia, or the Beneventan monk Taso, active in the central decades of the eighth century.[53] The bath house was the place, and collective bathing the time, of a levity and pleasure unsuited to such grave figures, for whom contact with society had lost its significance.

The bath from collective nudity to domestic solitude

The association of collective bathing with the gratification of the senses may have been one of the reasons for baths' gradual removal from the routine of the Italian urban population. Many pagan moralists saw baths as instruments of social corruption and advocated avoiding them as much as possible.[54] Tacitus, for instance, quickly identified communal bathing as the one aspect of Romanization most damaging to "noble" Briton moral excellence.[55] The Christian clergy, particularly the monks, replaced these voices in late antiquity. They were ambivalent but in general hostile to the custom of collective bathing in public or semi-public baths, for they saw it as spawning disorder and license. Hence, from earliest times, a vein of suspicion toward bathing and bathing complexes ran through the writings of Christian ascetics.[56] Clement of Alexandria's pronouncements on the subject of bathing are exemplary. He condemned the public nudity inevitable in baths, a sure path to sexual

[51] Gregory the Great, *Registrum Epistularum* 13.1, pp. 991–2.
[52] *LPR* 127, pp. 361–2, on Ravenna; *Chronicon Salernitanum* 65, p. 63. The Carolingian monk Gottschalk also refused to bathe (mourning over his captivity?) according to P. Riché, *Daily Life in the World of Charlemagne* (Philadelphia, 1978), p. 167.
[53] Ambrosius Auctpert, *Vita Paldonis, Tatonis, et Tasonis*, p. 553; Ennodius, *Vita Epiphani* 47, in *Opera*, ed. F. Vogel (Berlin, 1885), p. 90.
[54] J. Leclercq and F. Chabrol, "Bains," in *Dictionnaire d'archéologie chrétienne et de liturgie* II (Paris, 1925), pp. 73–4; Zellinger, *Bad und Bäder*, p. 36; Robinson, "Baths," p. 1073.
[55] Tacitus, *Agricola*, ed. E. De Saint-Denis (Paris, 1956), 21.3, p. 18. See also J. Delaine, "Recent Research on Roman Baths," *Journal of Roman Archaeology* 1 (1988), p. 11; Dunbabin, "'Baiarum,'" pp. 24–5.
[56] Incisive on this is Zellinger, *Bad und Bäder*, pp. 47–8; see also Berger, *Das Bad*, pp. 34–40; Leclercq and Chabrol, "Bains," pp. 73, 88–90; Delaine, "Recent Research," p. 22. For the later period, see Vigarello, *Le propre*, p. 43. Nielsen, *Thermae*, pp. 1, 138, 147–8, opines that Christian writers warmly espoused the baths, but overestimates the evidence.

excess, and also claimed that frequentation of such places led to ill-health because overassiduous bathing sapped energies.[57] To Clement and similarly austere men, baths represented one of the most insidious and decadent aspects of pagan society. In the end, the Christian ascetics of the East rejected the baths as pillars of the Roman lifestyle. Men who could abandon *civilitas* to live in tombs or caves in the remotest deserts would feel at best ambiguous toward one of *civilitas'* mainstays, the baths. The ascetic disapproval found its way into the early monastic literature and into Pachomius' regulations for monks.

Yet ascetic opinion was not unanimous even in the East, and St. Basil, for one, did not share this disapproving view.[58] Many other authorities did not resent cleanliness or washing as such, but took a more nuanced view. They objected to immoderate enthusiasm for the pleasures of bathing and especially to the ancillary activities which often surrounded the baths of antiquity: prostitution, theft, and alimentary excess.[59] Western ascetics, who inherited the Eastern traditions, treated the baths with similar circumspect ambivalence. St. Jerome's letters, pivotal documents in the transfusion of desert ideals westward, describe baths in far from flattering terms, and presented toleration of baths as the first step in the dissipation of a Christian maiden's virtue. Not even so dour a saint advocated dirtiness, though. His target was the social life surrounding baths and the bath as frivolous recreation. This tenacious guardian of Christian rectitude himself permitted urban priests to frequent the baths on the grounds that they were steeled against the temptations they would confront there.[60] Thus, Italian clerics of late antiquity absorbed a double attitude toward Roman bathing culture from the classics of Christian literature.

Consequently, the Italian rules for monks did not develop a coherently negative approach to the baths. The more moderate among them allowed the brothers to leave the monasteries to reach the baths. Among the secular clergy a similar double-edged approach prevailed. Italian bishops,

---

[57] Clement, *Pedagogue* 3.5.31.3, p. 70; 3.5.32.1–3, p. 72; 3.9.46.2, p. 102. Clement thought that repeated bathing waterlogged the body.

[58] On Basil, see Berger, *Das Bad*, p. 38. On Byzantine uncertainty about baths, see P. Magdalino, "Church, Bath, and Diakonia in Medieval Constantinople," in R. Morris (ed.), *Byzantine Church and Society* (Birmingham, 1990), pp. 166–72.

[59] On the seedy side of public baths, see *Digest* 47.17.1, p. 789; Clement, *Pedagogue* 3.5.31.2, p. 70; also E. Brödner, *Die römische Thermen und das antike Badewesen* (Darmstadt, 1983), p. 115; Yegül, *Baths*, pp. 41–2; Nielsen, *Thermae*, p. 145. It is interesting to note that the Talmud mirrors the ancient uncertainty on baths' valence: M. Hanoune, "Thermes romains et Talmud," in R. Chevalier (ed.), *Colloque histoire et historiographie: Clio* (Paris, 1980), pp. 256–7.

[60] St. Jerome, *Select Epistles*, ed. F. Wright (London, 1930), 117, 125, pp. 384, 428. For other Western reactions, see Zellinger, *Bad und Bäder*, pp. 68–74. Irish monks, less aware of Roman customs, were not averse to baths: M. Parsons Lillich, "Cleanliness with Godliness," in B. Chauvin (ed.), *Mélanges à la memoire du père A. Dimier* III (Aubois, 1982), p. 125.

for example, were among the earliest patrons of bathing complexes, perhaps as an attempt to create morally unobjectionable baths. Already, in the early 400s, Paulinus of Nola had built "chaste" baths for visitors at Cimitille.[61] What St. Antony or St. Pachomius might have said about the Thursday bath in common, which the popes allocated to the Romans through the *diaconiae*, or of the popes' private Lateran baths, or even of the myriad of monastic bath houses functioning in the eighth and ninth centuries, it is difficult to imagine. But since most overtly ungodly activities seem to have disappeared from early medieval baths, they might not have been too scandalized. For the importance of the recreational component of bathing and the attendant social relations was gradually reduced, and the ascetics had been uncomfortable primarily about these, though they did not approve of "relaxing" the body either.

Although the western Church embraced baths as a tool of charity and allowed them as "a necessity of the body," to quote Gregory the Great, a vigorous undercurrent of hostility toward baths flowed through the early Middle Ages. This residue of hostility was a factor in the transformation of baths and bathing customs in the early medieval period. It mattered when St. Gregory condemned baths taken out of voluptuousness, and suggested that the proper Christian bath was a straightforward one aimed only at washing the limbs. Other types of baths fell under a pall. Monks who went to the baths, even in self-vigilating groups of three, were aware that their act was somehow wicked if its object was not austerely practical and strictly regimented. The persistence of these opinions among clerics is visible even toward the end of the millennium, albeit applied to the new upstanding bathing styles. In a letter datable to 957 Bishop Rather of Verona defended his Saturday bath from venomous assaults by suspicious clerics.[62]

The negative conception of baths held by clergymen and ascetics could spill over to more secular writers as well. Even Justinian's supplement to Roman law codes presumed that illicit sexuality found its safest haven under baths' vaults.[63] In many literary works, from Procopius' *Gothic Wars* to the *Chronicon Salernitanum*, baths crop up in most sinister ways, as places of assassination, or wicked sedition, or illicit seduction.[64]

---

[61] Paulinus of Nola, *Carmina*, ed. G. de Hartel (Vienna, 1894), 28.188, p. 299. Ecclesiastical patronage is covered by B. Ward-Perkins, *From Classical Antiquity*, pp. 131–9.

[62] Rather, *Epistulae*, ed. F. Weigle (Weimar, 1949), 13, p. 68. Rather was then abbot of Alna, near Lobbes. He may have acquired his bath habit while at Verona. The *Capitulare Monasticum* of 817 (*MGH Legum Sectio II*, vol. I, ed. A. Boretius [Hanover, 1883], p. 344) allowed use of the baths only after the prior's consent.

[63] Justinian, *Novels* 22.16.1, p. 157.

[64] For baths and murders, see *HL* 2.29, p. 89; 5.11, p. 150; 6.20, p. 171; Jordanes, *De Origine Actibusque Getarum* 59.306, p. 136; *Guerra Gotica* II, 3.1, p. 218. For baths and sedition, see *Chronicon Salernitanum* 48, p. 49; *LPR*, p. 356 (the evil bishop burns docu-

Whenever a bath is mentioned in an early medieval literary work, something appalling almost automatically takes place. There were excellent social reasons why it might be easier to murder, or seduce, or conspire with someone at the baths, where people were vulnerable, beyond the security of their domestic walls, or at least available. But the bath scenes of early medieval literature end up being genre scenes, veritable *topoi*. Here the victory of the Christian ascetical ideology on baths is visible. Under this stout assault the practice of collective bathing was destined to sputter out. By the full Middle Ages communal baths had an established reputation as fearsome places.[65]

While collective bathing was faltering, other, modified forms of group bathing were becoming established in early medieval Italy. At the same time as collective bath houses waned, monastic baths, in effect semi-collective because they eliminated the presence of people from outside the monastic community but not the habit of bathing in groups, were being disseminated. In the monastic baths "voluptuousness" could be nipped in the bud and supervisors could enforce the use of water for cleansing only. In the sixth century few monasteries enjoyed the lavish endowment of Vivarium, where the monks had their own private bathing complex. At Eugippius' monastery near Naples, for instance, monks left the cloister when they required a bath. Even in the late eighth century nuns left the convent to bathe in Salerno.[66] However, by then the great monastic houses of Italy had caught up with the Joneses of Vivarium, and had begun to build themselves baths within the monastic walls; a parallel trend was at work north of the Alps, for the ideal monastery in the plan of St. Gall had four baths.[67] By the later eighth century the nuns of S. Sophia in Benevento had baths and their sisters at S. Salvatore–S. Giulia in Brescia under Ansilperga

ments in the baths' furnaces). Theophanes, *The Chronicle of Theophanes*, tr. H. Turtledove (Philadelphia, 1982), AM 6289, p. 154, proves that baths were conspiratorial in Byzantium too. (Early on, Diodorus Siculus, *Bibliotheca Historica*, ed. F. Vogel, vol. I [Stuttgart, 1964], 4.79, pp. 522–3, had united the *topoi* of murder and conspiracy in a story about one of Western civilization's ur-figures, Minos.) For baths and seduction, see *HL* 5.37, p. 137; *Miraculum S. Anastasii Martyris*, p. 236. See also Berger, *Das Bad*, p. 39 and, on the dangers of baths in antiquity, Dunbabin, "'Baiarum,'" pp. 35–6.

[65] Vigarello, *Le propre*, pp. 32–3, 39; Braunstein, "Dal bagno pubblico," pp. 523–9.

[66] Cassiodorus, *Institutiones* 1.29, p. 73, who thought baths restful, not cleansing; *Regula Eugippii* 1.119, pp. 12–13; *Capitula Domini Aregis Principis* 12, p. 209. Zellinger, *Bad und Bäder*, p. 69, remarks on Augustine's expectation that nuns would leave the nunnery to bathe.

[67] On St. Gall (which followed Rheims: *Vita Rigoberti* 5, *AS* January 1 [Brussels, 1863], p. 175, proves the canons had baths by 733), see Ariès and Duby, *Histoire de la vie privée* II, p. 54; Riché, *Daily Life*, p. 168; Parsons Lillich, "Cleanliness with Godliness," p. 123; C. Bond, "Water Management in the Rural Monastery," in R. Gilchrist and H. Mynum (eds.), *The Archaeology of Rural Monasteries* (Oxford, 1989), p. 84. S. Paolo outside Rome had a bath about 600, fed by a *noria*, according to an inscription: G. Tomassetti, *La campagna romana antica medioevale e moderna* V (Florence, 1979), pp. 101–2.

seem to have enjoyed this privilege too, thanks to the aqueduct. Farfa had built itself an aqueduct in the 770s, and had baths in the ninth century, so the construction effort is best interpreted as part of a simultaneous bath-building at a monastery whose importance in Carolingian policy was growing after 774.[68] Several other monastic houses, of varying size and splendor, equipped themselves with in-house baths, so that by the tenth century this luxury distinguished regular clerics.[69]

Semi-collective monastic baths were an intermediate step toward private, solo baths. They developed out of the fear of collective and public baths characteristic of monastic literature even in the rules which tolerated them. Like all worldly pleasures their enjoyment had to be limited and controlled as much as possible. At the same time monks and nuns realized that baths provided important hygienic services; not all could be expected to behave like the champions of the deserts of Egypt and Syria, who did not think washing, let alone convivial bathing, of any worth. Bathing was the best way to get "clean" in the early medieval peninsula. The Italian monastic baths succeeded in reaching a compromise. They separated the hygienic from the convivial functions in bathing complexes. Frequenting collective baths was a necessary evil in the early days of monasticism in Italy, when monasteries were simple buildings in urban centers, or even simpler huts thrown up around the dwelling place of a famous hermit like St. Benedict. Monastic bathing complexes were not possible in either of these types of rural environment in the heroic period, when water supply was inadequate for any but the most basic needs (witness Subiaco, or the cave of the hermit Martin, in Gregory's *Dialogues*[70]). In many late antique cities easier solutions had offered themselves, like the collective, public baths. By the eighth century both rich rural monasteries like Farfa, or very rich urban ones like S. Salvatore–S.

---

[68] Admirable excavations at S. Vincenzo al Volturno have not turned up baths though there were water-works (R. Hodges [ed.], *San Vincenzo al Volturno* I [London, 1993], p. 36). Farfa's excavation report (J. McClendon, *The Imperial Abbey of Farfa* [New Haven, 1987]) also does not consider aqueducts or baths, but for Farfa's bath see *Il Chronicon Farfense di Gregorio di Catino*, ed. U. Balzani (Rome, 1903), 1, p. 30, and for the aqueduct *CDL* V, 69–72:241–8. For S. Sophia's, see the charter in Vat. Lat. 4939, 39r, and B. Ward-Perkins, *From Classical Antiquity*, p. 136; for S. Salvatore, see *CDL* II, 151–3:66–72, whose archeology is treated by G. Brogiolo, "Trasformazioni urbanistiche nella Brescia longobarda," in C. Stella and G. Brentenghi (eds.), *S. Giulia di Brescia* (Brescia, 1992), pp. 202–5. On monastic baths, see Zellinger, *Bad und Bäder*, p. 74. Berger, *Das Bad*, p. 61, maintains that they were open to lay dependants in Byzantium.

[69] A Lucchese nunnery was endowed with a bath in 783: *M&D* IV, 92:146. After 808 another nunnery there also had its own bath: *M&D* V.2, 231:136 (789). Salerno's S. Grammatius had had its bath for some time in 1042: *CDC* VI 1000:198–9.

[70] Gregory the Great, *Dialogi* 2.5, p. 154: "ex his autem monasteriis [Subiaco], quae in eodem loco construxerat, tria sursum montis erant, et valde erat fratribus laboriosum semper ad lacum descendere ut aquam haurire debuissent"; and 3.16, p. 334, on Martin's disciples' difficulties.

Giulia could afford and justify the choice to build their own baths because these monasteries were concentrations of population and resources for which the construction of baths and aqueducts made sense.[71] As monasteries grew richer and larger they became centers of water consumption able to impose their needs on the allocation of water in their area, and hence able to build their own sober and chaste baths to satisfy the requirements of austerity. Their inmates no longer needed to go out to bathe.

Monastic baths were a new form of bathing complex, developed in the early medieval epoch. Private domestic baths, on the other hand, were hardly unknown to the Romans. These latter baths, however, gained popularity in Italy after they first crop up in the written record from Ravenna in the sixth and seventh centuries.[72] They are documented for several central Italian cities in the eighth century and for Naples in the 900s, a time when they were numerous in Gaeta and Ravenna, too.[73] The domestic baths in the Ravennan, or Tuscan, or Salernitan charters are the antithesis of the public, collective baths of imperial Rome, though they could be considered as a return to the Republican bathing style. This had been modest, reserved, and strictly domestic; according to Plutarch, Cato the Elder never bathed in the presence of his own son, let alone strangers. Seneca, during his fascinating nostalgic tour of Scipio Africanus' house, took time to ponder the moral excellence of the general's simple bathing style, compared to the decadent luxury of Nero's age. Seneca was mesmerized by the idea of the good old days when people washed only those limbs most exposed to soiling in a small basin of water.[74] Although

---

[71] On monasteries' water needs, see Parsons Lillich, "Cleanliness with Godliness," p. 129; Bond, "Water Management," pp. 83–5; C. Kosch, "Wasserbaueinrichtungen in hochmittelalterliche Konventanlagen Mitteleuropas," in *Geschichte der Wasserversorgung* IV (Mainz, 1991), pp. 89–146.

[72] On the prevalence of small-scale domestic baths in the Pentapolis, see P. Galetti, *Una campagna e la sua città* (Bologna, 1994), p. 70.

[73] For Ravenna, see *Papyri Italiens* II, 44:176; *Breviarium Ecclesiae Ravennatis (Codice Bavaro)*, ed. G. Rabotti (Rome, 1985), 64:31 (c. 700, Rimini); 69:34 (c. 840, Ravenna); 73:36 (c. 800, Rimini). For Naples, see *CDC* I, 146:187 (927); for Rieti, *CDL* V, 52:187 (768); 82:273 (778); for Lucca, *CDL* I, 25:97 (720); for Gaeta, *CDCajetanus* 19:33 (906). At Ravenna numerous *lavelli* were recorded in the tenth century (e.g. "Gli archivi," 227:476 [965]; 405:535 [994]; 407:536 [995]), which were private but may not have been for immersion, just as the *caldaria* of the charters may not have been.

[74] Seneca, *Lettres à Lucilius* III, ed. F. Préchac (Paris, 1957), 86.5, 86.12, pp. 139, 141. On early baths, see Leclercq and Chabrol, "Bains," p. 74, who cites Plutarch; and esp. R. Ginouvès, *Balaneutikè* (Paris, 1962), pp. 101–2, 225–6. Some imperial-period villas had baths (A. McKay, *Houses, Villas, and Palaces in the Roman World* [Ithaca, 1975], pp. 108, 112), and *Codex Theodosianus* 15.2.3, p. 815 (389), makes sparing concessions of water from public aqueducts to them, according to their *dignitas* (one wonders how much *dignitas* Piazza Armerina had). Interestingly, in the 460s Gaul's aristocrats were adding baths to their villas, newly useful as year-round refuges: Sidonius Apollinaris, *Carmina: Epistulae*, ed. W. Anderson (London, 1913), 2.9.8, p. 458.

such baths lost currency in urban centers during the grand period of Rome's hegemony, clearly the plain bathing style of postclassical private baths was no novelty for the peninsula.

Early medieval Italians may have been less extreme in their decency, but many of them matched virtuous Republicans in their desire for privacy during corporeal washing. An interest in private bathing had developed again in late antiquity, alongside a more demure attitude to nudity and being seen in a vulnerable and exposed position at the baths. Whereas in classical times the shared bath hall was the preferred site for cleaning the entire body before other people, late antique bathers began to seek out small chambers for solitary ablutions which did not necessarily involve all the classical phases nor the exposure of all body parts to water. Such shifts are readily comprehensible in a time when young Americans are shyly abandoning communal showering in public places, to the bewilderment of their more easy-going seniors. Changes in perception of the body and the meaning of nakedness affect bathing styles in the 1990s as much as they did at the end of antiquity. In the waning Roman Empire the changed ideology of nudity, and thus of the propriety of ablutions, was a Christian creation.[75] The desire for privacy reflected by the small domestic baths in the houses of the privileged Ravennans and other city folk of the Dark Ages was a response to Christian definitions of decency, adumbrated in the monastic rules.

The privileged Ravennans whose domestic baths the papyri and later charters describe may have derived a certain prestige from bathing in private at home, and not going to the baths and mixing in almost egalitarian nakedness with their peers, just as Antiochene aristocrats of the fourth century had underlined their social superiority by flaunting their perfect bodies at the baths. The comrades of Lupino, an Amalfitan potentate of the tenth century who bathed companionably, had not espoused the private ideology. But their "locker-room" camaraderie, in the final analysis, was not so different in function from the Ravennans' modesty. Like fourth-century Antioch and seventh-century Ravenna, in tenth-century Campania, the bath served to emphasize status although the bathing systems and the ideological value of bathing in public had changed drastically. The Ravennans who could afford domestic baths could afford to be better Christians than others. The Amalfitans who bathed together underlined their tight military bonds. In other words, altered methods of

---

[75] Its emergence has been well chronicled by Rousselle, *Porneia*; P. Brown, *Body and Society*, esp. pp. 315–16. On young Americans' refusal to shower companionably, see D. Johnson, "Students Still Sweat, They Just Don't Shower," *New York Times*, April 22, 1996, p. 1. The recent study of American notions of cleanness (S. Hoy, *Chasing Dirt* [Oxford, 1995]) is deterministic but does show that "clean" has meant different things to different ethnic and gender groups at different times.

bathing in the early Middle Ages left the bath its social significance. Bathing, exactly like its result, bodily "cleanliness," revealed social and ideological allegiances. That, perhaps, is why so many ways of bathing coexisted in early medieval Italy, even though overall the public communal bath lost ground to the private domestic one.

Bathless washing

As this analysis shows, the early Middle Ages were a period of change in bathing customs, as well as continuity from Roman times. Roman-style bathing complexes open to wide segments of the citizenry became fewer, and the custom of frequenting them fell from fashion. Other types of bathing complex were popularized. Personal hygiene need not have suffered from this change; certainly it did not in the perceptions of contemporaries. People without baths to visit, and even some who had them, performed their ablutions in other, to them equally effective, ways. The evolution of bathing habits tended to eliminate public bathing and total immersion in large pools, yet to be "clean" remained important even after communal bathing fell from favor. The *labrum*, or wash basin, in front of many postclassical churches, like the famous pine cone in front of Charlemagne's chapel at Aachen, demonstrates the willingness of people to wash their extremities in public even in the absence of baths. The bath, after all, was only one of many systems to wash the body, and washing operations were carried out in such basins everywhere. The saintly Taso knew that baths were but one way of washing; he distinguished between going to the baths and washing his "head," an operation which he could accomplish without bath houses. The Salernitan princess who had a field basin for her ablutions when she accompanied her husband on voyages, and Bishop Barbatus of Benevento, who scrupulously washed his hands after each mass, like that other southerner, Rabbi Sephatiah, all divided washing from frequenting the baths. Face and hands, the most conspicuous parts of the body, likewise received special attention from Lombard women in eighth-century Salerno. Similarly, tenth-century magnates cared about washing their hands, as Liutprand of Cremona avows. For early medieval people of the most diverse descriptions, the cleansing of face, hands, and feet, whether in public or private places, was distinct from bathing and was equally acceptable.[76]

---

[76] Paulinus of Nola's church at Cimitille had elaborate wash basins, aesthetic and functional: *Carmina* 28.33–6, pp. 292–3; 21.666–7, p. 180. The *labrum* in front of postclassical churches often had an inscription inviting the pious to wash their hands before entering, so that their prayers might be more acceptable: e.g. E. Diehl (ed.), *Inscriptiones Latinae Christianae Veteres* (Berlin, 1924), 1.1514 (Rome), 1.1557 (Blera, near Viterbo), pp. 289, 298. Ambrosius Auctpert, *Vita Paldonis, Tatonis, et Tasonis*, p. 553; *Chronicon*

Monastic rules written in late antique Italy also suggest that much washing was accomplished without bathing. Benedictine abbots were to offer water with which guests could wash their hands upon arrival at the monastery. The abbot was joined by the other brethren when the time came for a (ritualistic and Christ-like, admittedly, rather than functional and hygienic) foot-washing. The *Rule of the Master* obliged the monks whose week-long turn in the kitchen it was to furnish water for the brothers to wash their hands and faces in. At meal times, water was brought in several relays so the monks could wash their hands. Earlier still St. Peter Chrysologus admonished that the first elementary rule of hospitality was to offer the guest water that he might wash his hands.[77]

The monastic arrangements were not, of course, normative beyond the cloister but do reflect the expectations of sixth-century societies. The visible parts of the body (hands, feet, head) ought to be immaculate. Thanks to simple ablutions, a reasonable level of personal cleanliness might be attained even in bathless or bath-poor communities in the Italian peninsula, especially those rural ones where neither population nor economic resources were concentrated enough at any time to make a bathing complex feasible.

As we have seen, baths were a composite pleasure, involving far more than scrubbing down in the interests of personal hygiene. In urban societies like those of Salerno, or Byzantine Ravenna, or Lombard Pavia the baths enjoyed an uncontested role as places for the externalization of wealth, beauty, and status. Nevertheless, after the eighth century, collective baths became rarer, and with them recreational baths. Charles the Great in distant Aachen might still desire delight from bathing with his sons, optimates, hangers-on, and bodyguards, but such delight was shared by fewer and fewer Italians. The ideological blows wrought by Christian thinkers – as much as the economic decline usually indicated as the culprit – contributed to the decline of semi-public, collective baths; but the decline was not a fall before 1000.[78] Other more reserved, less

Salernitanum 76, p. 73; *Vita Barbati*, ed. G. Waitz, in *MGHSRL*, p. 558; *Chronicle of Ahimaaz*, pp. 83, 91. On face and hands, see *Capitula Domini Aregis Principis* 12, p. 209, which is close to Seneca's proper washing (n. 74); *Vita et Regula SS. P. Benedicti*, pp. 519–20. On hands, see *Chronicle of Ahimaaz*, p. 83; Liutprand of Cremona, *Antapodosis* 3.45, p. 97; "Vita Sancti Fridiani," ed. G. Zaccagnini, in *Vita Sancti Fridiani* (Lucca, 1989), 4.7, p. 170.

[77] On monastic ritual, see Kosch, "Wasserbaueinrichtungen," pp. 121–5; *Regula Benedicti* 35, p. 566, and 53, pp. 610–16; *Regula Magistri*, ed. A. de Vogüé (Paris, 1964), 19, 23, pp. 96, 114–16; Peter Chrysologus, *Collectio Sermonum*, ed. A. Olivar (Turnhout, 1975–82), 171.1, p. 1046. See also *Vita S. Hilari* 2, *AS* May 3 (Paris, 1866), p. 474. The passage of manual eating styles (Ariès and Duby, *Histoire* I, p. 428) may have diminished the need for constant hand-washing.

[78] Economic troubles are blamed by Berger, *Das Bad*, p. 34, Nielsen, *Thermae*, pp. 1–2, and B. Ward-Perkins, *From Classical Antiquity*, p. 148.

ostentatious ways of washing prevailed. Megalomaniacal bathing complexes such as graced so many Roman cities no longer existed by 550 or
so. Instead, the rich and powerful, whether in monasteries or in town-
houses, bathed in small complexes, increasingly in seclusion, and increasingly with the purpose of emerging "clean," not "relaxed" or
"rejuvenated." Others, when bishops' support for the "charitable" baths
had dried up, did not even have those, and contented themselves with
simpler ablutions (though we have seen that "public baths" could subsist
in so remote a town as Nocera into the tenth century). Both for the privileged and for the less fortunate in early medieval Italian societies, many of
the customs tied to bathing changed, exactly as the supply of water
directed at supporting these customs changed. But for both categories
much remained unchanged from antiquity, not least the desire to wash
the body. Hence the epithet "the thousand years without a bath" and the
scorn heaped on the filthy Dark Ages by obsessively scrubbed modern
people is misplaced.[79] It is not just that "clean" meant something
different to people in early medieval Italy than it had to their ancestors or
than it has come to mean in modern times. In postclassical Italy baths,
bathing, and water were valued and sought after even if the way of being
"clean" corresponded neither to ancient Rome's nor to the modern
West's.

[79] Pessimism regarding early medieval hygiene is expressed by G. Barni and G. Fasoli,
 L'Italia nell'alto medioevo (Turin, 1971), p. 622; J. Forbes, "Hydraulic Engineering and
 Sanitation," in C. Singer (ed.), *A History of Technology* II (Oxford, 1957), pp. 689–90; A.
 Schiavo, *Acquedotti romani e medioevali* (Naples, 1935), p. 28; N. Smith, *Man and Water*
 (London, 1975), p. 95 (ch. 8 is called "Fifteen Centuries of Neglect"); M.-S. Mazzi,
 Salute e società nel medioevo (Florence, 1978), pp. 21–4; A. Higounet-Nadal, "Hygiène,
 salubrité, pollutions au moyen âge," *Annales de démographie historique* (1975), p. 82; Ariès
 and Duby, *Histoire* I, p. 441. Ironically, this sort of judgment itself has a very varied
 history, for in Parisian medical faculties of the nineteenth century the Middle Ages were
 held up as models of cleanliness and hygiene to students: E. LeRoy Ladurie,
 "Introduction," in J.-P. Goubert, *La conquête de l'eau* (Paris, 1988), p. 12.

3   The wet and the dry: water in agriculture

Although this simple truth is sometimes overlooked, the primary concern of early medieval people, whose societies were agrarian, was the struggle to obtain food from the land. Agriculture was the single most important activity in virtually all European communities, even if how it was practiced varied widely from place to place. Thus, even communities like the Italian ones of the centuries after Rome's collapse, with their wealth of wild, uncultivated foodstuffs and endless resourcefulness at extracting products from uncultivated zones, confronted the problems of water management posed by their agriculture. The serfs on a manor in the Po's plain during the tenth century and urban horticulturalists in the sixth may have lived different lives, but as members of agrarian societies they shared concern for and interest in hydraulics. For throughout the Middle Ages, and indeed long thereafter, all Italian cultivation, planted or sown, annual or perennial, depended on the presence in the soil of the correct amount of water at the appropriate time.

When inclement weather tipped too much water onto the land, or when unseasonable drought sucked the fields and exploited wilderness dry, the prospects for everyone grew grim. In hopes of eluding the calamitous consequences for agrarian communities of too much or too little water, early medieval people developed two strategies. Either they adapted cultivation to the naturally occurring water, or they developed techniques of water control, designed to make it available where and when it was needed. Great landlords, peasants of various sorts, and horticulturalists all strove for a balanced, carefully dosed mixture of earth and water in tune with their ambitions. Flexible settlement and land-use patterns, drainage ditches, and irrigation schemes were the tools of this struggle. Offered here is an overview of the strategies employed to regulate water and soil, set, as much as possible, within the social contexts of the early Middle Ages. This overview discloses a major theme: the emergence of small-scale water-control systems in a peninsula whose states did not dabble much in hydraulics and whose waterways were patrimonialized, increasingly so after the eighth century.

Floods, drainage, marshes, and mentalities

Of the two grave problems, shortage and superabundance of water, the latter left deeper traces in the postclassical historical record. Flooding and its consequences are frequently depicted in the chronicles and other writings of late antique Italy, especially those pertaining to the sixth century. Descriptions of hydrological chaos come from the likes of Cassiodorus, Ennodius, Gregory the Great, and from those passages in the *Historia Langobardarum* which deal with sixth-century events.[1] In these alarmed accounts, the problem of flooding actually appears to have been more acute in the sixth century than it had been earlier or was to be later. Perhaps they exaggerated, investing the climate with moral significance so as to warn their contemporaries of divine displeasure with their actions. But to them the floods of that century were prodigious and unprecedented in scope and frequency.[2]

Frightening floods were, of course, well enough known to the ancient Romans, who uneasily watched the Tiber within their very capital and propitiated it with sacrifices, and dedicated their finest legal minds to the nuances and responsibilities of building barrages against floods.[3] Still, the floods of 589 described by Pope Gregory I and Paul the Deacon have few peers in the earlier literature. Reflecting on the sixth century's hydrolog-

[1] Cassiodorus, *Variarum Libri Duodecim*, ed. T. Mommsen (Berlin, 1894), 2.21 and 2.32, pp. 58, 65, displays disgust for flooded lands and discusses attempts to drain them. Both the *Novels* of Theodosius, 20.3 (*Theodosiani Libri XVI*, v. 2, *Leges Novellae*, ed. T. Mommsen and P. Meyer [Berlin, 1905], p. 47), and *Codex Iustinianeus*, 7.41.3, p. 314, reward marsh drainage, as Cassiodorus did. Ennodius, *Epistulae* 1.6.4–6, and *Carmina* 1.5, both in *Opera*, ed. F. Vogel (Berlin, 1885), pp. 16, 293, vivaciously, indeed a little preciously, describes Po floods. Gregory the Great, *Dialogi*, ed. A. de Vogüé and P. Antin (Paris, 1978–80), 3.10 and 3.18, pp. 291, 346–8, covered the events of 589, and the floods mastered by Bishop Fredianus of Lucca (3.9, p. 289). See also Paulus Diaconus in *HL* 3.23–4, p. 104, and Gregory of Tours (*History of the Franks*, *MGH Scriptores Rerum Merovingicarum* vol. I, ed. W. Arndt and B. Krusch [Hanover, 1884], 10.1, pp. 406–7), who claimed to have consulted an eyewitness. On the famous flood of 589, see A. Castagnetti, "La pianura veronese nel medioevo," in G. Borelli (ed.), *Una città e il suo fiume* (Verona, 1977), pp. 35–45.

[2] P. Alexandre, "Histoire du climat et sources narratives du moyen âge," *Le moyen âge* 80 (1974), p. 112; H. Ingram, "The Use of Documentary Sources for the Study of Past Climates," in T. Wigley et al. (eds.), *Climate and History* (Cambridge, 1981), pp. 184–5, 198, warn against the chroniclers' meteorology. Certainly weather was imbued with moral, theological significance in early medieval Europe. See, for example, P. Dutton, "Thunder and Hail over the Carolingian Countryside," in D. Sweeney (ed.), *Agriculture in the Middle Ages* (Philadelphia, 1995), pp. 111–37. K. Randsborg, *The First Millennium AD in Europe and the Mediterranean* (Cambridge, 1991), pp. 24–8, tackles (and tabulates: see figs. 10 and 12) the written descriptions of weather in late antiquity, but is unsure about the utility of such analysis.

[3] On Tiber floods, see J. Le Gall, *Le Tibre, fleuve de Rome dans l'antiquité* (Paris, 1953), pp. 29–32. On barrage building, see *Digest* 39.3.1.1–23 (Ulpian), and *Codex Iustinianeus*, ed. T. Mommsen (Berlin, 1870), 7.41.1, and 3, pp. 395–6, 314.

ical indiscipline, these writers told tales of the Veronese taking refuge en masse in a church when the Adige burst its banks, and peering out at a solid wall of water which miraculously left them unscathed; of the dogged attempts made by the Luccans to reconstruct the embankments of a local river which constantly inundated the crops in their fields; or of the fixation of entrepreneurs with draining flooded land, reclaiming it, and not paying taxes on it thereafter.

There are ample archeological data to corroborate what the sixth-century narrators described. Of course, there is often evidence of some hydrological instability in early medieval sites, even those dating from after the sixth century, for waterways in premodern times were far less well behaved than they have been forced to become. Thus, to give an example, tenth-century Taranto witnessed the filling by sedimentation of the inland lagoon alongside the city, but no chronicler recorded this change with horror.[4] Nevertheless, a remarkable number of archeological sites, especially but not exclusively in the Lombard plain, show traces of potent flooding at sixth- and seventh-century levels. In several instances the waters' exuberance caused settlements to be abandoned after centuries of steady occupation, though in others human tenacity overcame the problems of unregulated stream and river flow.[5] This seems to confirm the chroniclers' soggy image of the period when antiquity ended. But although archeological research echoes what the medieval literary record suggested, neither source has yet persuasively explained the causes for the increased incidence of flooding in the postclassical peninsula.

Using both literary accounts and archeological evidence drawn from the most disparate corners of the Mediterranean region, Vita-Finzi proposed that the collapse of the Roman order was connected to short-term changes in weather patterns. According to Vita-Finzi, beginning in the fourth century the new climatic pattern caused massive downpours, topsoil erosion in agricultural areas, deposition in river valleys, and flooding everywhere.[6] This theory has been much criticized and, indeed,

---

[4] "Schede 1993–4," AM 21 (1994), p. 453.
[5] Evidence of unusually grave hydrological disarray from late antiquity can be found in "Schede 1991," AM 19 (1992), on Genoa's steep hillsides (p. 590), at Martinoscuro near Teramo (pp. 594–5), and at San Benedetto Po near Mantua (p. 602). Violent and extensive flooding was also visited upon downtown Modena (S. Gelichi, "Le città dell'Emilia-Romagna tra tardoantico e alto medioevo," in La storia dell'alto medioevo italiano (VI–X s.) alla luce dell'archeologia [Florence, 1994], p. 592); and a station on the road from Pavia to Turin (M. Negro Ponzi Mancini, "L'insediamento fortificato altomedievale di S. Michele a Trino," in E. Herring et al. [eds.], Papers of the Fourth Conference of Italian Archaeology [London, 1992], pp. 195–8, 204). An excellent analysis of hydrological history (M. Cremaschi and A. Marchesini, "L'evoluzione di un tratto di pianura padana (provincie di Reggio e Parma)," AM 5 [1978], pp. 542–62) demonstrates that the area between the rivers Taro and Reggio was periodically flooded throughout the early Middle Ages.
[6] C. Vita-Finzi, The Mediterranean Valleys (Cambridge, 1969), esp. pp. 113–14.

there is little evidence that the ecological processes outlined by Vita-Finzi were at work in many areas where the Roman order collapsed as it did in Italy, or that climatic shifts are ever so deterministically related to historical "events" like Rome's decline and fall.[7] However, the exceptional hydraulic disorders in sixth-century Italy indicate that the early Roman stabilization of the waters, the deforestation of hillsides, and heavy agricultural use of the fertile land had shattered some equilibria and had replaced them with new patterns whose maintenance proved too difficult even for the late Roman state.[8] The colossal floods which washed over the banks of so many water courses of the Po valley and other regions, and which had created large marshes there by the eighth century, indicate that the problem of flooding had reached a breaking point in the 500s, although trouble had been brewing for some time before, engendered by Roman economic development.

For the portentous floods of late antiquity were not purely natural phenomena. They were certainly affected by human activity (or the lack of it) to a far greater degree than Vita-Finzi postulated. Especially in the late antique and early medieval Po basin, hydraulic difficulties greater than normal were confronted by governments that were weaker and populations that were smaller than those which had existed earlier. Though clearly there was no Wittfogelian "hydraulic society" in the Po valley, the strong, centralized, authoritarian state which could best maintain the water-control systems that undergirded the agriculture of the lowlands crumbled, together with the communities dependent on such agriculture.[9] The Gothic kings of the late 400s and early 500s were perhaps the last rulers until the emergence of the *comuni* with the authority, population, and resources to control the water systems of the Po valley. The Goths' successors did not attempt to control the floods of the Po and its tributaries. Certainly no Lombard king or Byzantine exarch had at his

---

[7] For sound criticism, see K. Butzer, "Accelerated Soil Erosion," in I. Manners (ed.), *Perspectives on Environment* (Washington, DC, 1974), pp. 67–8. Fine summaries of the question can be found in T. Potter, *The Changing Landscape of South Etruria* (New York, 1979), pp. 25–7; C. Delano Smith, *Western Mediterranean Europe* (London, 1979), pp. 275–320; Randsborg, *First Millennium*, p. 29; and J. Bintliff, "Erosion in Mediterranean Lands," in M. Bell and J. Boardman (eds.), *Past and Present Soil Erosion* (Oxford, 1992), pp. 125–31. A major reason for skepticism about Vita-Finzi's "younger fill" theory is that climatologists do not see the period as mutable or unstable: M. Pinna, "Il clima nell'alto medioevo," *Settimane* 37 (1990), pp. 435–40.

[8] See A. Giardina, "Allevamento ed economia della selva in Italia meridionale," in *Società romana e produzione schiavistica* I (Bari, 1981), pp. 108–9, on Roman land-use and floods.

[9] Actually, some of the ancient dikes were built by collectivities without state supervision: R. Thomas and A. Wilson, "Water Supply for Roman Farms in Latium and South Etruria," *PBSR* 64 (1994), pp. 190–1. P. Leveau, "Mentalité économique et grands travaux hydrauliques," *Annales ESC* 48 (1993), pp. 3–16, offers good treatment of the Roman state's involvement in drainage.

disposal the financial and technical means to govern the great water retention and diversion systems of the Po basin under assault by natural decrepitude and the accumulation of silt.

However, technological poverty and incapacity to marshal manpower need not have been the only restraint on postclassical rulers. After all, early medieval communities had the technologies and organization to carry out monumental flood-control projects when they were deemed necessary, for example in Frisia.[10] After the Goths, Italian rulers seldom attempted to control flooding in the Po region not merely because they lacked the wherewithal to accomplish this task, but for several other reasons as well. In the first place, no one ruler held sway over the entire region and, in this sense, the political fragmentation of Italy had hydraulic effects. Any efforts made to dominate the waters at one end of the valley would have been nullified by the lack of effort at other points of the hydraulic network which were outside their jurisdiction. Vast projects involving waterworks require the ability to exact cooperation throughout the extension of the hydrological system whose interconnectedness is unavoidable. Disorder on any segment of the Po basin was thus contagious. In concrete terms, the exarch of Ravenna had no interest in building or maintaining dikes, walls, runoff canals, and so on at the eastern end of the Po if no such works existed upstream in the Lombard territory, for his efforts would be in vain because of the lack of similar works upstream. A state divided into rebellious duchies and semi-autonomous marches like the Lombard one before Liutprand was unsuited to large-scale water-control systems, and this contributed to the disorderly flow of the early medieval Po.[11]

Also relevant may have been the early medieval tendency to view water as an exploitable resource, a privately ownable element which often fell outside the ruler's jurisdiction. Massive drainage works and sophisticated embankments had been under the jurisdiction of the Roman emperors because the Roman state undertook to guarantee the common use of "public" waters, which meant perennially flowing ones. Lombard and later Italian kings did not share this sentiment, and this may have influenced them when they decided not to intervene to control the rivers'

---

[10] W. TeBrake, *The Medieval Frontier* (College Station, TX, 1986), pp. 12–22, 211–21. Byzantine and Western rulers were perfectly able to deploy huge numbers of workers on hydraulic projects in the eighth century: *The Chronicle of Theophanes*, tr. H. Turtledove (Philadelphia, 1982), AM 6258, p. 128; *Annales Qui Dicuntur Einhardi*, ed. F. Kurze (Hanover, 1895), AD 793, pp. 93–5.

[11] The big canals at Heraclea, the Byzantine city settled in the northern Po delta around 640, indicate that some "old-fashioned" hydraulic works *were* carried out even in the darkest ages: P. Tozzi and M. Harari, *Eraclea Veneta* (Parma, 1984), pp. 90–102. The purpose of the canals the Lombard kings built at Cittanova is unclear, though the effort expended was considerable: "Schede 1985," *AM* 13 (1986), p. 476.

rampages. Kings of Italy, and southern rulers too, considered the aqueous fisc which they inherited from their Roman predecessors their personal property. It existed to provide revenue, exactly as terrestrial fiscal possessions did. Hence they meticulously taxed and took tolls from those who moved goods on "their" rivers, and even legislated to foster the profitable movements of traders along water courses (many of the ninth- and tenth-century mercantile privileges about which we know originated in Lombard concessions of the eighth). Throughout, these rulers conceived the waters as property to be managed for their own immediate benefit. Therefore they alienated it to their protégés and allies, especially in the late Carolingian period. For them what mattered was obtaining political or economic advantage from possession of their water courses. The rivers were not a public good, a responsibility of the ruler, something whose orderly flow he should monitor for the benefit of the ruled.[12]

Thus hydrological "disorder" in the early medieval Po lowlands, but also elsewhere, and the attendant flooding, was caused by a coalescing of three factors. To begin with, there seems to have been an objectively more difficult ecological situation, more flooding, deposition, and erosion than previously, especially during the sixth century. Secondly, the Po valley, whose waterworks were Italy's most imposing, was dominated by many

[12] On the north, see G.-P. Bognetti, "La navigazione padana e il sopravvivere della civiltà antica," in his *L'età longobarda* IV (Milan, 1968), pp. 541–53; G. Fasoli, "Navigazione fluviale," *Settimane* 25 (1978), pp. 565–6, 595–7; P. Racine, "Poteri medievali e percorsi fluviali nell'Italia padana," *Quaderni storici* 61 (1986), pp. 9–32. For Liutprand, *antiqua consuetudo* dictated terms with Comacchio (L.-M. Hartmann, *Zur Wirtschaftsgeschichte Italiens im frühen Mittelalter* [Gotha, 1904], pp. 123–4; and in the same volume his "Comacchio und das Po-Handel," pp. 74–90), as it did for Charlemagne (*Urkunden der Karolinger* I, 132:182). Some examples of royal alienation of watery resources: in 744 Hildeprand gave the old *lectum Padi* to the bishop of Piacenza (*CDL* III, 18:84). Around 772 Desiderius gave privileges to Farfa (*CDL* III, 43:251). Lothar (*Urkunden der Karolinger* III, 1:51–2 [822], a particularly wide-ranging grant; 22:93 [834]), Louis II (*Urkunden der Karolinger* IV, 1:68 [851]), and Berengar I (*Diplomi di Berengario*, ed. L. Schiaparelli [Rome, 1903], 51:148 [904]; 118:310 [918]; 67:182 [908]) all gave waterways to churches very generously. Yet the tenth-century *Honorantie Civitatis Papie*, ed. C.-R. Brühl and C. Violante (Cologne, 1983), lines 94–110, 118–24, pp. 20–2, still ascribes rights over the rivers to kings. On the south, see R. Poupardin, *Les institutions politiques et administratives des principautés lombardes de l'Italie méridionale* (Paris, 1907), p. 16 (drawing on such sources as *Sicardi Principis Pactio cum Neapolitanis*, ed. F. Bluhme [Hanover, 1869], 5 and 12 [of 836], pp. 219, 220). It may be significant that the return of state intervention on the region's hydrology by the *comuni*, in the eleventh and twelfth centuries, coincided with the return to vogue of Roman legal structures: D. Balestracci, "La politica delle acque urbane nell'Italia comunale," *MEFR. Moyen âge* 104 (1992), pp. 431–79, provides a useful summary. On the *comuni* and Roman law, see E. Besta, "Fonti," in F. Del Giudice (ed.), *Storia del diritto italiano* I (Milan, 1923), pp. 378–410. For examples of *comuni* tackling hydrological problems: C. Dussaix, "Les moulins à Reggio d'Emilie aux XIIe et XIIIe siècles," *MEFR* 91 (1979), pp. 117–19; F. Menant, *Campagnes lombardes du moyen âge* (Rome, 1993), pp. 174–83. There appears to be a link between management of fluvial "disorder" in Italy, generally by the state, and prevalence of Roman legal conceptions of public jurisdiction over the waters.

different powers after 568, and these powers were unable to impose disciplined upkeep of waterworks throughout the region. Lastly, the most important power, the Lombard kingdom and its successors, seems not to have included water and hence its management as part of the public domain. This attitude extended its sway with the demise of Byzantine power in the north.

After the sixth century, accounts of disastrous floods wane, and flooding itself may also have decreased, though we should assume that it did not cease altogether.[13] The reasons for the decline of flooding and especially of literary concern for the superabundance of water are interesting, for they open another dimension to the history of Italy's early medieval waterscapes. In environmental historiography the relations between human economic activities (defined very broadly) with a given ecosystem and the prevailing ideologies, particularly those concerning nature, are often singled out for investigation.[14] An analysis of early medieval flooding in Italy fits admirably in this scheme. In wondering why late antique writers were more worried, in general, about disordered hydrologies than early medieval ones, we should seek answers in which economic and ideological factors converge.

Flooding and the formation of wetlands did not preoccupy the writers of the eighth and later centuries for several reasons. A first part of the explanation for the retreat of flooding from the writers' accounts is that flooding was more easily confronted in the depopulated Italy of the early Middle Ages. At that time, land and space existed in great quantities, which allowed early medieval people some maneuverability: often enough in the Lombard plain of the Dark Ages, settlements and agriculture fell back toward safer ground, away from those areas most liable to inundation.[15] This retrenchment had the advantage of allowing river banks and flood plains to revert to their marshy condition, to the natural ambiguity of water and earth. Along the waterways of early medieval Italy, between the seventh century and the clearances around the turn of the first millennium, streams, especially those with susceptible geology

[13] R. Hoffmann's idyllic picture of cool, clear, regular stream flow in early medieval Europe ("Economic Development and Aquatic Ecosystems in Medieval Europe," *American Historical Review* 101 [1996], esp. 633), is not fully applicable to Italy.

[14] D. Worster, "Doing Environmental History," in Worster (ed.), *The Ends of the Earth* (Cambridge, 1988), pp. 289–307. D. Cosgrove, *Social Formation and Symbolic Landscape* (Totowa, NJ, 1984), pp. 13–38, also analyzes the relationship between environmental perception and material or social realities.

[15] V. Fumagalli, "Note per una storia agraria altomedievale," *Studi medievali* 9 (1968), p. 370; his *La pietra viva* (Bologna, 1988), p. 55; and his "Colonizzazione e bonifica nell'Emilia durante il medioevo," in *I 70 anni del consorzio della bonifica renana* (Bologna, 1980), p. 27. I. Di Resta, *Capua medioevale* (Naples, 1983), pp. 49–52, instead discusses the shift of Capua to the banks of the Volturno during the Dark Ages in strategic terms.

(impermeable substrata), became a strip of marsh. Along the banks of such rivers as the Po and its main tributaries, swamps became an ecological buffer capable of absorbing the rivers' rage during rains or snowmelts without causing huge damage to human cultivation, which kept a respectful distance.[16]

One consequence of this new demographic and settlement pattern was that the most horrifying literary descriptions of floods and attendant hydrological upheavals do not derive from writers of the Dark Ages. Instead, as we have seen, they come from fifth- and sixth-century pens. In that time people were numerous enough, and enough bound by Roman agricultural traditions, to seek to resist floods. Their writers reflected this, recounting floods with dismay. Such portraits are rooted in a consciousness which assumed land was scarce and was generally worth defending and rehabilitating for agriculture. The literary culture connected to this mentality actually outlived the social and economic conditions which gave it birth, so educated and classicizing men like Paul the Deacon, writing in the late 700s, still depicted river floods as unmitigated catastrophes.[17]

While the abandonment of farming on marginal farmlands most subject to flooding was certainly one strategy which postclassical people embraced to cope with overwhelming problems of water management, it was not the only one. Unchecked, during the early Middle Ages seasonal and exceptional flooding formed wetlands in places removed from river banks. Such swamps were not a total novelty, of course: the Romans had had to cope with the intractable Pontine marshes, after all. Yet while most Roman agricultural landscapes separated themselves from the wild marshes as gingerly as possible, in the postclassical period an anarchy of small swamps was comfortably interspersed in the cultivated fields. The

---

[16] Fumagalli, "Note per una storia," pp. 369–76; his *La pietra viva*, pp. 53–60; and his "Colonizzazione e bonifica," pp. 27, 34–5. Cremaschi and Marchesini, "L'evoluzione," pp. 561–2, maintain that geology was the prime determinant in marsh formation. The hydrological functions of riverine marshes are treated by D. Cosgrove, "An Elemental Division: Water Control and Engineered Landscapes," in D. Cosgrove and G. Petts (eds.), *Water, Engineering, and Landscape* (London, 1990), pp. 3–5; G. Petts, "Forested River Corridors," pp. 12–17, 22–4, in the same volume. Malaria, evidently, had nothing to do with early medieval wariness of settling very close to rivers. As far as can be determined, the early Middle Ages were a time of dormant malaria: M. Grmek, *Les maladies à l'aube de la civilisation occidentale* (Paris, 1983), pp. 390–402. For a case-study of a region later highly malarious, see J.-M. Martin, *La Pouille du VIe au XIIe siècle* (Rome, 1993), pp. 106–8.

[17] *HL* 4.45, p. 135 (c. 650); 5.15, pp. 150–1 (c. 670); 6.36, p. 177 (c. 720), describes floods of the Po and Tiber. Paul the Deacon's poem on Lake Como (*Die Gedichte des Paulus Diaconus*, ed. K. Neff [Munich, 1908], pp. 4–6) shows that floods were feared in the late 700s too (as in the Roman *LP* 1.512–13). On the failure to record floods after 600, Fumagalli, *La pietra viva*, p. 58, exaggerates a bit.

quiet assimilation of very different sorts of marshes (the Ravennan deltaic ones where salt and fresh water mingled, or those in the valley bottom along the Sele near Salerno, or the big wetland area, enclosed by mountains, in the southern Lucchesia, are examples), throughout the Italian agricultural landscape, is a sign of economic as well as cultural adaptability.

Early medieval cultivators, and even landowners, made more intensive use of the wetlands and their erratic wealth of resources than their predecessors had. From marshes fish, waterfowl, wood, twine, reeds, and pasture, as well as numerous mammals, could be and were obtained. Mindful of such bounty, landowners, as well as cultivators, adopted them as economically viable ecosystems.[18] To do this, they developed a more tolerant mentality than had been possible for Roman landlords and their governments. This outlook in effect normalized the wetlands. Hence, while riverine marshes were reassuming their ancient role as giant storm drains, early medieval people assigned to them more prominent economic roles than they had had for centuries. They were now assets to be husbanded rather than blights to be removed and deprecated. The study of place names suggests that this shift was not related to Germanic culture, for the Lombards were indifferent to marshes, or at least to their charms as places of settlement. Nor is there anything in the nature of Christian cosmologies that might have led to stronger affinities for over-watered land. Yet it was over the course of the sixth and seventh centuries, when Christianity triumphed and the barbarian settlements took root,

---

[18] Examples of early medieval marsh exploitation for wood and reeds can be found in: *I diplomi di Berengario* 67:182 (908); *I placiti del "Regnum Italiae"* 1, ed. C. Manaresi (Rome, 1955–60), 36:111 (824). For hunting, see *CDLangobardiae* 278:468 (878); *Monumenti* I, 43:168 (965). For fishing, see *Monumenti* I, 68:220 (992); Vat. Lat. 4939, 52v (834, near Benevento). For pasture, see *I placiti* 30:93 (818); *CDL* II, 162:104 (762). There are scores of instances of marshland whose use is not specified exchanged on equal footing with other types of productive land like vineyards or arable: *CDL* II, 137:32 (759); III, 11:48 (714); *Museo* 21 (774); *CDC* I, 47:58 (856), *salectis* sold near Salerno; *Papyri Italiens* II, 30:58 (536) and 31:66 (about 540), *salectis* sold near Ravenna; 34:98 (551), *paludis* sold there; *Breviarium Ecclesiae Ravennatis (Codice Bavaro)*, ed. G. Rabotti (Rome, 1985), 31:19 (724–48), *salecto* near Rimini sold; *Urkunden der Karolinger* I, 113:159 (776), *paludibus* donated near Modena; *CDL* I, 124:368 (757), *paludibus* near Pisa; *CDL* II, 129:12 (758), "salictis atque terra vacua"; 137:31 (759); 155:81 (761); 236:301 (769), *paludibus* sold and donated near Alfiano; 162:104 (761), *paludibus* near Motta donated; 203:208 (767), *paludibus* near Pistoia donated; 217:248 (768), *paludibus* near Viterbo exchanged; 236:301 (769), *palude* near Pisa exchanged; *CDL* V, 30:115 (761), *paludes* donated near Farfa; 55:196 (777); 58:207 (772), *paludes* donated near Rieti; XI:376 (772), *paludes* near Benevento; *Urkunden der Karolinger* III, 41:129 (840), *paludibus* near Vercelli; *Chronicon Vulturnense* I, ed. V. Federici (Rome, 1925), 29:235 (819). Solid treatment of the economic significance of marshes in Piacenza's post-classical hinterland is in P. Galetti, *Una campagna e la sua città* (Bologna, 1994), pp. 120–8.

that the surviving documents begin to show people who owned marshes, rented them, and otherwise exploited their irregular productivity.[19] This, it should be noted, was a shift in emphasis more than a revolution in sensibilities. Roman Italy had known its marshes, and despite the state-funded drainage projects and the suspicion of the agronomists, rural folk had lived companionably enough with them.[20] But in the wake of the Western Empire's dissolution arable agriculture lost the primacy it had long enjoyed and the watery wilderness gained importance in food and other essentials' production, as did the *incolto* generally. Early medieval wetlands were both more extensive on account of shifts in ecological equilibria and state hesitation to interfere with them, *and* more economically relevant than earlier (and later) ones. Although Roman and late medieval farmers, for whom grain production was paramount, also understood how useful overwatered lands could be, in the early medieval period new energies were directed at them. Not just peasants seeking subsistence, but also landlords and magnates, perceived the value of the peninsula's wetlands. All responded to new economic realities and modified their outlooks and expectations.

To sum up, the use of overwatered lands and thinking about them interacted during the postclassical centuries. A series of interrelated factors accounts for the progressive effacement of disastrous flooding in narratives after about 600. Drier weather after the seventh century and resurgent riverine marshes to absorb exuberant waters were important ecological facts. The decline in population levels and the greater availability of land in areas unafflicted by floods were likewise relevant. Moreover, after about 600 floods were less marvelous to chroniclers. Their world had both drawn back from the most floodable areas, as a snail tapped on its horns withdraws to the security of its shell, and had, at the same time, come to terms with the ambiguous zones where water mixed with land, now more conspicuous than they had been in the tidy agrarian spaces of

---

[19] For Lombard settlement and marshes, see G. Fasoli, "Inizio di un'indagine su gli stanziamenti longobardi intorno a Pavia," *Bollettino della società pavese di storia patria* 5 (1953), p. 11. On the marshophile mentality of late antiquity, see G. Traina, "Paesaggio e 'decadenza,'" in A. Giardina (ed.), *Società romana e impero tardoantico* III (Bari, 1986), pp. 713–14, 724–7. The idyll did not last forever: Nonantola attacked the Ostiglia wetlands in the 900s (V. Fumagalli, "Note sui disboscamenti nella pianura padana in epoca carolingia," *Rivista di storia dell'agricoltura* 7 [1967], pp. 140–1; and Fumagalli, "Uomo e ambiente," in his *L'uomo e l'ambiente nel medioevo* [Bari, 1992], pp. 7–12, on north Italian clearances in general). For a comparative perspective on how environmental change can accompany the redefinition of "acceptable" landscapes, see E. Melville, *A Plague of Sheep* (Cambridge, 1993), pp. 99–100, 113–14.
[20] N. Purcell, "Rome and the Management of Water," in G. Shipley and J. Salmon (eds.), *Human Landscapes in Classical Antiquity* (London, 1996), pp. 180–9, 195–6, describes Roman ambivalence to swamps. See also Leveau, "Mentalité économique," pp. 6–14.

Roman Italy, and endowed with economic prominence. For early medieval cultivators made a virtue of necessity; they frequented and used wetlands, and soon landowners too found them no less acceptable than vineyards or wheat fields. Perhaps their more flexible outlook and the willingness to place marshes and overwatered lands at the center of their land-use practice also meant that they were neither frightening nor engrossing topics to write about; almost certainly this mentality is related to the fact that the narrators rarely record them after the seventh century. This is a case, in other words, where literate culture was informed by a mentality of the illiterate, whose economic wisdom incorporated wetlands in the humanized landscape.[21]

Drainage

The new distribution of water in Italy's landscapes and the acceptance of these ecosystems' usefulness to those who knew their idiosyncrasies did not end all interest in drainage among the inhabitants of the peninsula. On the contrary, throughout the postclassical period landlords and cultivators strenuously exerted themselves to remove water from land they intended to sow or plant. The documents which reveal this tenacious combat with waterlogging are far more abundant for the ninth and tenth centuries than they are for the earlier Middle Ages, but this circumstance need not imply that drainage became relevant only then, as Italian population levels rose again and pressure on agricultural production rose accordingly (as revealed by the early clearances, of ninth-century date[22]). The vagaries of charter survival shape our understanding of the history of drainage as much as they do our understanding of other aspects of the early medieval past. *Fossata, fossae,* and, more rarely, *canales* probably existed uninterruptedly from Roman times as a rustic technique for the control of water flow.[23] They begin to crop up in contracts only from the

[21] C. Glacken, *Traces on the Rhodian Shore* (Berkeley, 1967), pp. 313–17, discusses how illiterate peoples' practices can shape literate ideas about nature.

[22] E. Sereni, *Storia del paesaggio agrario italiano* (Bari, 1984), pp. 67–72, dates clearances too late; there is evidence even in the seventh century, though most authorities agree that a large-scale movement to occupy wildernesses with permanent farming dates to the 900s. See P. Jones, "Medieval Agrarian Society in Its Prime: Italy," *Cambridge Economic History of Europe* I (Cambridge, 1971), pp. 353–4; C. Wickham, "European Forests in the Early Middle Ages," *Settimane* 37 (1990), pp. 540–3 (who links it to market production); B. Andreolli, *Uomini nel medioevo* (Bologna, 1983), pp. 140–3 (who associates it to demography, in the Lucchesia); Fumagalli, "Città e campagne," in his *L'uomo e l'ambiente*, pp. 7–12 (who ties it to a mentality).

[23] In modern Italian *fossa* and *fossato* can be natural water courses, but in early medieval charters the meaning of these terms seems closer to the one given by Justinian's *Digest* 43.11.1, p. 581: "fossa est receptaculum manu facta." For Roman lawmakers these trenches controlled both rain runoff (39.3.1, p. 395) and groundwater (8.3.29, p. 262).

early eighth century because the contracts themselves begin to appear only from that time on.[24]

In the 700s, drainage ditches were clearly an established feature of the landscape, whether in the plain of Lucca, the Sabine hills, the great valley of the Po, or the outskirts of Salerno. Their presence implies a commitment to agriculture despite the extra work their excavation and, particularly, their maintenance demanded. The landlords and peasants who had made them and repaired them understood the advantages such furrows brought. Even if they reduced the ease of movement of people and animals over the fields and stole some arable land, ditches drained rain runoff, limiting erosion, and seeped the groundwater from damp soils, conveying the unwanted liquid to places where it would be less of a nuisance. Ditches also improved the oxygenation and nitrification of most land and, by regulating the water table, enabled roots to delve deeper and plants to grow stronger. Ditches further improved soil workability, for they allowed soil to warm sooner and turned muddy fields into workable soil earlier in the season. Thus farmers concerned with productivity (not all farmers, therefore) saw in ditches many practical benefits. These latter counterbalanced ditches' disadvantages and justified the very laborious upkeep and the obligatory dependence on neighbors, or the cooperation among ditch-diggers, which ditch networks required.[25]

Columella, *Res Rustica*, ed. H. Boyd Ash and E. Foster (London, 1941–55), 2.2.9, p. 112, advised the excavation of *fossae*, as did other agronomists. On Roman ditches, see the excellent M. Spurr, *Arable Cultivation in Roman Italy* (London, 1986), pp. 20, 57–8, who notes that ditches alone make winter sowing of grain possible in many Italian plains. Menant, *Campagnes*, pp. 183–5, discusses the difficulties of early medieval terminology.

[24] *CDL* I, 28:102 (720, from Lucca), is the earliest *fossatum* (later ones include: *CDL* IV, 4:12 [746, Farfa]; *CDL* V, 9:44 [747, Farfa]; *Museo* 52 [830, Segrate]; *I diplomi di Guido e di Lamberto*, ed. L. Schiaparelli [Rome, 1906], 11:31 [891, Modena]). For Liutprand (*Leges Liutprandi*, ed. F. Bluhme, 150, p. 174) a *fossatum* should be dug (*cavere*, the same verb later charters use) only on private property and without damaging others' vines or trees. In late antiquity *fossata* were military trenches (Anonymus Valesianus, *Chronica*, ed. R. Cessi [Città di Castello, 1913], 12, p. 15; Vegetius, *Epitoma Rei Militaris*, ed. C. Lang [Leipzig, 1885], 1.24, p. 26). *Fossae* are documented slightly later: R. Cessi, *Documenti relativi alla storia di Venezia anteriori al mille* I (Padua, 1942), pp. 72–3 (819, near Venice); *I placiti* 1, 36:111 (824, Reggio); *Urkunden der Karolinger* III, 39:120 (839, Pavia). Agnellus (*LPR* 23, p. 289, 79, p. 331, 127, p. 361) was a connoisseur of *fossae*. *Urkunden der Karolinger* III, 39:120, is an early reference to *canales*, which were numerous in tenth-century Ravenna (as well as *fossae*), but also in the southern duchies (*CDC* II, 232:26 [965, Salerno]); *CDC* III, 469:27 (994, Salerno), where earlier *ballones* was the preferred term. *Vallum* was seldom used: *Le iscrizioni dei secoli VI–VII–VIII esistenti in Italia* II, ed. P. Rugo (Cittadella, 1975–6), p. 23.

[25] The pros and cons of ditches (for capitalist farmers) are weighed by L. Smedema and D. Rycroft, *Land Drainage* (Ithaca, 1983), pp. 39–40, 63–4. That maintaining ditches was hard work is suggested by the obligation to do so imposed on Ravennan tenants in the tenth century (e.g. *Monumenti* I, 4:90 [889]; "Gli archivi," 242:480 [967]; 385:528 [989]). *Digest* 39.3.2, p. 397, is revealing on the shared responsibilities ditches created for Roman cultivators.

A further, perhaps less obvious, important function of the *fossae* was border demarcation. Very many of the ditches recorded in the charters ran between property claims. Among early medieval boundary markers ditches were the most difficult to ignore: unlike notched trees, posts driven into the ground, or pierced boulders, which all established imaginary lines over the land, the grooves of ditches were perfectly visible and sensible, real boundaries in themselves. They were uninterrupted, unmistakable (particularly when reinforced with hedges, as in the Lucchesia, or with stone walls, as in Apulia[26]), and regulated access to a given plot of land exactly according to the owner's wishes. Thus it is not overly surprising to find that most ditch boundaries ran along the lands of mighty landlords, whose exclusive claim to possession the ditches made enforceable. Nor is it surprising that most ditches were associated with sedentary cereal agriculture and with reclamation of wilderness for that activity, for ditches impede the movement across the land inseparable from pastoral and sylvo-pastoral forms of agriculture. Drainage ditches probably always drew water from Italian fields, especially those with specialized cultivation, but they appear to have multiplied toward the end of the first millennium, when the powerful were winning more extensive control of landed property and when clearances for agriculture began to replace increasing expanses of woods and swamps.[27] But of course the redoubled efforts of ditch-diggers after about 800 may reflect the patterns of charters' survival rather than the agricultural intensification produced by lords and demographics.

If medieval cultivators dug ditches to cope with the excess of water on the land, that was not their only method for conveying water away from their fields. They also modified their plowing so as to allow their furrows to act as tiny canals along which rain water could flush without removing topsoil.[28] They did not, it seems, delve deep underground to create *cuniculi*, as did the Etruscans in overwatered enclosed valley-bottoms; and their rulers did not organize vast networks of water-regulating channels as

[26] For a hedged *fossa* near Lucca in 798, see *M&D* V.2, 269:158; for Apulian ditches, see Martin, *La Pouille*, p. 395.
[27] In the Lucchesia, around the end of the 700s, there were many ditches and few lords, however. There viticulture, more market-oriented than arable agriculture, justified the use of *fossae*: *M&D* V.2, 221:130 (788); 269:158 (798). The importance of ditches in the early medieval landscape is a subject I hope to take up in the future. See P. Squatriti, "Water, Nature, and Culture in Early Medieval Lucca," *Early Medieval Europe* 4 (1995), pp. 26–9; and the very enlightening discussion in L. Lagazzi, *Segni sulla terra* (Bologna, 1991), pp. 22–9, who considers the social forms associated with differing types of boundary markers in early medieval Italy. G. Comet, *Le paysan et son outil* (Rome, 1992), pp. 98–113, treats ditches and drainage in late medieval Italy informatively.
[28] B. Slicher Van Bath, *The Agrarian History of Western Europe, AD 500–1850* (London, 1963), pp. 54–62, whose focus is north European.

had the Romans.[29] Nevertheless, the removal of unwanted water and, equally relevant, the cohabitation with overwatered environments proved to be viable strategies for the early Middle Ages. Like the lack of effort to control the behavior of water in river plains, the struggle to make water behave in ways conducive to cultivation reveals that early medieval Italian communities found varied solutions to the challenges their environments posed.

Irrigation

In the fields where arable agriculture, arboriculture, and vineyards persisted, removed from the flooded and floodable space, the difficulties of water management were different. There the problem was irrigation, supplying sufficient water to soil where there might not be enough. Irrigation, the artificial application of water for the benefit of crops or pasture, has been almost ignored by historians of Italy who deal with early medieval agriculture, and indeed the early medieval evidence for this age-old, pan-Mediterranean practice is exiguous.[30] Early medieval Italian societies obviously were not based on the disciplined upkeep of irrigation channels and customs. Except in bone-dry places like Apulia, irrigation was instead complementary to "spontaneous" sources of water, especially rainfall, and the water brought by irrigators was integrated into a larger supply system as a component limb, not as the backbone. Climate has something to do with this. Unlike some of their Mediterranean col-

---

[29] A. Hodge, *Roman Aqueducts and Water Supply* (London, 1992), pp. 45–7; A. Malissard, *Les Romains et l'eau* (Paris, 1994), pp. 223–6.

[30] The definition is borrowed from C. Clarke, *The Economics of Irrigation* (Oxford, 1970), p. 1. On archaic irrigation in the Mediterranean, see R. Forbes, *Studies in Ancient Technology* II (Leiden, 1965), pp. 1–5; G. Argoud, "Le problème de l'eau dans la Grèce antique," in A. De Reparaz (ed.), *L'eau et les hommes en Méditerranée* (Paris, 1987), p. 209; and his "Eau et agriculture en Grèce," in P. Louis (ed.), *L'homme et l'eau en Méditerranée* IV (Lyons, 1987), pp. 26–32. Scholars of early medieval Italy hardly mention irrigation (or discuss it in terms of Arab technical contributions, as C. Parain, "The Evolution of Agricultural Technique," *Cambridge Economic History of Europe* I [Cambridge, 1971], pp. 146–7, and Sereni, *Storia*, p. 64, do), but see A. Lizier, *L'economia rurale dell'età prenormanna nell'Italia meridionale secoli IX–XI* (Palermo, 1907), p. 110; C. Carucci, *La provincia di Salerno dai tempi più remoti al tramonto della fortuna normanna* (Salerno, 1922), p. 168, for scattered comments. Late medieval irrigation is well studied: G. Fantoni, *L'acqua a Milano* (Bologna, 1990), pp. 27–49; A. Lanconelli and R. de Palma, *Terra, acqua, e lavoro nella Viterbo medievale* (Rome, 1992), pp. 17–24, 36–44; Menant, *Campagnes*, pp. 183–97. Iberian specialists have generated an impressive corpus of irrigation studies, e.g. T. Glick, *Irrigation and Society in Medieval Valencia* (Cambridge, MA, 1970); his *Islamic and Christian Spain in the Early Middle Ages* (Princeton, 1979), ch. 2; and his *From Muslim Fortress to Christian Castle* (Manchester, 1995), pp. 64–91; L. Bolen, *Les méthodes culturales au moyen âge* (Geneva, 1974); and her "L'eau et l'irrigation," *Options mediterranéennes* 16 (1972), pp. 65–77.

leagues, say in the Spanish *huerta* or in the Maghrib, the cultivators of Italy, particularly those on the Tyrrhenian side, could count on rain in the wet seasons when they planned their growing. For them irrigation was not a necessary substitute for rain but a seasonal support for those moments when the crops' water requirement was at its apex and rain was not expected or sufficient. Such moments could be avoided by planting grain in winter and harvesting before the parched season began. The irrigation systems created under these conditions were not the perennial ones based on kilometers-long water channels of Mesopotamia. They were humbler, limited, very local networks of storage tanks, ditches, and derivations, functioning on a seasonal basis and seldom applied to cerealiculture. They did not require a tightly run centralized state and did not leave many traces for archeologists to discover and discuss.[31] Though unprepossessing from a technical viewpoint, these smaller "part-time" irrigation systems were not irrelevant either technologically or socially. They required some knowledge of hydraulics and rather elaborate social agreements (cooperation at least among those who shared earthworks) in order to function properly. This is perhaps clearest in Italy's early medieval vegetable gardens.

Close to clusters of population or even inside the urban centers of Italy, easily accessible because of the frequent work they required, numerous *horti*, or vegetable gardens, were kept by a variety of people. Horticulture was an urban and suburban specialty but country people practiced it too. The *horti* were considered an integral part of the house to which they were appended (though some *horti* were not attached to any habitation). Their purpose was the replenishment of the household with an array of foods, such as onions, cabbages, and lettuces (which need much water) as well as legumes (which need less).[32] The *horti* were well suited to simple irrigation, not only because of the type of crops they grew (which needed more water than field crops, which were planted by scatter) but also because they were cultivated intensively, in all seasons, even the driest ones, without the respite of fallow periods after a harvest. Unlike the products of the fields, the products of the *horti* were not liable

---

[31] As Thomas and Wilson, "Water Supply," pp. 157–8, note.

[32] See B. Andreolli, "Il ruolo dell'orticultura e della frutticultura nelle campagne dell'alto medioevo," *Settimane* 37 (1990), pp. 175–211; M. Montanari, *L'alimentazione contadina nell'alto medioevo* (Naples, 1979), pp. 22–7, and his "I prodotti e l'alimentazione" in A. Carile (ed.), *Storia di Ravenna* II (Venice, 1991), p. 89, on *hortus* products. On the water needs of these vegetables, see A. Michael, *Irrigation* (New Delhi, 1978), p. 511; and Forbes, *Studies*, p. 44. On tax-exemption for *horti*, see G. Petracco-Sicardi, "La casa rurale nell'alto medioevo," *AM* 7 (1980), pp. 364–5; but esp. Montanari, *L'alimentazione contadina*, pp. 309–36. On Spanish horticulture and irrigation, see Bolen, *Les méthodes*, pp. 169–71.

to rents or other exactions, so the *hortus* became a prized possession cultivators exploited year-round. On this favored soil the cultivator was most willing to lavish his labor and his investments. Consequently, the gardens became islands of agricultural intensification where every increment of work which raised productivity had beneficial repercussions for the cultivator.

The *hortus* was thus worth improving with manure, fences, gates, channels, ditches, and a perennial water source, even an artificial one like a well. This combination of inducements made the *horti* the primary irrigated land of the early medieval period, although irrigated farming can be thirty times more laborious than dry farming and six times more so than viticulture.[33]

From earliest times, therefore, horticulture was connected to irrigation in Italy. Rome's agronomists, from Cato to Palladius, all advised the watering of gardens, and late antique redactions of Roman law expected it.[34] In the middle of the sixth century Cassidorus described the "irrigated *horti*" of his famed monastery, Vivarium, an interesting case of non-urban garden-keeping. Slightly earlier he had scolded the citizens of Rome for stealing water from the aqueducts to irrigate their *horti*, a shameful case of private interests encroaching on what belonged to the commonwealth, according to the Calabrian statesman and monk.[35] Cassiodorus' testimony is very specific and is hence precious. The *horti* he mentioned were irrigated with running water, led off from a stream or an aqueduct in apposite channels. At roughly the same time some apparently similar channels crossed Lucca's gardens, suggesting that selfish Romans and lonely monks were not the only ones doing such irrigating.[36]

After Cassiodorus the direct evidence becomes more nebulous. Irrigated *horti* are described but once, in a suspect royal charter presum-

[33] Delano Smith, *Western Mediterranean*, p. 172. E. Boserup, *The Conditions of Agricultural Growth* (New York, 1982; orig. 1965), pp. 40–1, has instructive things to say about irrigation, work, and demography.
[34] Cato, *De Agri Cultura*, ed. A. Mazzarino (Leipzig, 1962), 1.7, p. 7, considered *hortus irriguus* the second most profitable use of land. See also Columella, *Res Rustica* 10.1.40, p. 9; Palladius, *Opus Agriculturae*, ed. R. Rodgers (Leipzig, 1975), 1.34.2, p. 33; *Codex Theodosianus*, ed. T. Mommsen and P. Krueger (Berlin, 1905), 15.2.7, p. 816. Due to Ennodius' lyricism it is unclear whether the best-known late antique *horti* were irrigated: "De Horto Regis," in his *Carmina*, in *Opera*, ed. F. Vogel (Berlin, 1885), pp. 214–15. K. Butzer, "The Classical Tradition of Agronomic Science," in K. Butzer and D. Lohrmann (eds.), *Science in Eastern and Western Civilization in Carolingian Times* (Basel, 1993), pp. 549–54, summarizes ancient garden irrigation.
[35] Cassiodorus, *Institutiones*, ed. R. Mynors (Oxford, 1961), 1.19, p. 73, *hortos irriguos*, and *Variarum* 3.31, p. 95 (echoing *Codex Theodosianus* 15.2.4, p. 815).
[36] The archeologists G. Ciampoltrini and P. Notini, "Lucca tardoantica e altomedievale," *AM* 17 (1990), p. 569, are cautious with the evidence.

ably of the year 714 whereby the Pavian church of S. Pietro in Ciel d'Oro was confirmed its possession of lands near the river Trebbia, including a channel "for the irrigating of the *horti*."[37] Although the rest of the numerous *horti* in the sources are not explicitly said to be irrigated, many of them probably were. Irrigation is most likely to have occurred close to cities whose voracious appetite for their products compensated irrigators for the drudgery of labor in their gardens. It is not necessary to adopt a retrogressive, Annaliste methodology to prove this, as Toubert did in analyzing the *horti* of the Sabina.[38] Irrigation may be inferred from the location of the wells, adjacent to the *horti* in so many charters. Any Lombard wells that were at all like those Liutprand depicted as customary in his laws were structurally suited to irrigating a contiguous plot of land. Their props, swings, and apparent lack of protective walls meant they could function as a rudimentary pump, with a person lifting water from the underground reservoir or vein onto the surface where the bucket could handily be tipped into a channel, allowing it to trickle through the nearby *hortus*.[39] Even in the event that a well did not have a Liutprandian "swipe," its proximity to the *hortus* was useful. A person could get water to her or his plants, perhaps sprinkling them by hand as Walafrid Strabo recommended in the middle of the ninth century, avoiding a tortuous trip to a distant place.[40]

In the eighth century, as we have seen, the cost of a reservoir built by the masons of Como depended on its depth. Regardless, it was never cheap. The construction and maintenance of wells was so complicated and

[37] *CDL* III, 11:39, a charter which Brühl thinks substantially faithful, "et aquaeductus per nostram Baugam in eorum sit potestatem ad irrigandos hortos." The first and third persons plural in this interpolation add to its questionableness. *CDLangobardiae* 782:1375 (978) confirmed the donation.

[38] P. Toubert, *Les structures du Latium médiéval* I (Rome, 1973), pp. 236–41. Slicher Van Bath, *Agrarian History*, pp. 14–15, thought that *only* cities' demands for food provided peasants with inducements to irrigate in the *Intensitätinseln* around their walls. In this he was too restrictive.

[39] For the well, see *Leges Liutprandi* 136, p. 167. Some examples of wells next to *horti* can be found in *Papyri Italiens* I, 24:374: "hortus in integro qui est in pergulis exornatus cum usu cortis et potei" in Ravenna c. 650; *Breviarium Ecclesiae Ravennatis*, 65:32 and 71:35, rented in Rimini c. 750; 72:36, rented in Rimini c. 810, though only a portion; *CDC* I, 131:108, in Salerno, c. 900; *CDL* I, 30:109, "cum curte et puteo suo, orto, anditu" at Lucca in 722; 65:204, "cum orto seu puteo" in Lucca, c. 738; *CDL* II, 148:60, "orticellu, cum parte mea de puteu" at Lucca, 761; 229:283, "orto et medietatem puteo" in Lucca, 769; 276:391, "duabus portionibus de curte et puteo et orto" in Lucca in 772; *Urkunden der Karolinger* III, 97:236, in Pavia 846, "usum putei cum horto." Martin, *La Pouille*, pp. 74–7, notes the proximity of cisterns to gardens in high medieval Apulia.

[40] *Liber de Cultura Hortorum*, ed. E. Duemmler, *MGHPoetarum Latinorum Medii Aevi* II (Berlin, 1884), 3, lines 53–61, p. 337. Despite the protestations of accuracy in 1, in lines 15–18, p. 335, Strabo evokes Horace and Ovid in his description.

costly that even in the cities some wells attached to a *hortus* had more than one owner.[41] There were instances in which the owner ceded the right to use a well for his *hortus* but did not relinquish ownership of the well itself, so precious was the water.[42] In such cases the water was probably divided by time, so the owner and the user had turns, because this system avoided disputes over quantity, which is difficult to gauge, and because time lots are the accustomed system of division in irrigation arrangements in the Mediterranean. With the possible exception of the Ravennan "six *unciae* of the well" given along with a *hortus* (and which could be a time slot too), the "portions" of well sold with *horti* and houses probably represented time units, known to all the portion-holders, who were never overly numerous. Probably these time units were adjusted to take seasonal variations in the availability of water into account.[43] Regardless, such subdivisions of wells associated with gardens by time or by other methods are an index of the importance and value irrigable gardens held in special circumstances. Well-irrigation, today considered the most wasteful and costly way to irrigate, was a technique suited to soil which was very productive, to areas where markets might recompense the irrigator for the work, and to proprietors who were prosperous enough to invest in wells, which in early medieval Italy meant well-irrigation was best suited to cities and *horti*.[44] One advantage of this style of irrigation was that it created fewer ties of dependency and left irrigators in control of their water supply.[45] In general the wells used to water gardens were owned by the gardeners.

In places provided with aqueducts, canals, or springs, the *hortus* could be fed from these sources too. They substituted for or complemented wells. Cassiodorus thought taking water from an aqueduct before it had reached a fountain and become public was selfish and uncivil, but expected such theft for private *horti* and even wrote of cases where the

---

[41] Use of a well was shared by prominent Pavese in the ninth century (*Urkunden der Karolinger* III, 97:236) and by Ravennans in the seventh (*Papyri Italiens* I, 27:374). See also n. 43.   [42] *CDL* II, 289:423.
[43] *Breviarium* 72:36 ("sex unc. putei") employs *uncia* as a physical measurement of half (six-twelfths) of the well. *Codex Theodosianus* 15.2.3, p. 815, measures water in *unciae*. Few as they were, portion-holders still constituted irrigation communities, with sharing enforced by cooperation. For other partible wells tied to *horti*, see *Museo* 23 (766), which describes a Milanese *orto* with "use of the waters" presumably shared with others; *M&D* IV.1, 107:167 (792, Lucca); *Monumenti* I, 29:143 (957, Ravenna); 51:190 (975, Ravenna); "Regesto," 337:512 (979, Ravenna). It is strange that summer drought and spring abundance are not mentioned in documents about irrigation turns.
[44] Clarke, *Economics*, p. 58; Boserup, *Conditions*, p. 39.
[45] Glick, *From Muslim Fortress*, p. 65, sees this irrigation technique as widespread in rural Spain on farms of less than one hectare, but unlikely to create irrigation communities.

theft had been perpetrated for more than thirty years, becoming customary, so the state had to reimburse the thieves for depriving them of their established title.⁴⁶ Later, in eighth-century Brescia, Abbess Ansilperga expected her fellow citizens to attempt to steal her aqueduct's water, for their *horti* among other things. We know little of illicit derivations made by avid irrigators from the aqueducts functioning in the early medieval peninsula; yet it is unlikely that they were more civic-minded than their Roman counterparts, drawing water only after it had reached its destination.

Horticulturalists without wells (or cisterns, actually) at Ravenna were eager to be able to draw on the entirely public canals of the city for their irrigation water, and from very early on; a *hortus* without a well in Ravenna lay on just such a channel in the middle of the seventh century. There were several similar situations in the region from later times.⁴⁷ Nor was the Ravennate unique in this, by the 800s. In 894 the Lucchese bishop Gherardus leased to one Leuprand a suburban plot of land near the church of St. Fredianus "along with the channel or aqueduct which crosses that land."⁴⁸ Tuscan cultivators also found water channels advantageous. By the tenth century, further south, Salernitan monasteries were squabbling over access to water from an open channel just outside the city. Both abbots involved were interested in the water for horticulture and were willing to go to extraordinary lengths to obtain it. A court decision made them share it, though the abbot of St. Maximus, whose claim to the water had seniority, wrested some privileges.⁴⁹ Irrigation of gardens with water from urban canals is thus attested to in different places throughout the early medieval period.

Some gardens, removed both from wells and deposit-laden waterways

⁴⁶ Rights to water established by custom were venerated in Roman law (*Digest* 8.5.10.1 [Ulpian], p. 270; *Codex Iustinianus* 3.34.7, p. 141). Cassiodorus reluctantly admitted the need to pay thieves whose thirty years of tenure established *consuetudo* (*Variarum* 3.31, p. 95).

⁴⁷ *Papyri Italiens* II, 44:176; 38:134–6 (616–19), is similar; *Monumenti* I, 7:97 (896, Ravenna), and 27:139 (950, Ravenna), link access to flowing water to urban cultivation. Pope Gregory the Great's *Registrum Epistularum*, ed. D. Norberg (Turnhout, 1982), 24.14, p. 1087, also describes suburban *horti*, crossed by a stream and licked by the Tiber, just south of Rome.

⁴⁸ *M&D* V.2, 992:613: "una cum . . . albio [alveum] seo aquiducto quas per ipsa terra percurrit." For the location, see I. Belli Barsali, "La topografia di Lucca nei secoli VIII–XI," in *Atti del 5o Congresso internazionale di studi sull'alto medioevo* (Spoleto, 1973), p. 505. A *clavaca* (*M&D* IV.2, appendix, 16:24) in 815 seems to have flushed wastewater through the ring of gardens north of Lucca. Irrigation by sewage was a venerable Mediterranean tradition: D. Crouch, *Water Management in Ancient Greek Cities* (Oxford, 1993), p. 36.

⁴⁹ *CDC* III, 469:27, of about 994. Irrigation is the most logical use of the water, drawn from the Rafastia, which did not reach the monastery itself. Suburban irrigation, presumably of *horti*, is also the likeliest goal of the *ballonem* from about 850: *CDC* I, 44:54–5.

in cities, drew upon natural water courses, or at least their location alongside these sources of water makes such a deduction legitimate.[50] In this
the *horti* resembled less intensively cultivated fields and orchards, which
seldom relied on wells but often appear in intimate connection to natural
water courses in the surviving charters.[51] The irrigation of arable fields, of
pastures, and of orchards is even more difficult to trace than that of
gardens, yet there is enough circumstantial evidence to suggest that this
practice was not unknown. For example, in the Sabina of the eighth
century, "our water which is in our farm" could be donated to a religious
house, which can only mean that the water was beneficial to the farm's
activities. Likewise, when at Varsi in 736 or again near Farfa in 766 we
learn that there were fields close to "the rivulet which flows from the
living spring" or "the rivulet which comes out of the cistern," the conclusion that we are before the time of rural irrigation systems becomes
inescapable.[52]

The notarial phrase so often attached to documents recording transactions of land, "with the use of the waters," a great favorite in the Cava
charters but a staple throughout Italy, is inexplicable unless the use of the
waters was relevant to the people who drew up the contracts. Even in
those instances where this was a formula, it was a formula with a
meaning.[53] This meaning derived from the fact that it was desirable to
associate land and "use of the waters." The most plausible explanation for
this desirability is irrigation. Use of the waters, as well as outright control
of springs and streams, was bought and rented and sold because water

---

[50] *CDL* I, 38:132 (726), where Gumfonis' *hortus* is on the Brana torrent north of Pistoia;
the almost contemporary charter in Vat. Lat. 4939, 69v (724), describes Zacharias'
property at Ponticellum, including "alo horto qui esse videtur iuxta fluvium Sabbato."
In eleventh-century Apulia, gardens had similar locations: Martin, *La Pouille*, p. 349.
Early medieval Iberian examples of such irrigation are known: Glick, *From Muslim
Fortress*, p. 69.

[51] There are instances of wells in rural agricultural (not horticultural) contexts: *CDC* I,
24:27 (844), where the well serves an arable field and a house near Salerno; *CDL* II,
130:150 (758), where "use of the well" is tied to the *arboribus* near Piacenza; *CDL* III, 1:6
(613), where well and field are linked near Bobbio.

[52] *Il regesto di Farfa* II, ed. I. Giorgi and U. Balzani (Rome, 1879), 114:99 (778), "aquam
nostram quae est in casale nostro Musella." Charter 101:92 of 777 might indicate that
the water was destined to Farfa's aqueduct, however. But 66:66 (766), where a "rivus qui
exit de cisterna" can only be an irrigation system. For Varsi, see *CDL* I, 59:188: "caput
tenente in riolo qui exeunt de Funtana Viva."

[53] I agree with the general point made by B. Andreolli, "Formule di pertinenza e paesaggio," *Rivista di archeologia, storia, economia, e costume* 5 (1977), pp. 7–18, that formulas in
early medieval Italian charters are more varied and less formulaic than they are thought
to be, and that they describe a reality. Menant, *Campagnes*, p. 184, decided *usibus
aquarum* in the 900s in eastern Lombardy are too vague to prove anything. See also B.
Schwineköper, "Cum aquis aquarumve decursibus'," K. Jäschke (ed.), *Festschrift für H.
Beumann* (Sigmaringen, 1977), pp. 22–56.

was convenient, and in some seasons necessary, to anyone who grew crops. Production was lower if one's land had no access to water, and even farmers for whom productivity was not the primary concern lessened their risk of shortfall or catastrophe by retaining rights to a nearby source of water.[54]

The entitlement to use a spring or stream could become a commodity, as it did in Spain. In early medieval Italy, however, it never circulated separately from the land to which the right pertained. "Use of the waters," together with land, was exchanged by people who practiced arboriculture in fruit orchards; by people whose fields were made to grow meadows for pasture; and by people whose arable fields mainly produced grain.[55] The peculiarities of the root-systems involved made the need for a supplement of water more acute for arboriculture, pastures, and for any crops that had to pass through the summer without withering, something the infusion of water made more feasible.[56] The practice of intercultivation (more picaresquely called promiscuous cultivation), with its interwoven types of husbandry, may account for the interest in water sources exhibited by

[54] L. Bussi, "Terre comuni e usi civici," in G. Galasso (ed.), *Storia del Mezzogiorno* III (Naples, 1990), p. 213, interprets the formulas as expressions of common rights. But these surely did not require written expression and, as not all contracts have them, the right to "use of the waters" was not all that common.

[55] A sampling of land used for arboriculture with access to water can be found in: *Papyri Italiens* I, 20:346 (about 600); 2, 35:108 (575), both with springs; *CDC* I, 12:13 (822), for chestnuts near Salerno; 47:58 (856), for vines and fruit trees near Salerno; 89:114 (882), for vines, woods, and pastures with water rights near Salerno; *CDC* II, 232:26 (965), vines on "aque que de canali descendit" near Salerno; *CDL* I, 84:249 (about 744), near Volterra; *CDL* II, 129:12 (758) and 195:189 (766), for vines near Lucca; *CDL* IV, 5:14 (746), near Farfa. For pasture on watered land, see *Breviarium* 18:13 (about 815), "pratum cum formis suis," and 27:17 (c. 750), near Rimini; *CDC* I, 144:185 (926) "pascuis et aquis" near Salerno; *CDL* I, 95:275 near Como; *CDL* II, 155:80, near Lodi; *CDL* V, 34:304 (762), near Rieti. *Museo* 72 (843) records the sale near Verona of a "pascuo vel aquario," highly suggestive of irrigated pasture of the type discussed by R. Baird Smith, *Italian Irrigation* (Edinburgh, 1855), pp. 86–8, and by Milan's 1346 "Statuti delle strade delle acque del contado di Milano fatti nel 1346," ed. G. Porro Lambertenghi, in his *Miscellanea di storia italiana* VII (Turin, 1869), 2, pp. 375–7; the *Sicardi Principis Pactio*, 45, p. 217 – "de aqua, herba, et collata" – links water and pasture in an interesting way. For watered arable, see Vat. Lat. 4939, 69v (724), 106r (833) near Benevento; *CDC* I, 30:35 (848), 63:78 (866), and 66:86 (869), near Salerno; *CDL* I, 54:178 (735) and 59:188 (736), at Varsi; 60:185 (737), 64:202 (737) near Piacenza; 78:230–1 (742), near Pavia; *CDL* II, 142:47 (760) and 225:270 (768) and 249:327 (770), Piacenza; 155:80 (761), where "campo ad pisina Anspert" stands for an artificial tank next to the field; 179:49 (764), at Lucca; 271:380–1 (772), near Bologna; 293:435 (774), Bergamo; *CDL* III, 24:117 (c. 750), Modena; *CDL* IV, 24:70 (776) and 25:73 (776), *cum aquis*, and 37:111 (783), near Farfa; *CDL* V, 47:171 (766), *cum rivis*, and 100:322 (786), *clausuram et lacum*, near Rieti; XIV:385 (783), XV:388 (784), near Benevento.

[56] See Michael, *Irrigation*, pp. 502–11, on how root-systems affect irrigability. Varro, *Rerum Rusticarum Libri*, ed. W. Davis Hooper (London, 1934), 1.31.5, p. 254, said fruit orchards needed drink.

people who were acquiring land not ostensibly in need of irrigation, where grains grew and were supposed to yellow in early summer.[57] The irrigation of cereals was uncommon in the western Mediterranean, and even more so in Italy. Nevertheless, it was not wholly unknown in Roman times, when the elder Pliny noted that the farmers of Sulmona watered their grain fields.[58] By the fifth century, bishops anxious to smooth down feathers ruffled by their acquisitive water-management schemes did so by promising that everyone's fields could be irrigated thereby. Paulinus of Nola's public relations campaign for his aqueduct indicates that the possibility of irrigation was seductive to Campanian landlords and cultivators.[59] Limited in scope, perhaps applied only in exceptional places and in exceptionally cold or dry years, when crops matured later in summer, the incidence of irrigation in early medieval Italy should not be minimized.

Certainly the evidence for irrigation in early medieval fields is circumstantial and scantier than it is for ancient and late antique times. Even on farms whose borders skirted water courses (which provided useful boundary markers and therefore were often mentioned in records of property exchanges) some plots of land whose borders (*capita* or *latera*) lay on water courses were probably irrigated, but this is never specified. Still, when the "head" or "side" of crop-bearing fields is described abreast a water course (in contracts from south Italy, the mid-Po valley, the Lucchesia, and from the Sabine hills), the descriptions ascribe a direction or proper orientation to the fields. Such a method of imagining the fields, with an orientation, depended on local microtopography, on inclination or gradient, and on the most efficient and convenient direction of plowing and arranging furrows. Of course these factors will have been different in a north Italian plain or subapenninic hill. But all plots of land with their "head" in a stream or other source of water were excellently placed for furrow irrigation, a system whereby water is allowed to flow into furrows that previously have been planted with crops whose roots are liable to

[57] In late antique north Africa, for comparison, the olive trees growing in fields turned over to other crops were diligently irrigated: B. Shaw, "Lamasba," *Antiquités africaines* 18 (1982), p. 85; D. Gilbertson, "The UNESCO Libyan Valleys Survey VIII," *Libyan Studies* 15 (1984), p. 68.

[58] The early imperial inscription from Venafro (*CIL* 10, 4842), which deals with arable irrigation, is discussed by Shaw, "Lamasba," p. 74; W. Eck, "Die Wasserversorgung in römischen Reich," in *Geschichte der Wasserversorgung* II (Mainz, 1987), p. 80. On Venafran farming, see G. Chouquer et al., *Structures agraires en Italie méridionale* (Rome, 1987), pp. 28–94. Pliny was clearly surprised by Sulmona: see Spurr, *Arable Cultivation*, p. 20; Butzer, "Classical Tradition," p. 547. Irrigation of fields took place at Tusculum and elsewhere in Italy: Hodge, *Roman Aqueducts*, pp. 246–50.

[59] Paulinus of Nola, *Carmina*, ed. G. de Hartel (Vienna, 1894), 21.653–830, pp. 179–85. *Carmina* 27.486, p. 284, is evidence of rain-fed irrigation near Cimitille.

develop fungal rot if the water is allowed to stagnate or stay on the soil for long periods; the furrow's gradient ensures adequate drainage and prevents harmful waterlogging.[60]

In the *bassa* around Pavia, where water courses dig deep beds for themselves, it was probably no use to have a watered "head," for early medieval Italians do not appear to have used Archimedean screws or the other ancient water-lifting devices without which raising water from a low-lying stream to an elevated earthen plane would be prohibitively difficult (it might require long derivation canals originating upstream at a point a little higher than the field into which the water would flow, which is exactly what the *aquaria* near Abbiategrasso in 742 may have been).[61] Likewise furrow irrigation would be impractical in torrents which ran dry in summer, as many Apenninic torrents do, precisely when their services were most needed.[62] But that still leaves a respectable number of early medieval fields whose location and orientation might suggest that their furrows carried water.

[60] Furrow irrigation is explained by Michael, *Irrigation*, p. 611. Examples of land with *caput* on water sources in the 700s can be found in: *CDL* I, 59:188 (736); 60:189, "de utraque capita quoerente rivoras" (737, Piacenza); 95:275 (748, Como); 106:304 (747, Lucca); *CDL* II, 142:47 (760, Piacenza); 179:149, 249:293 (764 and 770, near Lucca). For examples from the ninth century, see *M&D* V.2, 305:180 (803, Lucca); 459:275 (824, Lucca); 718:431 (855, Lucca). Border irrigation – whereby water is permitted to trickle into areas parallel to the water course (land with watered *latera*, that is), not at right angles to it, and is then left for some time before being admitted to the next parallel area alongside using gravity – is a technique adapted to crops sown by scatter which have little propensity to be ruined by root fungi, such as wheat. It may have been the preferred "use of the waters" of landowners whose fields lay between parallel water courses such as *CDL* I, 60:189; *CDL* IV, 24:70 (776, Farfa); *Breviarium* 136:76 (about 840, near Osimo); Vat. Lat. 4939, 69v–70r (724, near Benevento). On border irrigation, see Michael, *Irrigation*, p. 586.

In a few extreme cases, ditches formed a quadrilateral of borders around a plot of enclosed land (*clausuria*), "near the river," and evidently would enable the owner to flood his soil when he wanted to, since he had the right to use the waters: *CDL* II, 241:311 (770, Lucca); *Il Chronicon Farfense di Gregorio di Catino*, ed. U. Balzani (Rome, 1903), 1:158 (about 774). Sometimes *insula* meant floodable land, too: S. Caucanas, *Moulins et irrigation en Roussillon du IXe au XVe siècle* (Paris, 1995), p. 23. *CDL* IV, 5:14 (746), describes land with four watered borders, but the meaning of *aquam traversam* is obscure. *Regesto di Farfa* II, 30:41 (736), also refers to a water-bearing ditch called *aquam traversam*. Acqua Traversa is a toponym still in use.

[61] On the stream beds of the *bassa*, see R. Pracchi, *Lombardia* (Turin, 1971), p. 131. R. Chevalier, *La romanisation de la Celtique du Pô* (Paris, 1980), p. 63, discusses their impact on Roman settlement. Delano Smith, *Western Mediterranean*, p. 183, wisely notes that relief is conducive to irrigation. *CDL* I, 78:231 (Milan, 742), mentions the *aquaria*, a very rare term. The amount of neighborly consent long channels require discouraged their construction.

[62] "Mediterranean" stream regimen is explicated by D. Ruocco, *Campania* (Turin, 1976), pp. 163–74; E. Churchill-Semple, *The Geography of the Mediterranean Region* (New York, 1931), pp. 103–9. In parts of south Italy the erratic stream regimen was alarming even to as "Mediterranean" a man as Procopius: *Guerra Gotica* III, 4.35, p. 260.

As we have seen, the rural landscape was scarred by many earthworks, drainage ditches designed to improve soil workability and enhance crop growth. Some ditches, like the *ballones* in Salerno's suburbs, led water to crops, not away from them. The *aquaria* occasionally mentioned by charters, the earliest in 742 near Abbiategrasso on the Ticino, and others from the ninth-century Tyrrhenian south, also seem to have been irrigation channels. The channels called *seriolae* which led stream water through the grain fields in the vicinity of Bergamo in the 900s certainly were.[63] There were, then, some certified irrigation channels, but their relative rarity corroborates the impression that irrigation of farmlands was not a universal practice in Italy, even on land owned by major proprietors. Irrigation was, however, a possibility, and one whose realization was determined by circumstances such as the economic interests of landowners, the ease of reaching the water, the techniques available, and the presence of incentives to raise productivity (in the form of urban markets as lively as those of Pavia in the 740s or Salerno in the ninth century).[64]

Irrigation always obliges people to agree on rules, to cooperate with each other. Even the humble irrigation systems of early medieval Italy evoked social relations of this sort. The very wells which watered *horti* were sometimes divided among several gardeners, whose sharing had to be organized. The construction of channels was a laborious task, best undertaken through cooperative efforts by the various people whose land stood to gain once the furrow was finished, and neighbors' toleration was a sine qua non even for privately dug individual ventures; as Justinian knew, rivalries derived from sharing waterworks. Thus the small-scale irrigation systems of postclassical Italy, inevitably, created social relations, so the relative silence of the early medieval sources concerning cooperative mainte-

---

[63] *Ballonem* is in *CDC* I, 11:11–12 (821, Lucera); 43:53 (856); 44:55 (856, Salerno). The formula in many rulers' donations which included *decursibus* or *ductibus* for (irrigation?) water is illustrated in *Regesto di Farfa* II, 89:83 (764); 92:86 (775); 169:141 (801); *Urkunden der Karolinger* III, 29:105 (836); 41:129 (840). *Aquarium* is repeated in *CDC* I, 61:76 (865, Salerno, not for irrigating), and *CDC* III, 469:27 (994, Salerno, where it is an irrigation channel). *Aquariis*, probably irrigation channels, went with land in *CDCajetanus* I, 15:25 (890). An *aquario* near Parma in 919 (*CDLangobardiae* 482:832) led to a mill. For *seriolae*, see Menant, *Campagnes*, pp. 185–6, who teleologically assumes they are the *beginning* of a bright agricultural future.

[64] On the commercial bent of much Salernitan agriculture in the ninth and tenth centuries, see H. Taviani-Carozzi, *La principauté lombarde de Salerne IXe–XIe siècle* I (Rome, 1991), pp. 415–19; B. Kreutz, *Before the Normans* (Philadelphia, 1991), pp. 106–15. Pavia was the goal of much Po trade. On commercialization of agriculture in east Lombardy, see Menant, *Campagnes*, pp. 287–90, who dates "true" market production to the 1100s. Caucanas, *Moulins*, pp. 26–8, describes new irrigation canals made by major landlords in the Roussillon during the 800s. The area's environment was quite "Italian," but in Italy social conditions seem to have inhibited such initiatives.

nance and orderly use of irrigation systems (even in the form of disputes about them) is perplexing. In Roman Italy inscriptions and laws such as those in Justinian's *Digest* encoded the preoccupation of a more irrigation-prone society over ditch maintenance, ditch-neighborliness, and water-sharing, but there is no parallel early medieval legislation. Liutprand's law on ditches, which curtailed indiscriminate digging, does not add up to a policy on water management.[65]

Yet Liutprand's attempt to protect the public roads and the private vines and trees of individuals against water-bearing ditches is revealing, even in its muteness, and may hold a key to understanding early medieval irrigation communities and their practices. For his law depended on a tight interpretation of the inviolability of private property, of which water channels were one part. In Lombard law, in other words, irrigation ditches were principally small individual ventures over which individual landowners had rights. This conception may have attenuated the ambiguities surrounding the responsibilities of the users of a collective ditch, which could give rise to disputes. It did not, obviously, eliminate disputes altogether; as we have seen, the Salernitan monasteries of St. Maximus and St. Laurentius were embroiled in a nasty controversy over an irrigation channel in the last decade of the first millennium.

The absence of other evidence of irrigative cooperation and the perplexing lack of disputes among irrigators raise the question of who had a title to the water in the ditches and channels, and also, by extension, in streams, springs, and rivers, and hence who controlled the possibility of irrigating. The answer is many-faceted and depends to a large extent on chronology. In Roman law, which held sway in much of Italy even after 568 and was formally the law of Byzantine Italy, the right to derive water from a water course considered perennial (and thus public) was held by all cultivators. In consequence there was a generous open-handedness toward digging channels for irrigation in the *Corpus Iuris Civilis*. These

---

[65] See *Digest* 43.20.26, p. 598, on *rivales. Leges Liutprandi* 150, p. 174: "Si quis fossatum in viam fecerit et ipso loco suo provare non potuerit, componat solidos sex et ipsum fossatum restaurit, et damnum si in vitis aut in arboriis ipsum fossatum cavendum fecit, componat sicut anterior edictus contenit." See also *Edictus Rothari*, ed. F. Bluhme, 305, p. 71, whose ditches are defensive, since sometimes they are purposely hidden. Liutprand's provision implies that earlier *fossatum*-makers had suffered few restrictions, and confirms Justinianic requirements that cultivatability in the land through which channels passed not be spoiled: *Digest* 43.13.2, p. 580 (Pomponius); 43.20.3.1, p. 598 (Pomponius). 43.21.1 (Pap. Iust.), pp. 599–600, and *Institutiones* 2.3, p. 13, show Roman willingness for ditches to be made freely; and 39.3.2.1–10, p. 397 (Paulus) and 8.3.15, p. 260, give rules for ditch neighborliness. 43.20.1.11, p. 595; 8.3.2.1–2, p. 258; 8.6.16, pp. 274–5, regulate irrigation turns. Ancient Greek laws granted extensive rights of channel passage through private property (Argoud, "Le problème de l'eau," p. 215), and *Digest* 8.5.18, p. 271, is explicit in defense of the would-be irrigator.

norms ran against the grain of Lombard conceptions, which gave primacy to private rights over common ones, so that by the eighth century charters recorded the sale of "that water" or someone's portion thereof (the rural context means "that water" was probably used in agriculture).[66] The patrimonialization of rural water rights in Italy, visible in Lombard law, may have begun in late antiquity or with the Lombard conquest, but it becomes truly measurable only when charters' survival rates improved in the 700s.[67] In the course of the eighth century, alongside the kings and dukes, other landowners possessed water courses, or tracts of rivers.[68] Their private and exclusive control of water had inevitable effects on irrigation in Italian agriculture. When the *potentes* acquired water sources they reduced the options open to other cultivators. To the extent that use of the waters was important to local cultivators, they became more dependent on the water's owner, who was likely to own a lot of land in the locale as well. Thus the patrimonialization of water in the countryside was an important component of the diverse lordships

[66] G. Longo, "Il regime delle concessioni e delle derivazione di acque pubbliche nel diritto romano classico e giustinianeo" in *Studi in memoria di G. Zanobini* V (Milan, 1965), pp. 361–84. A few examples of eighth-century transactions of water (not its use) can be found in: *CDL* I, 124:368 (springs near Pisa, 757); *CDL* II, 271:381 (springs near Bologna, 772); *CDL* IV, 25:73 (Tuscany, 776); 37:111 (near Farfa, 783); *CDL* V, 72:248 (Farfa, 777); *CDC* I, 144:185 and 179:232 (near Salerno, 926 and 950); *Urkunden der Karolinger* I, 156:211 (Benevento, 787); *Codice diplomatico del monastero di S. Colombano di Bobbio* I, ed. C. Cipolla (Rome, 1918), 27:130 (774).

[67] Justinian's *Codex* 3.24.2–7, p. 141, gave a more restrictive interpretation to the rights of irrigators to water than did the *Digest*. Even in classical antiquity non-perennial water sources could become the property of individual landowners.

[68] The assumption that all major water courses originally belonged to rulers (Poupardin, *Les institutions*, p. 16; Lizier, *L'economia rurale*, p. 24; Bognetti, "La navigazione padana," pp. 547–8; and, more timidly, Dussaix, "Les moulins," p. 114) is founded on the belief that these had been part of the imperial fisc that rulers inherited (but C.-R. Brühl, *Fodrum, Gistum, Servitium Regis* [Cologne, 1974], does not treat water courses as fisc). Indeed, the rulers of the peninsula did give away rights over a lot of water. But also other magnates held such titles by the time the surviving charters were drawn up (*rivis* are exchanged in *CDL* II, 137:31; 155:81; 162:104; 225:270; 249:327; 271;381; *CDL* V, 30:115; 47:171). There are no general statements of rulers' jurisdiction over the waters from the early Middle Ages. If Prince Sicard controlled the Volturno and Minturno around Capua in 836, this does not mean that all rivers belonged to the fisc (see G. Galasso, *Il mezzogiorno nella storia d'Italia* [Florence, 1977], p. 29), but rather that Sicard wanted peace for traders, and that his monopoly of fishing applied in those specific places and times. And if King Hildeprand donated "the river bed of the Po where before this time it flowed and now has left, near Piacenza" (*CDL* III, 18:84), to the local bishop in 744, he need not have been claiming jurisdiction over the whole river. Hildeprand may have owned the land on the river banks at that place and thus owned the bed when it freed itself of water (as Roman law allowed: *Digest* 43.12.1.7 [Ulpian], p. 579). Thus the control of water courses by rulers appears not to have been the only pattern. It cannot be assumed. When tenth-century rulers referred to *publicas aquas* (*Urkunden Konrad I.*, 265:378, of 964), they thought these to be only one of several types of water.

which, after at least a century of gestation, became so vital in late Carolingian Italy.[69]

An interesting early example of how the private control of water resources by mighty landlords could affect a rural society, and of how water courses could become the focus of rustic disputes, is hinted at in a charter from Farfa, dated to 783.[70] Duke Hildeprand of Spoleto donated to the monastery of Farfa "that portion of water at Septepontium which Autichis held, and had been owned by the monastery and had been taken away from the same monastery by duke Teudicius." The situation described in this matter-of-fact way was quite complex. There had been a contested, perhaps forcible, perhaps legal, seizure of water from the owner (Farfa) by a powerful man, Hildeprand's predecessor Theudicius. Both Farfa and Theudicius seem to have accorded the enjoyment of the waters to Autichis, a water tenant whose tenancy neither the seizure by Theudicius nor the reinstatement by Hildeprand imperiled. Duke Hildeprand then granted the water to the monks. The end result of all of this was that Farfa tightened its grip over local resources, including aqueous ones (Hildeprand's generosity to Farfa was doubtless encouraged by the Carolingian authorities, for whom the monastery was a valuable outpost). In this case, we do not learn much of the opinions of people at less lofty social levels, though the usurpation of water must have been one of the recurring fears of Sabine farmers in the eighth century. Yet it transpires that everyone – the dukes and the monks and even Autichis – considered the water ownable, an exploitable property like land.[71]

---

[69] Glick, *From Muslim Fortress*, p. 87, suggests that all irrigation systems tend "toward patrimonialization and privatization of water rights." On the origins of rural lordship in Italy, see P. Toubert, "L'Italie rurale aux VIIIe–IXe siècles," *Settimane* 20 (1973), pp. 95–132. Recent interesting contributions to the huge literature on lordship are T. Bisson, "Medieval Lordship," *Speculum* 70 (1995), pp. 743–59; and C. Violante, "La signoria rurale del secolo X," *Settimane* 38 (1991), pp. 329–85. Neither considers the impact of lordship on water or the impact of control of water on lordship. For a case study of east Lombardy, see Menant, *Campagnes*, pp. 395–485. In Roussillon very similar patrimonialization processes resulted, by the ninth century, in private ownership of water: Caucanas, *Moulins*, pp. 40–1, 259–60.

[70] *CDL* IV, 37:111: "similiter donamus . . . aquam illam in Septepontio portionem quam Autichis tenuit et ab ipso monasterio possessa est et Teudicius dux de ipso monasterio eam abstulit."

[71] A possible exception might be Theudicius, whose capture of the water might be seen as a reassertion of public, rulerly rights over water the monks had furtively appropriated. When unsuccessful, appropriations like this near Farfa were known as *invasio*, the illicit takeover of water (or non-aqueous property). Watery *invasio*'s circumstances are never quite as clear as in the Farfan document. For eighth-century instances of invasion of water, see *CDL* I, 24:95 (a bath, not irrigation); *CDL* III, 11:49; *CDL* V, 90:293; Vat. Lat. 4939, 70v. Some milder requisitioning than that of Theudicius also existed; it was temporary, a kind of borrowing, rather than an outright permanent assault on the possession of the water of the rightful owner, and occurred in the suburbs of Salerno: *CDC* I, 61:74 (865).

Tensions around water in agricultural areas, where the water's most important function would have been irrigation, could erupt in other ways too, with humble people as protagonists. They become visible in an extremely interesting, albeit anomalous, document from Carapelle, in the southern Apennines where S. Vincenzo al Volturno had vast estates in the eighth century.[72] The document refers to the *invasio* made by the local peasantry on the *terraticae* of S. Vincenzo, and "concerning the *aquarico*, which they subtracted." Whereas *terraticae* appear in other documents as rents paid on land, *aquaricum* has no contemporary parallels. It must refer to a rent the peasants had to pay the monastery for the right to use its waters in the rented fields; this would explain why it is paired with the rent on the lands. Not far from Carapelle, in the early tenth century, *aquarica* were a special rentable right, like *piscatio*, that the owner of the local water course held. This, too, suggests that the Carapellan *aquarico* was an early impost on the use of water which the monks who owned the water rights wished to exact from the cultivators.[73]

Though Carapelle is rather high, the area is limestone and parched in summer, so irrigation of crops which matured during or after that season was worthwhile to the cultivator, even if paid for. Any reader of Ignazio Silone's novels, in particular *Fontamara*, whose peasants battle fiercely for control of the local spring, can understand the value of water in the Abruzzi. Indeed, irrigation of arable was one of the area's distinguishing traits when Pliny the Elder wrote his *Natural History*, for he remarked that, although grain could be cultivated without irrigation, in the vicinity of Sulmona "there they even irrigate grain, and amazing it is."[74]

The arrangement hidden behind the term *aquaricum* was felt by the peasants of Carapelle to be an unjust imposition contrary to age-old custom because their mountains, a marginal zone if ever there was one,

---

[72] *CDL* V, 90:293. All the Carapellans had made *invasionem* and refused to pay *terraticas* but Tedemar and Sinderad pushed their *invasio* as far as "de aquarico, quod subtraxerant." The epilogue to this episode is implied in 95:308.

[73] The affair is studied by C. Wickham, *Studi sulla società degli Appennini nell'alto medioevo* (Bologna, 1982), pp. 20–1, who explains *terraticae* but is mystified by *aquaricum*. *Aquarica* are included among the rights of the owners of the waters of the Beneventan Calore at one place held over the waters in the tenth century (Vat. Lat. 4939, 119r). F. Arnaldi, *Latinitas Italicae medii aevi lexicon imperfectum* (Brussels, 1939), lists *aquaticum* as "tributum pro iure aqua utendi." In Berengarius' charters *aquaticum* is always paired with other taxes, and seems to have been a tax on water use. The earliest other reference I have found to it, from faraway Asti, is from 885 (*Diplomi di Berengario* 51:148, repeated by Otto I in 969: *Urkunden Konrad I.*, 374:514). DuCange gives *aquaria* as rent in fish "at non ita certa est." Taxes and dues often ended in -*aticum*: F. Ganshof, *Frankish Institutions Under Charlemagne* (Providence, RI, 1968), p. 45.

[74] They still do: Spurr, *Arable Cultivation*, p. 20. See Pliny, *Naturalis Historia*, ed. L. Ian and C. Mayhoff [Stuttgart, 1967], 3, 17.26.41, p. 136: "in Sulmonense Italiae agro, pago Fabiano, ubi et arva rigant mirumque."

had remained untouched by the trend toward the privatization of water rights which had been developing in the lowlands. Perhaps these peasants had irrigated by arrangements current at least since Pliny's day. S. Vicenzo had only recently come into possession of the region and was imposing the innovation, trampling on rooted traditions with its efficient administration. The monks sought to transform water the local resource into water the rent-producing commodity. Their *aquaricum* and the dispute over it must remain mysterious to some extent, but, like the Farfan incident of 783, it is a polished mirror reflecting the tensions which the patrimonialization of water could entail. For eighth-century rural central Italians, water was a resource worth using, and hence worth owning. To Carapelle's peasants it was worth an ill-fated struggle in the Carolingian courts.

There are few such formal disputes about which we know. It took pluck to confront a major landlord as she or he or it turned running waters into private property. More typical, perhaps, of how such affairs went in the rural areas is the uncontested appropriation of water S. Vincenzo carried out at Venafro, just downstream from the monastery in the Volturno valley, on a hillside overlooking that valley at the edge of the Campanian plain. Coincidentally – but perhaps this is a meaningful coincidence – Venafro is the town where the most complete Roman inscription in Italy recording water allocation agreements was carved.[75] One might imagine very ancient water allocation arrangements behind the systems described in a rare run of charters from Venafro, preserved by the monk John when he compiled the *Chronicon Vulturnense* in the twelfth century. The documents show that between 807 and 836 the monks of S. Vincenzo became the sole proprietors of land in an area close to the river Volturno which previously had been shared by at least twenty proprietors.[76] The monastery was particularly eager to gain possession of a local spring and the rivulet "from whence the water flows" through the land. In 833 the monks triumphed with the acquisition of land "where the Ravennola [probably today's Rava torrent] begins to gush out" from Prince Sicard, who further extended S. Vincenzo's holdings three years later with much land he had confiscated from ten landowners "on account of their guilt."[77]

---

[75] On Roman Venafro's farming, see Chouquer et al., *Structures agraires*, pp. 289–94.

[76] *Chronicon Vulturnense* I, 31:245 (810); 35:252 (815); 37:254–5 (817); 50:273 (807); 52:278 (817); 58:293–4 (833); 59:295 (836). S. Vincenzo's land policies are elucidated by L. Feller, "Les patrimoines monastiques dans les Abruzzes (VIIe–Xe s.)," in M. Fixot and E. Zadora-Rio (eds.), *L'environment des églises et la topographie religieuse des campagnes médiévales* (Paris, 1994), pp. 150–5.

[77] *Chronicon Vulturnense* I, 58:294, "unde incipit orire iam dicta Ravennola"; 59:295, "terras et servos . . . pro culpe eorum meritis, ad sacrum nostrum palacium devenerunt."

The water, allocated to the contiguous plots of land in an unparalleled way, "per tempus," was obviously crucial to rendering the fields fruitful. The phrase "whence by time the water flows" is common to all the charters. It should be interpreted as a recognition of local irrigation customs in which water was divided as it was in many Mediterranean irrigation communities, by turns dictated by time slots. By 836 S. Vincenzo had graduated from being one member of this small community to controlling much of the area and most of its precious water. This small but emblematic success came in a time and place where smallholders and their claims over resources were still strong, and big landlords struggled to create manors and lordships. The monks obstinately pursued their watery objective over three decades because they could perceive the benefits in such a fertile arrangement. The sufficiently watered land of the valley floor, so close to the monastery's warehouses, was probably more productive than the average, and the surplus its workers produced could fill the storage rooms of the monastery without long and difficult hauling. As all the water's time became monastic property at Venafro in the early 800s, it followed the course of much other aqueous wealth in Italy. For the main beneficiaries of the watery patrimonialization during the eighth and ninth centuries were religious houses, though this impression is based on monastic archives.

Probably the events witnessed at Venafro were more normal than those of Carapelle. Unlike the belligerent Carapellans, the Venafran irrigators found the thrust toward patrimonialization and signorialization of water and water rights irresistible, perhaps even attractive. No resistance was offered and on the contrary many Venafran proprietors spontaneously donated their land and water. No doubt the new lords continued to have the subject peasants irrigate the fields "per tempus." Thus, for the people on the land, involved in irrigating routines along the banks of the Volturno, disruptions were limited, and reasons to resist the appropriations few. Even the Carapellans who unsuccessfully resisted an increase in surplus extraction by the owners of the land and, finally, its water, did so only because their day-to-day livelihood was endangered. When powerful lords determined that they could exert dominion and control over a water course, lesser cultivators and peasants would have acquiesced. The rulers who profligately gave away rights over these waters certainly did.[78] This combination of rulers willing to devolve water rights onto their supporters and irrigators unable and unwilling to prevent appropriations created a situation of private control of water resources in much of the peninsula.

---

[78] However, B. Rosenwein, "The Family Politics of Berengar I (888–924)," *Speculum* 71 (1996), pp. 247–89, teaches that such profligacy was good statesmanship.

The Lucchesia, where water appears not to have been patrimonialized until after 1000, and then only in a limited way, was an exception.[79]

The history of the struggles among irrigators (and the absence of such struggles), like the history of irrigation and the history of attempts to govern the "uncultivated" waters in early medieval Italy, is shadowy and at times elusive. A careful analysis reveals only the salient characteristics of these histories, and casts dim beams of light on related matters of agricultural technique and social hierarchy. Nevertheless, the history of the agricultural adaptations of water emerges from total obscurity with outlines matching the more significant developments visible in the administration of water by early medieval societies. The mounting tendency to include water among the various types of exploitable property, perhaps the salient theme of the story of water management in the period, is detectable in the *horti*, and in the fields and woods, just as it is in the aqueducts and, in a different way, in the baths of the cities. Something similar is visible in early medieval fishing practices.

[79] Explained in Squatriti, "Water," pp. 30–3.

4   Water, fish, and fishing

In the middle Po valley of the tenth century fishing was a highly complex and carefully organized activity. The *Honorantie Civitatis Papie*, the document attesting to this organization, refers to a substantial association of fishers at Pavia who selected one of their number to be chief magistrate and principal interlocutor of the royal government.[1] The fishers also maintained a sizable fleet of boats (at least sixty of them) from which to fish and with which to reach fisheries and traps set in the Po's waters, whose regimen suited numerous fish species. The association collectively paid a monthly tribute in money to its magistrate, presumably a fraction of the income generated by the sale of the fishers' daily catch. The magistrate was supposed to handle this fund in such a way that the royal table in the capital city could be supplied with fresh fish delicacies on demand. The "magister" did not take fish tributes from fishers "in good standing" because of the perishable nature of this commodity. In fact the complicated taxation scheme of the *Honorantie* aimed at flexibility for the rulers, who preferred incorruptible silver coins paid regularly to payments in fish which might not always be needed. Thus the *Honorantie* reveals a sophisticated world of inland, fresh-water fishing in Italy's greatest river at the close of the period under consideration in this study. There were specialized workers and techniques, developed markets and taxation, elaborate hierarchies, and complex consumption patterns, all attuned to the riverine ecosystems of the area. The *Honorantie* is uniquely detailed, but similar fishers' brotherhoods appear fleetingly in roughly contemporary documents from Lucca and Ravenna. Taken together with the charters and with narrative accounts in which private fishing rights play a prominent role, a picture emerges in which fishing is virtually a full-scale industry in the peninsula of the 900s.

Naturally, in a peninsula fishing is always a prominent occupation. Already in Roman times fishing had been a keenly developed industry.

---

[1] *Die Honorantie Civitatis Papie*, ed. C.-R. Brühl and C. Violante (Cologne, 1983), lines 104–10, p. 20.

But there were several novelties to tenth-century Italy's fishing, which this chapter will investigate. To highlight the originality of Italian fishing before the end of the first millennium requires description of the historical background to the tenth-century situation. Therefore some delineation of the evolution of fishing from Roman through early medieval times will be presented. The links between the history of fishing in early medieval Italy and changes in the aqueous environments in the peninsula, as well as changes in the structure of Italian societies (like shifts in the legal status of water, changes in who had access to its bounty, and cultural reorientations deriving from the success of Christianity), will be the principal objects of this analysis. Yet it is not enough to ask "how was the Pavian situation reached?" without also asking "to what extent was the Pavian experience representative in early medieval Italy?" Hence this chapter investigates the variety of methods by which people set about the task of making the diverse waterscapes bear fruit by fishing in them, showing the essential unity of fishing customs in various environments in Italy.

The Roman heritage

For several centuries before the *Honorantie Civitatis Papie* was drawn up, Pavians and other Italians had hauled fish out of their waters, stored them, and eaten them. It was on this ancient foundation that early medieval fishing relied. In Roman Italy fishing secured culturally and economically important food supplies. Fish and fish products like the infamous *garum* (the Roman equivalent of ketchup, though there were several types of *garum*, unlike ketchup) contributed to the caloric intake of ordinary citizens and represented one of the most used condiments for and accompaniments to bread, staff of imperial life.[2] Furthermore, fish of certain species, sizes, and shapes, deemed rare and wonderful by members of the Roman elite, took on a cultural meaning far greater than that attributed to everyday fish. All elite gastronomy was politically charged, but among Roman aristocrats it was fish like mullet and lampreys that were the most favored luxuries. Eating them signaled the shared assumptions of the eaters, their refinement, and "home-grown" fish (brought from the host's own fishery) had even greater semantic clout. Special sea creatures were sought after and fetched astronomical

---

[2] A. McCann, "The History and Topography," in McCann (ed.), *The Roman Port and Fishery of Cosa* (Princeton, 1987), pp. 17, 37. On the *garum* factory and fishing at Cosa, see also, in the same volume, E. Gazda and A. McCann, "Reconstruction and Function," pp. 137–59. *Garum* was still produced in the 700s, at Comacchio and Genoa: M. Montanari, *Alimentazione e cultura nel medioevo* (Bari, 1988), pp. 153, 165.

prices in urban markets because their consumption reinforced and perhaps even created social distinctions. Rome's fishes, therefore, had political and social meanings as well as economic roles. Roman fishing was a correspondingly sophisticated industry.

Much of what we know about the organization of Roman fishing derives from Latin literature and technical handbooks from after 100 BC, which teem with information on the fishing practices which most interested the literate. It is important to bear in mind that these practices were only one part of the Roman fishing world; subsistence fishing and "ordinary" market fishing received far less attention from Roman writers but were certainly significant. The fishing which did interest Roman writers took place in artificially created maritime environments, *vivaria* or *piscariae*. There, fish or sea mollusks of the preferred species were stored after capture and bred, allowed to reach maturity, and culled. While many sea-coast fisheries were run as economic ventures and sent catches to urban markets, many others were mainly recreational facilities for their happy owners, who turned some fish into pampered pets while also keeping a supply of prestigious home-grown fish handy for the glory of their dinner table. Thanks to the resilience of Roman *caementum*, these fisheries have left some vestiges of their former grandeur behind, particularly along the Tyrrhenian coast close to large cities.[3] At Cosa, for example, archeological remains demonstrate how Roman fishers combined the seasonal pursuit of tuna and other species with the breeding in captivity of prized species in complexes where processing for transport and sale was possible. Like the literary sources, these archeological traces suggest that the preference of the Roman elite for sea fish shaped the Roman fishing industry enough that its most visible, glamorous activities focused on the Mediterranean Sea and the salt-water creatures living therein.[4]

Though this maritime industry dominates the surviving data, Roman agronomists, acknowledging that inland fisheries were less "noble" than

---

[3] McCann, *The Roman Port*, documents a fine example. See also G. Schmiedt, *Il livello antico del mar Tirreno* (Florence, 1972), pp. 215–36; R. Zeepvat, "Fishponds in Roman Britain," in M. Aston (ed.), *Medieval Fish, Fisheries, and Fishponds in England* (Oxford, 1988), pp. 17–18; W. Radcliffe, *Fishing from Earliest Times* (New York, 1921), pp. 205, 223; *Paulys Realenzyklopädie* (Stuttgart, 1950), 14, pp. 1783–4, and Supplementband 4 (Stuttgart, 1924), p. 459.

[4] Tuna fishing was the object of *Digest* 8.4.13. In general on the environmental impact of Roman fishing, see J. Hughes, *Pan's Travail* (Baltimore, 1994), pp. 21–2, 103–5. On Roman appetite for sea fisheries: see *Paulys Realenzyklopädie* 14, pp. 1783–4; Columella, *Res Rustica*, ed. H. Boyd Ash and E. Foster (London, 1941–55), 8.16.1, p. 402. See Radcliffe, *Fishing*, p. 203, on the Roman love of sea fish (even emperors without *vivaria* bought them: *Codex Theodosianus*, ed. T. Mommsen and P. Krueger [Berlin, 1905], 14.20.1, p. 797).

coastal ones, also knew that fresh-water fisheries could be very lucrative.[5] Thus, the aristocratic predilection for certain sea fish, which led the ruling class to build, use, and celebrate so many coastal fisheries, did not preclude sensible investments in inland fisheries too. We are far better informed about ornamental fisheries on the Tyrrhenian coast than on Roman fresh-water fisheries, but should not underestimate the diffusion and elaboration of the latter. In the hinterland of Rome, for instance, numerous villas had small seasonal fresh-water fisheries to stock and rear captured fish. They functioned until the dog days of summer (and increased evaporation) made their water too precious to use in this way. In late antique documents there is further evidence of the normality of fresh-water fishing in Italy. In Diocletian's *Edict* sea fish cost twice as much as "the best" river fish, but river fish were still worth listing, a sign that fresh-water fishing mattered. Rutilius Namantianus, who remarked on the Tyrrhenian fisheries as he passed them returning to Gaul, probably would also have remarked on less aristocratic and prestigious fishing structures removed from the coast, had these had any literary and cultural allure for his refined audience.[6]

Both this less remarked-upon style of fishing from ponds and river-banks and the Roman fisheries along the coastline of the peninsula depended on the basic Roman legal concept that the use of the navigable waters was free, open to all comers, public. Roman law codes enunciated and embellished upon this concept. It was the bedrock upon which all Roman fishing depended. The *Institutes* (2.1.2) proposed that "the right to fish in harbors and rivers is common to all," while the *Digest* (1.8), building on early pan-Mediterranean custom, stated that the sea and its shores were open to everyone. For Rome's lawyers the waters were "res publica extra patrimonium," or things over which the Roman state exercised jurisdiction but not property rights, simply ensuring that their use be available to citizens. The fish within these waters differed slightly from the waters themselves; although no one owned them they were capable of becoming the object of ownership rights through capture (*Digest*,

---

[5] Varro, *Rerum Rusticarum Libri*, ed. W. Davis Hooper (London, 1934), 3.17.2, p. 522. Macrobius, however, despised all cultivated fish: *Saturnalia*, ed. F. Eyssenhardt (Leipzig, 1893), 3.15.4–10, 3.16.1–10, pp. 202–4, 207. For archeological data, see R. Thomas and A. Wilson, "Water Supply for Roman Farms in Latium and South Etruria," *PBSR* 64 (1994), pp. 164–7.

[6] Thomas and Wilson, "Water Supply," pp. 164–6, provide an important survey of central Italian fishponds of imperial date, suggesting the gap separating the literary image and the archeological reality of fresh-water fishing. See also *Diokletians Preisedikt*, ed. S. Lauffer (Berlin, 1971), 5.1–12, p. 108. In 416 Rutilius Namantianus noted several fisheries on the coast north of Rome: *De Reditu Suo*, ed. E. Doblhofer (Heidelberg, 1972), 1.379, p. 116.

41.1.1).[7] Fishers and builders of fisheries were citizens who chose to exercise rights which everyone held but not everyone exercised. Fishers in open waters converted fish into property by seizing them. Instead, by building a fishery the builders went a step further and removed from the public sphere small areas of coast or river, and the fishes swimming inside the fisheries ceased to be "property of no one," belonging to the owner of the fishery. Roman fishery practice, in other words, circumscribed the theoretical openness of all waters to all people. The limitation of the publicness of waterways by fisheries was temporary, lasting only as long as the fishery withstood the wear and tear of the elements (though the ruins show that could be a very long time indeed). Thus all Roman fishing, including the style which employed fisheries, relied on the theory of water's natural publicness. It was in this area that the most important developments were to occur during the early Middle Ages.

As noted earlier, large-scale subsistence fishing in both fresh and sea water, which underlay the legal idea of water's publicness, must be presumed, for the subaltern people who practiced it left few traces of their activity. Indeed, throughout the history of fishing in Italy, the evidence is richest for the practices which concerned elites. This surely distorts our understanding of how people fished, but our image cannot elude the evidence, with its focus on elite fishing. Thus, the salient characteristics of such fishing during the Roman period are the distinction between salt- and fresh-water fish, so important to Flavian aristocrats, and a corresponding separation between fishing that was principally commercial, practiced widely in the inland waters of the Italian peninsula, and a more ornamental fishing, which could also have commercial outlets, designed to increase the status and renown of the fisher or fishery-owner, carried out mostly in the sea, close to the coast, or in artificial habitats. During the late imperial period the aristocratic class whose culture gave rise to these distinctions encountered increasing economic and political difficulties, and floundered. The demise of the urban aristocracy coincided with the erasure of the distinguishing characteristics of imperial Roman fishing. Hence, in the fourth century, Palladius did not discuss fisheries in his guide to proper husbandry, whereas before him agronomists did, a sign of diminished aristocratic concern for *vivaria*.

---

[7] P. Fenn, *The Origin of the Right of Fishery in Territorial Waters* (Cambridge, MA, 1926), pp. 3–14, 20; G. Mira, *La pesca nel medioevo nelle acque interne italiane* (Milan, 1937), pp. 1–2. A clear statement is in *Institutiones*, ed. P. Krueger (Berlin, 1872), 2.1.2, p. 10: "flumina autem omnia et portus publicae sunt: ideoque ius piscandi omnibus communis est in portubus fluminibusque." Roman law codes are not always consistent about which waters (all? perennial? navigable?) should be always public and which ownable.

What survived best into the early medieval period was the tradition of inland fishing. Inland waters provided fish for people too far from the coasts to benefit from their bounty or too poor to afford the luxury fish cultivated in coastal *vivaria*. As we shall see, there were other, less economically rational reasons for the resilience of inland fisheries, which were admirably adapted to the food regimens of (inland) monastic communities. Meanwhile, coastal and open-sea fishing, known to have been practiced into the third century from ports such as Cosa's, dwindled. Late antique fishers, however, *were* occasionally active in the sea, for example in Istria, and erudite men knew most about sea fish. In zones of Italy under the control of Byzantium Roman traditions of fishing survived well beyond late antiquity: at Reggio Calabria salvage excavations uncovered a fish-processing plant that survived earthquakes and inundations and produced fish preserves into the eighth century. Here the cultural continuity facilitated by Byzantine authority gave coastal fishing unexpected resilience.[8] But sea fishing also endured into the early Middle Ages in parts of Italy whose coastal lagoons and/or exceptionally meager fresh-water hydrology created special environmental conditions. Still, the aridity and flat coastlines of Apulia were not the norm. The fresh-water ecosystems of postclassical Italy were in general adequate suppliers of fish. Consequently, fishing as it is portrayed in our documents was very seldom a marine activity during the period.[9]

This medieval change did not, however, separate classical fishing from its successor altogether. While Christian alimentary norms changed the meaning of fish on the tables of believers, some fishing patterns that emerge from the postclassical sources closely reflect the Roman past. For example, even though they did not make a fetish of fish as certain Romans

---

[8] Isidore of Seville, *Etymologiarum sive Originum Libri XX*, ed. M. Lindsay (Oxford, 1911), 12.6.1–64, represents late antique piscatory learning. See R. Spadea, "Lo scavo della stazione 'Lido' (Reggio Calabria)," *MEFR. Moyen âge* 103 (1991), pp. 689–707, who suggests that Reggio's environmental conditions, favorable to tuna, made the fishery work; he neglects cultural expectations. Very scanty bone evidence from early medieval Naples (a city in the Byzantine *oikumene*) indicates that "ancient" fish species were consumed there: A. Frezza, "Resti di pesci dal monastero medievale di S. Patrizia, Napoli," *AM* 22 (1995), pp. 611–17.

[9] This does not apply to subsistence fishing, of course, but too little is known about it. Some seas were thoroughly exploited; Constantinople's fishers plied the Bosphorus' waters in the early Middle Ages: G. Dagron, "Poissons, pêcheurs, et poissonniers de Constantinople," in G. Dagron and C. Mango (eds.), *Constantinople and Its Hinterland* (Aldershot, 1995), pp. 58–61. *Ostrea* were fished in Istria and Campania in the sixth century, according to Cassiodorus, *Variarum Libri Duodecim*, ed. T. Mommsen (Berlin, 1894), 12.22, p. 378 (also 9.6, p. 272, on Baiae's fisheries). On Apulia, see J.-M. Martin, *La Pouille du VIe au XIe siècle* (Rome, 1993), pp. 402–8. See also R. Hoffmann, "Economic Development and Aquatic Ecosystems in Medieval Europe," *American Historical Review* 101 (1996), p. 647.

did, early medieval elites were perfectly capable of perceiving social value in special fish.[10] The sixth-century occupants of fortifications above Como, a military elite, consumed mostly large pike, but also some trout, eels, and fish of the carp family. In rent contracts and inventories of Carolingian date the largest fish of a catch, or the harvest of particular fish like trout or eels or pike, could be reserved for potentates.[11] Surely one function of these payments was to elevate the gastronomy of the powerful from anonymity, exactly as the "home-grown" mullet of the Flavians did. For while transportation systems and settlement patterns in early medieval Italy precluded the possibility that sea fish retain their cultural meaning for elite consumers living far from coasts, nevertheless the fish remained a creature whose size and species communicated messages of power.

The new fishing patterns

The history of fishing in early medieval Italy illustrates both the dialectic between continuity and innovation typical of the postclassical centuries and the dialectic between nature and culture characteristic of all environmental history. If the *vivaria* of ancient Rome survived, duly adapted, there is much in eighth-century Italian documents that no Roman fisher could have recognized. Some of the novelty arose from new ecological conditions. The waterways of the peninsula were far less regulated and humanized in AD 700 than they had been four hundred years earlier, and this made a difference for the communities of fish dwelling in them. (Though the specific situation varied considerably from locality to locality, in general there was probably more water flowing more gently, due to climatic fluctuations, to the growth of wetlands capable of absorbing floods, and to increased forest cover; there was probably more shade along riverbanks and more tree trunks floating in the water, helpful for spawning many species; thanks to the marshes, there were likely more

---

[10] La *"Carta Piscatoria" di Ravenna*, ed. G. Monti, in his *Le corporazioni nell'evo antico* (Bari, 1934), pp. 217–19, allows the archbishop to take for himself the largest of some fish types: size, not just species, mattered (see also H. Zug Tucci, "Il mondo medievale dei pesci tra realtà e immaginazione," *Settimane* 31 [1985], pp. 319–20; and J. Verdon, "Recherches sur la pêche et la pisciculture en Occident durant le haut moyen âge," in *Actes du 102e congrès national des sociétés savantes: section d'archéologie et d'histoire de l'art* [Paris, 1979], p. 339).

[11] For fish remains from the castle at Monte Barro (Como), see "Schede 1991," *AM* 19 (1992), p. 600. See *M&D* V.2, 787:475 (866), for pike; trout are specified in the polyptych of *S. Colombano di Bobbio*, ed. A. Castagnetti, in *Inventari altomedievali di terre, coloni, e redditi*, ed. Castagnetti et al. (Rome, 1979), p. 138, on eels and trout. Some fish payments symbolized the property rights of landowners who delegated the use rights to others (who paid the symbolic fish).

algae suspended in the waters, vital to the aquatic food chain; there were probably fewer barriers to migration built by humans, and, of course, fewer fishers to deplete stocks.[12])

The later 700s appear to have been a time of accelerated change in water use in Italy, partly because there survive more charters for the decades after 750 than for earlier times. These charters show Italy's greater landowners focusing more and more attention on the procurement of fish. The nature of their demand determined some innovations. To supply regular amounts of fish at specific times of the year became an increasingly acute need. To this end, landowners built and maintained inland fisheries, thanks to which the accessible waters became productive and through which their productivity could be controlled and regularized. Together with these structures, and related to their dissemination, came exclusive privileges to fish in specific places.[13]

There is some ambiguity in the documents' use of the technical terms for fishery and private fishing preserves. The right to fish, usually called *piscatio* in early medieval Italy, was exclusive. It was different from the fishery (generally called *piscaria*) by which the right was exercised. In south Italy, however, particularly in Apulia, this distinction was not maintained. As occurred in southwestern France and in some regions of north Europe, in Apulia *piscaria* and *piscatio* signaled the same thing, a fishery. Moreover, local usages could vary, and even within the same locality usage was not always consistent. On occasion, even the classical word *vivarium* was still used, sometimes to describe a hatchery and sometimes a storage basin.[14] Behind all this semantic slippage lies the fact that most fisheries did hold the exclusive right to exploit determined tracts of water even when donors or renters did not bother to spell this out, perhaps considering it self-evident. But in many charters, especially those pertaining to the Po valley, the redactors appear to have made an effort to separate the right to fish in a specified body of water, a right that they could exploit

---

[12] An edifying study of early medieval conditions is furnished by M. Cremaschi and A. Marchesini, "L'evoluzione di un tratto di pianura padana (provincie di Reggio e Parma)," *AM* 5 (1978), pp. 542–62. For a general treatment of fresh-water biology, see A. Outwater, *Water: A Natural History* (New York, 1996), pp. 26–65, who may exaggerate the relevance of forests to water regimens (see M. Newson and I. Calder, "Forests and Water Resources," *Philosophical Transactions of the Royal Society B* 324 [1989], pp. 283–98). The only survey of the impact on medieval fish of human activity is Hoffmann, "Economic Development."

[13] The relatively sudden surfacing of fisheries (*piscariae* is the most usual term) and fishing preserves (generally called *piscationes*) is due to the patterns of Lombard document survival.

[14] E.g. "Placiti del 'Regnum Italiae,'" ed. R. Volpini, in *Contributi dell'istituto di storia medievale* III, ed. P. Zerbi (Milan, 1975), 9:311 (972). See also P. Skinner, *Family Power in Southern Italy* (Cambridge, 1995), p. 78. On Germany, see E. Cahn, *Das Recht der Binnenfischerei im deutschen Kulturgebiet* (Frankfurt, 1956), p. 33.

haphazardly, from the fishery proper, where a commitment of labor and an investment in physical structures involved the proprietor in permanent and not just whimsical exploitation of resources.

With different rhythms in different parts of the peninsula (quite suddenly in the 780s in the Byzantine-influenced Exarchate, partially and only late in the 900s in the Lucchesia), fisheries and private fishing rights became a standard feature of most waterscapes in the ninth century. Thus inland fisheries (*piscariae*) and extensive exclusive fishing preserves (*piscationes*) were the crucial element of the new, post-Roman piscatory world. They accompanied the concentration of wealth and power in the hands of the few and indeed were an important component of the process by which large landed properties, fortified with numerous exclusive rights, spread across the countryside. For the formation of ever-larger estates, often run as manors by powerful proprietors, was contemporary with the advent of *piscaria* and *piscationes*. The new landholding patterns appear to have affected "waterholding" patterns, as rights over water often depended on owning contiguous land in Germanic custom and early medieval practice.[15]

The *piscaria* mentioned in the contracts of the eighth century and later may represent a revival of Roman-style piscatory administration or only renewed interest in such structures among the literate. In either case, they differed from their Roman counterparts because they clustered along the banks of inland waters by preference. In propitious environmental circumstances some early medieval sea fisheries existed. Near Siponto on the Adriatic in the late eighth century Benevento's S. Sophia owned a fishery, as did S. Vincenzo al Volturno in 812.[16] But overall, even when the sea was not far, early medieval fisheries shied from its salty waters. Perhaps the more important departure from Roman conditions was represented by the extensive presence of fishing preserves and exclusive fishing rights in certain waters, for these restricted the public waterscapes in ways Roman law did not admit. These too were primarily an inland and fresh-water phenomenon, though the rulers of tenth-century Gaeta controlled fishing rights in the Pontine islands.[17]

This reorientation of large-scale fishing activities – which was only

---

[15] Cahn, *Das Recht*, pp. 26, 73–86; M. Venditelli, "Diritti e impianti di pesca degli enti ecclesiastici romani tra X e XIII secolo," *MEFR. Moyen âge* 102 (1992), p. 389.

[16] For Siponto, see Vat. Lat. 4939, 41r (774). *Chronicon Vulturnense* I, ed. V. Federici (Rome, 1925), 42:263 (fake?), records a fishing zone at Siponto "ad sippie prindendum," the only instance I know of squid fishing from the time. On south Italian sea fishing, there is also J.-M. Martin, "Città e campagna," in G. Galasso (ed.), *Storia del Mezzogiorno* III (Naples, 1990), p. 334.

[17] For Gaeta, see Skinner, *Family Power*, p. 78. In the 830s poachers fished in the Patria coastal lagoon, evidently a preserve with salty water: *Sicardi Principis Pactio cum Neapolitanis*, ed. F. Bluhme, 33, 37, p. 217.

partial, since less-documented fresh-water fishing *was* practiced in Roman Italy – has several concomitant explanations. Quite aside from technological considerations (early medieval ships were small, unsuited to the high seas, and the ever-more-common water mills were natural springboards for inland fisheries) and environmental factors (it was easier to catch fresh-water fish, which were then more abundant), inland fisheries and fishing preserves reflect a medieval taste for fresh-water fish.[18] To be more specific, the abundance of *piscaria* in the documents which survive reflect the predilections of the early medieval archivists, almost all of whom were monks. For them, the Biblical distinctions between the Christ-like fresh-water fish and the demonic sea fish of the sort the Apocalypse promised were important. Though early monastic legislators were uncertain on the subject, in the course of the early Middle Ages regular clergy embraced the idea that fishes, especially those swimming in fresh water, were ideal, pure food, suitable replacements for the meats of the *potentes* which the monastic vocation abhorred. The eighth century was the time when fish attained the fateful status of not-meat.[19] Monastic alimentary customs and the enforcement of ascetic, non-carnivorous practices among monks thus influenced the dissemination of private fisheries and fishing preserves in early medieval Italy.

Already the bigger sixth-century monasteries, such as Vivarium in Calabria, had pioneered the field of systematic water-exploitation by monks.[20] Vivarium illustrates the intense interest exhibited by late antique monastic communities in the maintenance of fish supplies, even though fish had not yet become the monastic flesh of choice. Other smaller, poorer communities without powerful patrons also confronted the problems of conforming to Christian dietary restrictions and their bloodless ideal. All monastic houses, rich or poor, shared certain characteristics relevant to the history of fishing: a sizable group of mouths to feed, regular requirements for certain foods at specific times of the week and year, and a dominant culture in which ritual observance was paramount. The great awakening of Italian monasticism during the eighth century brought with it increased standardization of practice and

---

[18] M. Montanari, "I prodotti e l'alimentazione," in A. Carile (ed.), *Storia di Ravenna* II (Venice, 1991), p. 96. A fine example of monastic houses *choosing* to fish in a river though the coast was accessible comes from Rome: Venditelli, "Diritti e impianti," p. 389. The argument lately made in favor of a revision of the view that fresh-water fish predominated on medieval tables (Aston, *Medieval Fish, Fisheries, and Fishponds in England*, p. 3) has some applicability to early medieval Italy.

[19] Zug Tucci, "Il mondo," pp. 292–3, 296–9; Montanari, *Alimentazione e cultura*, pp. 47–8; Hoffmann, "Economic Development," p. 638.

[20] Cassiodorus, *Institutiones*, ed. R. Mynors (Oxford, 1961), 1.29, p. 73. The Calabrian monastery overlooked the Gulf of Schillace and Vivarium's fisheries contained sea fish; hence they did not become the model for early medieval *piscaria* to follow.

more rigorous imposition of norms of culinary behavior. The revival induced monasteries, larger and more populous than ever before, to seek out secure and predictable supplies of the foods they needed, with fish increasingly prominent on the list. The special consumption needs of the new and re-founded communities were characterized by rigid and inelastic demand. Large quantities of fish were becoming essential at rigidly fixed times.[21]

The monks' desire for alimentary purity felicitously coincided with the desire of patrons to acquire the favor of the monks and their saintly protectors. Eighth-century patrons responded to the demands of the revitalized monastic communities with enthusiasm, donating scores of fisheries and extensive fishing rights.[22] This response was possible because by then the legal apparatus of the Roman state, and the type of fishing which had

[21] On the rebirth of Italian monachism in the 700s, see G. Penco, *Storia del monachesimo in Italia* (Milan, 1983), pp. 131–60; on the south, M. Del Treppo, "Longobardi, Franchi, e Papato in tre secoli di storia vulturnense," *Archivio storico per le provincie napoletane* 73 (1953–4), pp. 37–8. On monastic fishing in general, see C. Kosch, "Wasserbaueinrichtungen in hochmittelalterliche Konventanlagen Mitteleuropas," in *Geschichte der Wasserversorgung* IV (Mainz, 1991), p. 117; and, in the same volume, C. Bond, "Mittelalterliche Wasserversorgung in England und Wales," p. 165. C. Bond, "Monastic Fisheries," in Aston, *Medieval Fish, Fisheries, and Fishponds in England*, p. 73, is overly optimistic on observance of dietary restrictions prior to 1200. Monks were members of the carnivorous elite in that time, and brought their culture into the cloister. C. Dyer, "The Consumption of Freshwater Fish in Medieval England," in the same volume, pp. 27–38, estimates monastic fish consumption (but uses late, idealized household management guides for nobles to do so). C. Currie, "The Role of Fishponds in the Monastic Economy," in R. Gilchrist and H. Mynum (eds.), *The Archaeology of Rural Monasteries* (Oxford, 1989), p. 154, states that ten monks ate 875 pounds of fish per year, but assumes that only fish was eaten on fast days.

[22] Emblematic of the large holdings ecclesiastical foundations held by the 900s is *CDLangobardiae* 782:1374–5 (978), where Otto I confirmed properties to S. Pietro in Ciel d'Oro. Examples of transactions ending with churches or monasteries in control of fisheries can be found in: *CDL* V, 66:232 (776); *I placiti del "Regnum Italiae"* I, ed. C. Manaresi (Rome, 1955–60), 10:29 (798); 36:111 (824); 40:126 (830); Vat. Lat. 4939, 52v (834); *Urkunden der Karolinger* III, 41:129 (840); 157:337 (c. 830); polyptychs of S. Giulia in Brescia and S. Colombano at Bobbio (*Inventari altomedievali di terre, coloni, e redditi*, pp. 84, 138); *I diplomi italiani di Lodovico III e di Rodolfo II*, ed. L. Schiaparelli (Rome, 1910), 9:29 (901); *I diplomi di Ugo e Lotario, di Berengario II, e di Adalberto*, ed. L. Schiaparelli (Rome, 1924), 10:323 (958); 30:93–4 (932). For fishing rights, see: *CDL* III, 40:237 (771); 44:258 (772); *CDL* IV, 11:29 (750); *CDL* V, 46:169 (766); Vat. Lat. 4939, 41r, 53v (834), 55v (841); *I placiti* 17:53 (804); 30:93 (818); *Urkunden der Karolinger* I, 113:159 (776); *Urkunden der Karolinger* III, 22:93 (834); "Gli archivi," 211:470 (963); *Diplomi italiani di Lodovico III*, 13:42 (901); *S. Giulia da Brescia* polyptych, in *Inventari altomedievali di terre, coloni, e redditi*, pp. 58, 61, 75, 86 (the "lacora ad piscandum" of this last document [pp. 75, 80] and the "condome ad piscandum" of Vat. Lat. 4939, 41r, are *piscaria*, or artificially created fishing sites). On monasteries and fisheries, see Radcliffe, *Fishing*, p. 291; M. Montanari, *L'alimentazione contadina nell'alto medioevo* (Naples, 1979), p. 283. H. Fichtenau, *Living in the Tenth Century* (Chicago, 1991), p. 281, suggests that the location of early medieval monasteries could actually be dictated by availability of fish. Fichtenau exaggerates the paucity of fish in tenth-century Europe, however.

flourished under it, had crumbled. The result was that inland fisheries and extensions of water in which a sole proprietor could fish proliferated. Fresh-water fisheries were disseminated in growing numbers in waterways as close as possible to the owners' central place of consumption, preferably in different ecological zones, so that when a mishap, a frost or drought or disease, struck one fishery, fish from other sources remained available to the nuns and monks.[23]

The gastronomic choices, the technological limitations, the social and religious forces, the economic laws, and even the ecological factors which fostered the extension of private fishing zones in the streams, lakes, and rivers of the Italian peninsula were intimately related to changes in the legal status of the waters. Early medieval fishing in Italy differed from classical fishing also because the medieval fishing preserve was predicated on the un-Roman notion that the private individual could reserve for his own use a body of flowing water. The early medieval fishing world was the outcome of the progressive patrimonialization of the inland waters in the opening centuries of the Middle Ages. The waters which the Roman state had guarded for the use of all came increasingly under the tutelage of local landlords who exploited them and the fisheries in them according to their local interests. This shift from a culture in which some resources are public and common to all inhabitants to one in which even the waters are property affected the organization of fishing as much as did the disappearance of the Roman aristocracy and its voracious taste for sea fish or the new stream regimens determined by depopulation, afforestation, climate change, and the attendant evolution of aquatic ecosystems.

It is relevant that the emergence of this new world of private inland waters and fishing preserves occurred in a period when fish were plentiful in Italian water courses and lakes.[24] In light of this, the hypothesis that restrictions and inhibitions on the exploitation of the wilderness were introduced only when resources were thinning out and becoming precious for the elite because of depletion loses credibility.[25] Cultural norms regarding property played the larger role in the formation of the post-

---

[23] Ennodius describes the Alpine tributaries of the Po, where later many monastic fisheries arose, as positively arctic: *Vita Epiphani*, in *Opera*, ed. F. Vogel (Berlin, 1885), 147, p. 102. On the iced-over and dried-up Migliarina fishery in the 900s, see Montanari, *Alimentazione e cultura*, p. 36.

[24] This is impossible to know with precision, but Mira, *La pesca*, p. 89, makes some reasonable estimates. Hoffmann, "Economic Development," also postulates an early medieval phase of copious fish.

[25] The notion is ubiquitous, especially applied to hunting and hunting rights; see T. Glick, *Islamic and Christian Spain in the Early Middle Ages* (Princeton, 1979), p. 109; and esp. H. Savage, "Hunting in the Middle Ages," *Speculum* 8 (1933), pp. 34–5. See also Montanari, *L'alimentazione contadina*, pp. 254–6, who applies it to fishing on pp. 280–2.

classical piscatory environment, its private fisheries, and the attendant fishing rights.

The rise of private fishing rights

In the charters *piscatio* was seldom a right with loose boundaries. Normally it was strictly delimited, though the southern Lombards tended toward greater specificity than their northern counterparts, measuring out in paces how far a *piscatio* extended, or limiting another to only the islets protruding from a river.[26] Some north Italian donations of fishing rights also restricted the privilege to the water surfaces "pertaining to" a given manor.[27] In the 960s the monks of Subiaco also sought confirmation of their meticulously measured fishing rights in the Aniene's headwaters.[28] In both the Kingdom of Italy and the southern principalities rulers became rather less exact in their piscatory generosity after about 800. The donation of fishing preserves in early medieval Italy seems to have worked much as it did in medieval England, where periods of strong central authority coincided with periods when *piscationes* were carefully circumscribed. The more nebulous grants of Italy's rulers were made during spells of anemic central rule.[29] For example, King Desiderius, whose position in Italian politics was often precarious, gave to his favorite foundation, S. Salvatore in Brescia, very extensive fishing rights in 772, so that "it be permitted to the men of this convent to have and to exercise the right of fishing in all the lakes and rivers within the borders of the cities aforementioned [where the convent owned land]."[30] Similarly, the embattled Carolingian emperor Lothair gave a Pavian monastery the right to fish anywhere on the Po or Ticino.[31] But wideranging grants such as these, or like that confirmed by Berengarius to Cremona's bishops, which included exclusive fishing rights on the entire course of a large river like the Adda, remained rare.[32] In the end, most

---

[26] Vat. Lat. 4939, 41r (c. 775), gives a *piscatio* 300 paces wide, sandwiched between two other *piscationes*; 53v (834), a 200-pace one; 52v (834), a mile-long, 200-pace wide concession.   [27] For instance, *Urkunden der Karolinger* I, 113:159 (776).
[28] *Urkunden Konrad I.*, 336:451.   [29] Bond, "Monastic Fisheries," p. 79.
[30] *CDL* III, 44:258: "ut liceat homines ex ipsa monasteria in ipsa iudiceria omne in tempore piscatione habendum et faciendum per omnes locoras [for lacoras?] et fluminis in finibus predictis civitatis."   [31] *Urkunden der Karolinger* III, 22:93 (834), an impractical gift.
[32] *I diplomi di Berengario* I, ed. L. Schiaparelli (Rome, 1903), 112:289 (916): "piscaria quoque eiusdem ecclesie a Vulparolo usque in caput Adduae cum molendinis at portubus transitoriis eidem episcopio confirmamus iure proprietario usque in perpetuum"; see also 73:198 (910) which suggests that Charlemagne originated the grant. For wideranging concessions, see *CDLangobardiae* 278:468 (879), in which Carloman gave S. Zeno "piscaciones et venaciones per totas ripas lacus" on the Garda, "a meridie ... usque Sermionem et Piscariam"; and *Diplomi italiani di Lodovico III*, 13:42 (901).

grants of *piscatio* were restricted to the territory of a given community or to a specified water course. The temporary right to fish in the Badareno from the sea upstream to a fixed point, "the location called Pensulus," in Ravenna in 943, was more typical.[33]

According to the documents which survive, the main beneficiaries of these grants of fishing rights were ecclesiastical institutions, but laymen presumably also took advantage of rulerly profligacy whenever they could. The *hypatoi* of Gaeta, actually, donated fishing privileges at Ponza to (related) laymen in 1019.[34] These concessions of *piscationes* by rulers raise the question of the origins of these rights. Huge, topographically vague fishing rights are consistently associated with the highest secular authorities by early medieval Italian documents. The kings, dukes, and princes donated and alienated rights which their fiscs appear to have inherited from Roman emperors.[35] For the postclassical rulers, what had been *publicum* was their personal property, to be administered, used, or alienated as they saw fit. In the process by which once-public water resources of the peninsula became private property of individuals and churches, the incorporation of the imperial fisc in the private, personal property of the post-Roman rulers was a crucial step. During the last decades of the Lombard monarchy and under the Carolingians, particularly those whose authority was feeblest, the royal fisc shrank in size. Rulers increasingly lost control of natural resources like rivers.

The grants and concessions by which Italy's various rulers allowed others to appropriate water and fish resources do not dictate that rulers alone had rights over all waters. In the early Middle Ages no legal thinker enunciated the principle that all waters pertained to the governing authorities, and indeed even the Justinianic code made exceptions to this Roman idea for non-perennial water courses. Thus, when we discover powerful individuals in early medieval charters receiving water rights and *piscatio* rights from kings or emperors we may be witnessing a use of stately grants as retroactive justification for, or additional insurance against others' usurpation of, rights long exercised de facto.

The powerful did not control all the *piscaria* or *piscationes* recorded in the documents. Two very striking charters from the region of Rieti show

[33] The *Carta Piscatoria*, p. 218, gives use of the river Badareno "et tendente da locus qui dicitur Pensulus da usque in mare . . . habemus piscare" (yet *Monumenti* II, 4:11 [858], from the annals of Camaldoli, records a vague concession from Ravenna's archbishop to a monastery "omni tempore quando volueritis piscari"). Though dated 943, the *Carta Piscatoria* incorporates older agreements. Another good example of a "limited" grant, on the Marta north of Rome in 820, can be found in J. Raspi Serra and C. Laganara Fabriano, *Economia e territorio* (Naples, 1987), p. 257.   [34] *CDCajetanus* 135.

[35] C.-R. Brühl, *Fodrum, Gistum, Servitium Regis* (Cologne, 1974), pp. 282–3; G.-P. Bognetti, "La navigazione padana e il sopravvivere della civiltà antica," in his *L'età longobarda* IV (Milan, 1968), pp. 547–8.

that simple laymen owned fisheries and even *piscationes* in the 760s and 770s.[36] Obviously the monopoly of fishing by the local *potentes* was not quite total even in the Sabine hills in the late eighth century. Likewise in the ninth-century Ravennate some ordinary people owned fisheries and fishing rights, though nowhere near as extensive as those the archbishops held.[37] This suggests that fishing rights, and by extension fisheries, were not always the prerogative of the ruler, and even when monasteries, bishoprics, or secular lords controlled them we cannot assume that this was thanks only to a prior donation by the local secular authorities. Perhaps only rulers could grant wide-ranging fishing rights over huge extensions of water, but the lowly Scambert and Lupo of Rieti held equivalent though far smaller rights too. If lesser landholders could possess fisheries and fishing rights over small bodies of water in central Italy, it is possible that in some cases entitlement to exclusive fishing in a given body of water derived from ancient common rights exercised by local farmers.[38]

Admittedly, the Reatine example is uncommon. The development of *piscaria* and *piscationes* in eighth- and ninth-century Italy was inimical to men such as Scambert and Lupo. Fisheries run by a subject class of fishermen for great landowners, especially monastic ones, who controlled the exclusive right to fish, a result of the new vision of water as private property, became the norm by the tenth century. Some friction was inevitable while the powerful jostled for position along the waterways of Italy, spearheading the transition from a Roman world of fishing as a common right and waters as public resources to an early medieval world of private, exclusive rights over the inland waters. Quarrels and legal disputes arose from the imposition of private, patrimonial claims over the waters.

The clash between lesser cultivators (often represented as collectivities in the Italian *placita*) and the champions of the *piscationes* and large fisheries appears to have flared up in the decades around 800, surely a tribute to the efficiency of the Carolingian courts and their record-keeping. In the duchy of Spoleto, in 798 Carolingian *missi* ruled in favor of the monks of Farfa (a Carolingian protégé anyway) against the rather pusillanimous Duke Guinichis who claimed ignorance of the affair and

---

[36] *CDL* V, 46:169 (766; since C. Brühl does, I am inclined to accept this charter's authenticity, though a mere Scambertus owning *piscationibus* is odd); 66:232 (776).

[37] *Monumenti* I, 7:99 (896). Ravenna, in a wetland area, was not a "normal" place. In medieval England a variety of people controlled fisheries: Currie, "Role," pp. 147–51.

[38] On the commons in ancient and early medieval Italy, see L. Bussi, "Terre comuni e usi civici," in Galasso, *Storia del Mezzogiorno* III, pp. 213–15, on the south; G.-P. Bognetti, "I beni comuni e l'organizzazione del villaggio nell'Italia superiore fino al mille," *Rivista storica italiana* 77 (1965), pp. 469–99, on the north. Documents like *Urkunden Konrad I.*, 348:475 (near Verona, in 967) – which accords the right "in suis praeterea aquis nemo presumat piscari," but adds the provision "nisi sicuti antiquitus licentia fuit" – are tantalizing references to old, perhaps common fishing rights.

left his men to take the blame for an assault on the *piscaria* of Farfa.[39] Guinichis' men, who "broke the nets of the monastery and stole the fish and beat its men" in what was probably not an act of random vandalism but rather a backlash of the traditional notion that such *piscaria*, to use Cassiodorus' terms, deprived the local public of what ought to benefit all. The Spoletan thugs did not act to defend a shimmering ideal, but their violence, carried out methodically in several different places, is best read as an attack on Farfa's (recently established?) right to fish and organize *piscaria* for the benefit of the monks alone. As the area of Spoleto moved from a theoretically open, casual way of organizing fishing to the rigid demarcations of the *piscaria* and *piscationes*, old customs were overthrown, and tensions boiled over.

Similarly, the Istrians whose case the *missi* heard at Ričana in 804 saw a deep injustice in the duke's establishment of private fishing preserves in their territory.[40] The Istrians complained that in the places where "the whole people communally fished, now we scarcely dare to fish because they [the men of the *dux*] beat us with sticks and cut our nets." The duke retorted that he had assumed the waters were his to dispose of. The Istrians were temporarily successful in their plea, but their case's principal revelation is the obliviousness to common rights over the waters of powerful men. Other *placita* from the Lombard plain a few decades later further illuminate the difficulties encountered by fishers who attempted to continue fishing as they had long done, freely, after the dissemination of patrimonial fishing rights. The inhabitants of Fiesso, like the fishers defeated by the abbey of San Fiorenzo in Fiorenzuola near Piacenza, lacking the requisite charters to uphold their claim to common fishing rights, lost the court cases.[41] These instances, like the Istrian and the Farfan contests, are interesting because they come from a period when this question had not

[39] *I placiti* 10:29: "homines suprascripti Guinichis ducis contenderent piscarias iam dicti monasterii, quas habet per singula loca ducatus Spoletani, et retia ipsius monasterii rupsissent et pisces tulissent et homines eius vapulassent." 30:93 (818) records disputes between powerful proprietors who agreed on how to exploit the waters, but not on who should. J. Steane, "The Royal Fishponds of Medieval England," in Aston, *Medieval Fish, Fisheries, and Fishponds in England*, p. 48, links political disorder to fish theft.

[40] *I placiti* 17:53–4: "mare vero publica, ubi omnis populus communiter piscabant, modo ausi non sumus piscari, quia cum fustibus nos cedunt et retia nostra concidunt." See H. Krahwinkler, *Friaul im Frühmittelalter* (Vienna, 1992), pp. 200–14; Fenn, *Origins*, pp. 3–31, supplies some legal background against which to understand this famous case.

[41] *I placiti* 36:112 of 824 (whose mention of Aistulfan *piscarias* is one of the oldest such mentions in the documents after Rothari's – though Mira, *La pesca*, p. 2, singles out a Romualdine grant of 711 as the oldest of all) records the defeat of the "men of Fiesso" by Nonantula, whose rights over extensive *piscarias* near Reggio Emilia the Fiessans impugned "malo ordine et contra legem." 40:126 of 830 records how the priest Ursus and his men, who claimed they and their ancestors had always fished in the "pischaria illas ad pissina Fischina," were thwarted by S. Fiorenzo because they lacked documents to prove their claims.

been definitely settled in Italy in favor of the incorporation of water, water rights, and, in consequence, of fishing rights within the sphere of private property.

When the matter was settled, and during the transitional period too, it was settled to the advantage of the powerful. As mentioned before, from the moment fishing rights and fisheries begin to be mentioned in the surviving sources, most of their owners are of very high status. Dukes, magnates, and particularly abbots and bishops had a stranglehold on *piscaria* and *piscationes*. They tightened their grip on both in the ninth and tenth centuries, when even kings treated fishing rights as their personal, private property, disposing of them according to their immediate interests, usually for the benefit of just such secular and clerical grandees, who could offer loyalty, service, or spiritual aid. But the willingness of the rulers of Italy, in the south and north, to grant such rights to supporters created a patchwork of competing exclusive fishing preserves over which the rulers themselves held no further sovereignty. The conception of *publicum* as the personal property of the individual ruler led to the atomization of the watery part of the royal demesne during times of political turmoil and to its subsequent control by mighty private persons.[42]

The administration of fishing

From Rome north, *piscationes* (the rights) sometimes existed without any clear connection to actual fisheries. They appeared separately in contracts because they had economic and social value. The forms this value took varied. Some fishing rights were prized because their owners themselves wanted to fish by intensive or less structured means. But in some cases the owners both fished in the water over which they held exclusive rights and rented out this privilege as well.[43] Throughout Italy until roughly the middle of the ninth century, renting *piscationes* was less widespread than it later became. This, presumably, was because owners found it more convenient to exploit their right directly, but also because private fishing preserves were not enormously common yet. Thereafter, as the richest landlords' *piscatio*-holdings outstripped their capacity to consume the benefits, they permitted others to fish within the confines of the

---

[42] Dagron, "Poissons," pp. 64–6, describes a similar process in Byzantium around 1000.

[43] The polyptych *S. Giulia da Brescia*, in *Inventari altomedievali di terre, coloni, e redditi*, p. 75 ("illa piscatio tota ad monasterium erit ducta") suggests that parts of a *piscatio* were conceivable too. On some manors, like Iseo's (p. 58), S. Giulia's *dominica piscatione* was separate from the tenants' *piscatio*: fishing rights on manors may have been allocated to the lord and workers according to the pacts which governed the distribution of the other capital resource, land. In *Monumenti* I, 43:168 (965), the archbishop obtained money for ceding *piscatione* rights in the wilderness of Palazzolo, north of Ravenna (see also 68:220 [991]; and *Monumenti* V, 28:249 [977], where a *vilicus* rents for twenty denarii).

fishing preserves, with or without the help of traps, dikes, sluices, and water-control mechanisms. Sometimes the income from renting *piscationes* was monetarized: in the environs of Bologna one *piscatio* sent the nuns of S. Giulia a pound of silver annually.[44] Evidently the monastery used its *piscatio* in those waters to generate rent, or gathered a toll from the locals who fished. In a similar fashion, in the Bientina swamps near Lucca a local abbey rented fishing privileges out after receiving them in a generous Ottonian grant; and in the equally fish-rich Tiber delta several ecclesiastical foundations rented out *piscationes* in the tenth century, as did one of the contemporary Po delta's greatest "fishlords," Ravenna's archbishopric. Indeed, renting *piscatio* appears to have been normal usage in many corners of the western Mediterranean by 1000.[45] This is also what appears to have happened with regard to some fisheries. In the early tenth century, for example, the archbishop of Ravenna exacted one-fifth of a rented fishery's catch, presumably not piecemeal but at a single time (when the fish were harvested). The archbishop sent his own workers to gather the rent, which accompanied the agrarian dues owed by the same Ferrarese couple.[46]

Renting was not the only option open to the owners of fishing rights or fisheries. Everywhere and at all times, the management of fisheries posed problems which tended to connect owners and operators to markets and systems of exchange, though the latter did not exist everywhere and at all times. The ecological balance of the fishery encouraged the consumption of the "mature" fish each year, especially when reproduction cycles of reared fish or the seasonal migration of wild species like eels created temporary surpluses. The result of this cyclical overabundance was that the great landowners, who were also the great fishery-owners, unable to consume all the product and unable to store it effectively for long periods, involved themselves in selling their excess bounty. (This was preferred to selling or exchanging the fisheries, a "means of production," for another asset.[47]) In other words, the pursuit of a stable supply engendered interest

---

[44] Polyptych *S. Giulia da Brescia*, in *Inventari altomedievali di terre, coloni, e redditi*, pp. 84, 86: "piscaria una qui redidit in anno solidibus V" and "piscatio una unde venit de argento libra I in anno." The locals must have had to rent the right to fish, which produced the silver.

[45] For Lucca, see A. Onori, *L'abbazia di S. Salvatore a Sesto e il lago di Bientina* (Florence, 1984), pp. 55–60 (and *Annales Camaldulenses*, ed. G. Mittarelli and A. Costadoni [Venice, 1755], 1, p. 357). For Rome, see Venditelli, "Diritti e impianti," p. 422; for Ravenna, "Gli archivi," 313:505 (977); 361:821 (c. 980). For Catalonia, see P. Bonnassie, *La Catalogne du milieu du Xe à la fin du XIe siècle* I (Toulouse, 1975), p. 92.

[46] "Gli archivi," 86:427 (906); also *Monumenti* V, 28:249 (977).

[47] Though this too happened: in 887, S. Ambrogio of Milan traded its "porcionem de piscaria que est prope fluvio Addua" with Arnulf's land (*Museo* 153). Hoffmann, "Economic Development," p. 656, singles out Italy as the first place where fishing rights became a market commodity.

in fisheries whose desirability depended on the predictability of their supply. But interest in and desire for fisheries, when successful, led to excess supply of a delicate product for some great proprietors, and interested them in exchange systems.

Around 800, north of the Alps, as the *Capitulare de Villis* (chs. 21, 65) shows, there were secular owners who owned so many fisheries disseminated through so many regions that they could not consume the production directly. Such owners sold the surplus fish. Similarly, S. Salvatore–S. Giulia seems to have marketed fish from its *piscaria* near Cremona in the late ninth century; though the fishery was close to the convent, it was expected to produce *solidi*, not fish, for the refectory.[48] Because of their location on waterways, which were major axes of medieval communication, and because of the nature of their production, early medieval fisheries were often connected to commercial networks.[49]

Thanks to enterprising traders like the Comacchians, salting fish was possible quite far from the sea, and smoking or drying, though undocumented, was too; sale of excess fish harvested from fisheries was therefore not the only alternative to eating it. The monks of ninth-century Bobbio arranged for the salting of their excess production in faraway fisheries, and the same process may be inferred for the fishery Arechis gave to S. Sophia around 775.[50] Extolled in most unmodern fashion by the fifth-century Ravennan archbishop Peter Chrysologus as "a healthy condiment if used with measure . . . it gives flavor, improves the intellect, generates prudence, widens the heart, increases ingenuity" (among other things), salt facilitated the long-distance transport of fisheries' product.[51] Unfortunately, there is no way of telling whether the salted fish was supposed to be marketed or simply sent to the monastery for consumption: the salted fish may have been transported to the proprietors' main center, in Liguria or Benevento.

[48] Polyptych *S. Giulia da Brescia*, in *Inventari altomedievali di terre, coloni, e redditi*, pp. 84, 86.

[49] For the Po, see F. Menant, *Campagnes lombardes du moyen âge* (Rome, 1993), p. 289.

[50] In a polyptych, *S. Colombano di Bobbio*, in *Inventari altomedievali di terre, coloni, e redditi*, p. 138, salt is distributed to the *piscaria* "propter pisces." Vat. Lat. 4939, 41r (c. 775): "et condome tres ad piscandum & ad salem faciendum." Ready availability of salt was the advantage of lagoonal and sea fisheries; "Gli archivi," 375:525 (897), suggests that Palazzolo's salt pans made fishing there especially advantageous (on Palazzolo, see G. Pasquali, "Economia e paesaggio rurale dei 'deserta' alle porte di Ravenna," in his *Agricoltura e società rurale in Romagna nel medioevo* [Bologna, 1984], pp. 53–60). See also Zug Tucci, "Il mondo," pp. 310–12.

[51] Peter Chrysologus, *Collectio Sermonum*, ed. A. Olivar (Turnhout, 1975–82), 125.1, p. 766: "salubre est condimentum si mensura non desit . . . dat saporem, intellectum parit, prudentiam generat, cor dilatat, auget ingenium, maturat dicendo, audienda componit, fitque sibi dulci, fit degustantibus tota dulcedini plenitudo."

Early medieval fisheries and their techniques

Several techniques of fishing coexisted in the large and varied post-classical peninsula. However, the subsistence fishing which may have been most relevant to coastal dwellers and the occasional capture of fish by inland dwellers seeking to vary their agrarian diets have left fewer traces than the structured fishing methods employed by the mighty. This obliges us to focus attention on the latter. Italy's elites had begun to own water sites and to exploit them in consistent fashion by the eighth century. Their *piscationes* and *piscariae* became the most obtrusive fishing method in Carolingian and later Italy.

The constructions related to an early medieval fishery could, in fact, be quite prominent. Though they are somewhat shadowy, since the charters seldom describe fisheries from a technical standpoint, they are worth considering in detail so as to emphasize the extent to which early medieval fishing created artificial habitats for fish rearing and storage, and not primitive, ephemeral traps only.[52] This is obvious in allusions to fisheries made by some ninth-century documents. In 852 Amalric, bishop of Como, won from Louis II the right to rebuild a lake fishery destroyed several decades earlier, and when he "restored" it, he built a solid and imposing structure. Similarly, in 860 another *piscaria*, on the Mincio near Lake Garda, had a complex construction suited to the fast-flowing waters of this river. In the more murky, sluggish water of the Po delta, at the end of the 900s another fishery had complicated water-intake systems with sluices and gateways.[53] Even the smaller fisheries, with fewer fixed structures and more movable equipment like nets and wicker traps, altered stream flow. The impact of early medieval fisheries on hydrology was strong, especially when they were annexes to water mills and their dams, as occurred near Bergamo in 924.[54] Fisheries like these also altered the navigability of a water course, and hence determined commercial routes.

[52] The tendency to minimize the economic, ecological, and social impact of early medieval practices seems to me to be wrong-headed.
[53] *Urkunden der Karolinger* IV, 10:82–3, with the words "destructa" and "restaurata" bearing particular significance; 31:131 describes a fishery which was once "novum opus edificatum" and now "perstruimus." A "piscaria . . . que vocatur Augusta" near Comacchio in 977 had channels and water intakes as part of its endowment: *Monumenti* V, 28:249.
[54] *CDLangobardiae* 503:866; or, from just east of Rome, *Urkunden Konrad I.*, 336:451 (967). Because mills required water-controlling devices which could be used by fisheries, the latter often piggy-backed on mill-sites. See S. Caucanas, *Moulins et irrigation en Roussillon du IXe au XVe siècle* (Paris, 1995), p. 144, for a southwestern French example; Bonnassie, *La Catalogne* I, p. 461, for a Catalan one; Bond, "Mittelalterliche Wasserversorgung," p. 165, on Britain. P. Rahtz and D. Bullough, "The Parts of an Anglo-Saxon Mill," *Anglo-Saxon England* 6 (1977), p. 25, observe that the same Old English word applied to fish-weir and mill. Hoffmann, "Economic Development," p.

The larger *piscaria* of early medieval Italy's inland streams sometimes made use of walls, basins, enclosures, weirs, and artificial canals to regulate in- and outflow of water. They also used man-made ponds ("lacus ad piscandum").[55] However, no early medieval text explicates the functioning of the fish ponds, so a reconstruction must rely on later evidence. Medieval fish ponds manipulated the natural hydrology to suit the lifestyles of desired fish species. They kept fish of different ages separated, thus curtailing the depletion of minnows which free mixing with their big brothers inevitably causes.[56] Whether natural or created by diverting the water of a stream or river into a low enclosure alongside the banks, ponds could be governed by sluices. These gateways enabled fishers to decrease or increase the water, thus regulating light and oxygen levels and hence conditions in the water (nutrients, temperature, etc.). Ponds with sluices were used wherever medieval fishers harvested their fish by draining the ponds. (If this was done in spring, around Lent, when demand might peak, the fisher had to cope with the highest water levels of the year in much of the peninsula.) This drastic fishing method was advisable in the long run on account of the depletion of food in the water, as well as of the need to aerate the soil and liberate the sluices from accumulated sediment.[57] The *vasum* or *vadum* seems to have been a pond-like enclosure of smaller dimensions, also used for fishing. These too were sometimes set in the shallows of a river's waters or along its banks. Like the artificial, regulatable ponds they were an instrument of pisciculture.[58]

Weirs (probably of wicker), traps, and nets were also staple parts of the technical structure of early medieval fisheries. They occur already in

641, stresses the ecological "blockage" mill dams created on Europe's waterways after 1000. S. Vincenzo seems to have widened the Volturno's bed to make a fishpond: R. Hodges (ed.), *San Vincenzo al Volturno* I (London, 1993), p. 38.

[55] For ponds, see polyptych *S. Giulia da Brescia*, in *Inventari altomedievali di terre, coloni, e redditi*, pp. 75, 80; *I placiti* 40:126 (of 830, near Florence, a very early mention of such a *pischina*; in England they appear later: Bond, "Monastic Fisheries," p. 92). R. Morris, "Dispute Settlement in the Byzantine Provinces in the Tenth Century," in W. Davies and P. Fouracre (eds.), *The Settlement of Disputes in Early Medieval Europe* (Cambridge, 1986), p. 141, mentions a pond at Taranto in 981. The "lacibus duobus eorumque flumine" of *Urkunden Konrad I.*, 336:451 also functioned as "piscariis."

[56] A hatchery (*vivarium*) operated in the riverine marsh ponds near Piacenza in the 800s: P. Galetti, *Una campagna e la sua città* (Bologna, 1994), p. 122.

[57] On pond management, see R. Hoffmann, "Fishponds," in J. Strayer (ed.), *Dictionary of the Middle Ages* V (New York, 1985), pp. 73–4; B. Roberts, "The Rediscovery of Fishponds," in Aston, *Medieval Fish, Fisheries, and Fishponds in England*, pp. 8–13. Apulia and Campania used natural lagoons much as Lombardy used fresh-water ponds.

[58] For *vadum* and *vasum*, see *Diplomi di Ugo*, 30:93–4 (932, on the Ticino); *CDLangobardiae* 503:866 (924) "vasum aque et piscacionibus"; 782:1375 (978), a confirmation of older possession of "vada ad piscandum quae sunt in Ticino in rivo Polonus Morasca, seu vadum quod dicitir Laude Marii, costam Teveredum, et aliud quod dicitir Sextemascum, cum illo medio quod Sepem dicitur et illud quod Adaunella nuncupatur sed etiam illa vada quae sunt in Pado."

Rothari's *Edict* but, as in later sources, the details of their use in early medieval Italy are obscure.[59] The fishery Bobbio owned near Lake Garda worked when "crates" (wicker traps) were "placed" in the Mincio's current.[60] Weirs could be used in flowing waters to direct fish into traps or enclosures where their capture was easier. Although they wore out quickly and had to be replaced often, once in place they gave good returns for minimal labor. Their effective use depended on accurate knowledge of the seasonal habits and movements of fish, a type of knowledge peculiar to fishers. In the Po delta, where the water was sluggish and could not be relied upon to drive fish against the weirs, fishers were traditionally creative in the development and deployment of weirs. Comacchio's fishers' skill and knowledge of eels' migratory patterns made their weirs highly successful. The Comacchians were famous purveyors of *garum* to north Italy by 715, and the manufacture of this specialty must have been related to the supply of fish from local traps.[61]

Nets could serve similar functions, but also could help in waters far removed from fisheries. Fishing nets were worth legislating about in the 640s. Later, in 798, the tearing of the nets of Farfa's fishers by the duke of Spoleto's men put the abbey's *piscaria* out of commission and caused a legal battle between the monks and the duke. To "draw the nets" was the standard technique of the fishery "called Burbure" near Brescia in 860 and Tiber fishers of the late 800s used nets to sift the river's flow – on one famous occasion they caught a dead pope in them. At Lucca, fishers active in the Serchio used nets cast from the river banks to catch fish in areas lacking fisheries, according to an eleventh-century text.[62]

Hook-and-line fishing was presumably practiced too in fisheries or "wild" waters, though the sources which attest to this are literary.[63] Another "instrument" employed in fishing, the islands, sometimes artificial ones, often mentioned in connection with fisheries, increased the range of the fishers' activities by giving them a foothold far from the river banks. This was valuable in seasons when fish which spawn in gravelly bottomed shallows clustered close to the banks, where the water was

[59] For wicker weirs (*nassas*), see *Edictus Rothari*, ed. F. Bluhme, 299, p. 70.
[60] *Urkunden der Karolinger* IV, 31:131 (860), "crates ponere."
[61] See L. Hartmann, *Zur Wirtschaftsgeschichte Italiens im frühen Mittelalter* (Gotha, 1904), pp. 122–3.
[62] For nets, see: *Edictus Rothari* 299, p. 70; *I placiti* 10:29 (798); 17:52 (804); *Urkunden der Karolinger* IV, 31:131 (860), "retia trahere." "Vita Sancti Fridiani," ed. G. Zaccagnini (ed.), in *Vita Sancti Fridiani* (Lucca, 1989), 4.8, p. 171, confirms the archeological traces of net weights in the Lucchesia; *Vita S. Cethegi, AS* June 2 (Antwerp, 1698), p. 692, includes an improbable anecdote of nocturnal net-fixing near Pescara; Liutprand of Cremona, *Antapodosis*, ed. J. Becker (Hanover, 1915), 1.31, p. 24, on Rome.
[63] See Gregory the Great, *Registrum Epistularum*, ed. D. Norberg (Turnhout, 1982), 9.29, p. 785; Liutprand of Cremona, *Antapodosis* 1.26, p. 22.

warmer and favored the young. The islands could also serve as illusory refuges for edible birds, whose nests could be raided when the catch or crop of fish was unsatisfactory.[64]

Its conspicuous technical structures set the fishing establishment apart from the run-of-the-mill manors which often had the same owners. So did its location on the edge of lakes, streams, and other bodies of water. But in effect, the *piscaria* looked much like another farm, with several buildings clustered around an open space. There could be woods, pastures, vineyards, and fields in *piscaria* just as there were in a purely agricultural manor.[65] This endowment provided fisheries with the necessary wood, twine, and canes for making the fishers' equipment; it also fleshed out the subsistence of those who worked the fishery.

The fishers

Piscaria could be managed in several ways, depending on the needs, wealth, and watery endowment of the owners. Most *piscaria*, whether harvesting for markets or for the consumption of the owner, depended on the work of specialist fishers. The history of this category in postclassical Italy may be reconstructed from several sources. To begin at the beginning, in Cassiodorus' day there were still respectable fishers who were independent entrepreneurs and who fished wild fish (*res nullius* available to anyone, unlike the "cultivated fish" from fisheries). They were not bound to fish at one site only and were protected from abuses by the state. Cassiodorus, desperately attached to the affectations of the leisured Roman squire, considered these fishers' main utility the provision of delicacies for his and other aristocratic tables, and hence defended them from attempts to divert their labor to other purposes.[66] Though he had a soft spot for fishers in general, the Calabrian statesman did reprimand fishers who clogged rivers with their equipment. Forced to choose between delicacies for his table and the navigability of rivers on which the state's messengers might need to travel, Cassiodorus had no doubts – navigability

---

[64] For islands, see: Vat. Lat. 4939, 55v (841); *Urkunden der Karolinger* IV, 53:171 (871); *I diplomi di Guido e di Lamberto*, ed. L. Schiaparelli (Rome, 1906), 2:6 (890); *Diplomi italiani di Lodovico III*, 9:29 (901); their utility is explicated by Roberts, "Rediscovery," p. 10; D. Brinkhuizen, "Some Notes on Recent and Pre- and Protohistoric Fishing Gear from Northwestern Europe," *Palaeohistorica* 25 (1983), pp. 15–25. Caucanas, *Moulins*, p. 23, considers them a variety of irrigated land.

[65] For buildings in *piscaria*, see: Vat. Lat. 4939, 41r (c. 775), 52v (834), 78r (743); *CDL* IV, 35:108 (781); *CDL* V, 46:169 (766). For agricultural or arboricultural land (the latter shaded the water, affecting breeding: Roberts, "Rediscovery," p. 10) with *piscaria*, see: Vat. Lat. 4939, 78r; *CDL* IV, 11:29 (750); 35:108.

[66] Cassiodorus, *Variarum* 5.16, p. 153. See also 12.24, p. 380, where subsistence fishing is alluded to.

came first (in any case, like most self-respecting Roman gentlemen, he did not like fresh-water fish much). On navigable water courses, and indeed in general, Cassiodorus thought the traps and enclosures and barrages of net made by fishers pernicious and immoral, and above all egoistical. He ordered their removal, in compliance with Roman law, and asked that fishers fish "by normal means," which meant by non-permanent, non-structural ones. The enclosures and barriers so typical of later inland *piscaria* were a sign of greed and deprived the commonwealth of "what might benefit many" to the exclusive advantage of a few avid private professional fishers.[67]

Cassiodorus' letters add colorful details to the portrait of the fisher of the middle of the sixth century. The Cassiodoran fisher seems to have been a free man who built dikes for himself and fished anywhere he thought it worthwhile and advantageous. This fishing environment, which we could call "Romanized," survived longest in areas under Byzantine control. Though the fishers of Rome itself followed the peninsular trend, and were mostly slaves in the eighth century, in the Ravennan region, where Byzantine–Roman authority was most effective, free, professional fishers clung to their lifestyle.[68] At Ravenna, even in 725, the late antique fishing environment was intact: Agnellus' description of the pollution of the Badareno's waters in the early eighth century reveals that fishing concerned the entire Ravennan citizenry.[69] The "Romanized" conception of fishing as everyone's free prerogative still prevailed. But the legalities of the *ius piscandi* changed within a few decades, for the Frankish regime extended to the Exarchate's placid waters new conceptions of ownership. In 787 Charlemagne granted fishing rights to a Ravennan church, and the city's prelates tightened their hold on some of the richest fishing zones of the diocese in the course of the ninth and tenth centuries.[70] Interestingly, this shift in the status of the waters did not totally transform the status of

[67] Ibid., 5.17, p. 154; 5.20, p. 155, where he says "quantum ad multos poterat pervenire" ought not to fall into the hands of one avid man. For norms to protect navigability, see *Digest* 43.12.1–2, pp. 579–80. Justinian expected irrigators more than fishermen to harm navigability.

[68] Venditelli, "Diritti e impianti," p. 426, who also notes that Rome's fishers, again following peninsular trends, gained more autonomy in the tenth century. Liutprand of Cremona, *Antapodosis* 1.31, p. 24, depicts Tiber fishers doubling as undertakers.

[69] *LPR* 153, p. 377. *Digest* 1.8.4–5, p. 11, orders fishing not be restricted (on sea and river shores); 43.14.1, p. 581, excepts fishing that hampers navigability. See also E. Costa, *Le acque nel diritto romano* (Bologna, 1919), pp. 17, 31–2; P. Bonfante, "Il diritto delle acque dal diritto romano al diritto odierno," *Archivio giuridico* 87 (1922), p. 8.

[70] In this process papal concessions had a big role: *Monumenti* V, 36:266 (997); *Johannes Papae X Epistulae*, ed. J. Migne (Paris, 1853), 5, 6, pp. 804–6. Also P. Fabbri, "Il controllo delle acque tra tecnica ed economia," in Carile, *Storia di Ravenna* II, pp. 12, 15; the archbishops had fishing rights by 858 (see *Monumenti* II, 4:11, and Pasquali, "Economia e paesaggio," pp. 44, 46).

all the Ravennans who fished in them. Ravenna indeed remained a bastion of free fishers until much later, even after the right to fish had been privatized. A local association of fishers made contracts for the exploitation of the Badareno and other branches of the Po with the new owners of the fishing rights on those water courses, the archbishops of Ravenna, perhaps as early as 843, as the *Carta Piscatoria* discloses.[71]

Actually, the Byzantine segment of the peninsula was not unique in this respect. The Lucchesia, where comital powers, balanced by episcopal ones, kept their vigor up to the turn of the millennium, also enjoyed a free fishing regime. There peasants expected to fish without impediments, and the appropriation of the waters by the local magnates took place haltingly. This suggests that it was not only Roman law and culture, nor even appropriate environments where all water was navigable, that maintained "Romanized" fishing conditions, but the survival of public powers and an effective state too.[72]

Removed from Ravenna, in parts of the peninsula where Lombard influence was stronger and public power weaker, people turned to other systems for the exploitation of water after the eighth century. A different type of fisher was created by the new fishing systems. The fishers in the charters of Lombard Italy are often bonded men, given away or acquired like the stones of their houses and the islets of land protruding from the streams in which they worked.[73] Fishers of the eighth, ninth, and tenth

[71] In 896 one Engelrada owned land outside Ravenna "cum omnibus piscationibus et venationibus": *Monumenti* I, 7:99; see also "Gli archivi," 211:470 (963); 361:821 (c. 980). On the similar fishing climate of the Byzantine south, see Martin, *La Pouille*, pp. 402–5. On Byzantium itself, where Leo VI's *Novels* illustrate the incipient privatization of fishing, see Dagron, "Poissons," pp. 61–6.

[72] On the Lucchesia, see P. Squatriti, "Water, Nature, and Culture in Early Medieval Lucca," *Early Medieval Europe* 4 (1995), pp. 29–39; also "Vita Sancti Fridiani" (eleventh-century redaction) 4.8–10, p. 171. Lucca's bishops, unlike Ravenna's, did not rent fishing privileges. But some renting did occur in the Bientina depression after 996 (Onori, *L'abbazia di S. Salvatore*, pp. 55–60), and the Lucchesia was not wholly immune to private fishing preserves.

[73] For examples of unfree *piscatores*, included in donations of fisheries and fishing rights as if they were cogs necessary to the fishing machinery, see Vat. Lat. 4939, 78r (743): "condoma nomine Palumbo peccatore cum uxorem filios & filias & cum onia eorum ptinentia cum casa vineas terras cutis & incultis movilia peculia"; 41r (775): "condome tres ad piscandum"; 55v (841): "homines de ipsa ecclesia" expected to fish; 52v (834): "piscatorib"; *Chronicon Vulturnense* I, 42:263; *CDL* IV, 11:29 (750): "hominem nomine Sindulum cum uxore et filiis atque portiuncula sua unde piscationem facere visum est"; 23:67 (c. 774): "piscatores in Marsis in loco qui dicitur Secundinus"; 36:108 (782): "filii Baroncioli piscatori, idest Anscausu et Fuscari"; *CDL* V, 46:169 (766): "Petrum piscatorem cum tota domo sua"; *Il regesto di Farfa* I, ed. I. Giorgi and U. Balzani (Rome, 1879), 134:113 (776): "piscatores in Marsis tres"; "Placiti" 9:311 (also in the Marsica, in 972); *Urkunden Konrad I.*, 336:452 (Subiaco, 967), "cum Ursulo piscatore et aliis servis"; 249:357 (near Ferrara, 962), "cum duodecim piscatoribus de villa que nuncupatur Ueterana."

centuries are the most frequently named specialized serfs in the extant documents. Such fishers formed a subordinate, powerless class obliged to haul fish out of a determined water-site for their overlords, who disposed of them, their fish, their labor, and the water as they wished. Thus, in most of the peninsula the growing popularity of manorial systems of land and labor management accompanied both the decline of the concept of free rights to fish in any water body and the decline of the free, entrepreneurial fisher familiar to Cassiodorus.

The documents which define the status of the subject fishers derive from large estates in Lombard and later Carolingian Italy, and ignore many social realities along Italy's water courses, such as the small-scale subsistence fishing which surely took place. But they do portray the subaltern fishers fully. They were a varied group, fissured by hierarchies and variations in social position. For instance, some eighth-century fisher families were urban, lived in Rieti, and exercised the trade nearby. Other fishers were rural and lived close upon the waters whence came their livelihood, in houses belonging to the *piscaria*.[74] While some *piscatores* cultivated the land and tended animals, others inhabited fisheries not provided with these ancillary means of sustenance (which of course absorbed their work).[75] Many on the lordly *piscaria* also had to immerse themselves in further "non-piscatorial" activities, ranging from packaging to transportation of the harvested fish.

Just as these different levels of exploitation of the fishers' energies demonstrate social heterogeneity among fishers of north and south Italy, so too do the methods of rent payment among Po valley fishers. Rents due to S. Giulia in the 880s show how the nuns devised different systems for exactions from different fishers, whose status defined their exploitability. Ten *piscatores*, probably serfs, from the manor of Iseo paid 1,200 fish to the convent, all hauled out of the demesne's *piscatio*. This was a fraction of their estimated annual catch, an average calculated by the nuns so as to stabilize their supply.[76] S. Giulia left the ten men the option to decide what to do with any fish harvested beyond the 1,200 mark, indeed to decide whether to catch any beyond that number, but these fishers had to bring the fish to the nuns. Where geographical or other hurdles interposed themselves between the lord and the fisher, the fisher was not sub-

---

[74] *CDL* IV, 36:108 (782, Rieti); *CDL* V, 46:169 (766); Vat. Lat. 4939, 78r (743), 41r (775), 52v (834); *Chronicon Vulturnense* I, 42:263, all show fishermen with houses at the fishery.
[75] For examples of fisheries with land to use, see: Vat. Lat. 4939, 78r (743), 52v (834); *CDL* IV, 11:29 (750); 36:108 (782); "Gli archivi," 408:536 (995, near Faenza).
[76] Polyptych *S. Giulia da Brescia*, in *Inventari altomedievali di terre, coloni, e redditi*, p. 58. As the fishes' size and species is not stated, the amount of edible flesh reaching the convent must have varied.

jected to the imposition of hauling the catch to the lord. Tribute in coins or a weight of bullion replaced the duty to transport the fish rent to the lord's chosen place, rather as Charlemagne required of his manorial fishers when production exceeded consumption.[77] These latter arrangements suggest a more complex situation where the fishers were also merchants, marketing their catch so as to generate the required medium of exchange. North Italy's subaltern fishers were thus far from constituting a homogenous class.

In Tuscany, professional fishers were rare but many cultivators nevertheless contributed token fish to ecclesiastical landlords' residences. Such part-time fishers, in the Lucchesia of the 700s and 800s, owed symbolic payments designed to clarify relations of power and authority. In the Lucchesia of the 800s, the tribute of a single fish appears to have been more a statement that the tenant-peasant owed his fruition of fishing to the landowner than a real economic burden.[78] By the eleventh century, as stated earlier, the region also supported an association of professional fishers whose willingness to donate fish to the clergy the *Vita* of S. Fredianus extols. Both of these Lucchese fishing arrangements suggest a situation different from the *piscaria-* and *piscatio*-rich Italy which lords constructed in this period. Atypically, in Lucca's territory, subject fishers running fisheries were uncommon. Elsewhere, from Salerno to the Po, such situations prevailed, especially in ecclesiastical endowments.

As commercial fishing for a living practiced by free entrepreneurs declined, and serfs multiplied among those involved in capturing fish (specialized serfs, to be sure, whose special knowledge and skilled labor separated them from agricultural laborers), the prestige of fishers and their occupation dimmed. Not even the apostolic associations of fishing redeemed its practitioners from a lowly place in the opinions of the literate. Unlike hunting, the favored occupation of the early medieval aristocracies, fishing was not a reputable occupation in the postclassical period. The fishers' prey was thought bloodless, which may have robbed it of some allure. Fish had not always been second-rate prey. In the fifth century Sidonius Apollinaris appears to have enjoyed angling and to have practiced it himself. He also appears to have thought that this pastime

---

[77] Ibid., p. 58. I assume that the *piscatores* who worked in the *piscaria* (likely, but not specified) had to convert the fish into money, since the documents mention only fishers in association with fisheries and no merchants.

[78] *M&D* V.2, 639:381; 640:381; 739:445; 745:449. In the late 800s Lapulo of Arena (near Pisa) owed "pisces VII" to Lucca's archbishop, while everyone else there paid labor, crops, or money: *Vescovato di Lucca*, ed. M. Luzzati, in *Inventari altomedievali di terre, coloni, e redditi*, p. 220. See also B. Andreolli, "I prodotti alimentari nei contratti agrari toscani dall'alto medioevo," *AM* 8 (1981), p. 123.

could increase his reputation among the Gaulish aristocrats who constituted his primary audience, for he publicized it in his letters.[79] But after
him, until the twelfth century, few members of the upper echelons of
European societies indulged in fishing.[80] Although *milites* fished illegally
in Lake Patria in the early 800s, their activities did not enhance their position in southern society. In fact, Liutprand of Cremona, epitomizing a
common attitude, could think of no better way to ridicule the weakling,
degenerate Romans of his day than to accuse them of wielding their
fishing poles rather too skillfully, obvious sign of their military ineptitude
and perhaps lacking virility.[81]

The loss of freedom of most fishers active in eighth- and ninth-century
Italy and the parallel loss of social standing for the activity of fishing are
surely related phenomena. The emergence after the 800s of associations
of (apparently) free fishers in Ravenna, Lucca, and Pavia did not
promptly rehabilitate fishing, either. Another two centuries would elapse
before upstanding medieval people would happily admit that they hauled
fish out of the waters. Angling and all other fishing, in the early medieval
centuries, was an occupation fit for humble people (even saints, as the
bronze doors of San Zeno in Verona show), not for landholding *potentes*.

By the tenth century, fishing took various forms in the subalpine peninsula, but few matched the mold Rome had pressed on this occupation. All
the early medieval developments affected the plant and animal communities living in the waterways or along their productive edges, for they
altered human demands on the fresh-water ecosystems (in general
human impact on these waters intensified after 700; perhaps coastal and
marine creatures were grateful for their new-found obscurity).
Meanwhile the piscatory world created by Italy's large landholders after
the seventh century redefined the legalities of fishing and extended
private property rights over the peninsula's waterscapes, changing who
had access to fish and under what circumstances. The emergence (or

---

[79] In Sidonius Apollinaris, *Carmina: Epistulae*, ed. W. Anderson (London, 1913), 2.12.1, p.
470, Sidonius turned down an invitation to go fishing with a friend to nurse a sick child (I
am grateful to R. Hoffmann for this citation). Sidonius enjoyed watching fishing too
(2.2.12, p. 426), and was, in general, a lover of fresh-water fish (e.g. 2.2.17, p. 432; 4.8.2,
v. 2, p. 90). See also Verdon, "Recherches," 347; Mira, *La pesca*, p. 9.

[80] R. Hoffmann, "Fishing for Sport in Medieval Europe," *Speculum* 60 (1985), pp. 900–1.
Louis the Pious was an interesting exception: Astronomer, *Vita Hludowici Imperatoris*, ed.
E. Tremp, *MGH Scriptores Rerum Germanicarum i.u.s.* LXIV (Hanover, 1994), 46, 52, pp.
466, 492.

[81] The ninth-century *milites* who fished in Lake Patria north of Salerno according to the
Sicardi Principis Pactio 33, 37, p. 217, were probably poachers; Liutprand of Cremona,
Antapodosis 1.26, p. 22 (a citation of Perseus). See also his *Relatio de Legatione
Constantinopolitana*, ed. J. Becker (Hanover, 1915), 51, which considers fishers a vile
group.

perhaps reemergence) of fishers' cooperatives before the end of the first millennium injected further dynamism into this picture, though fishers' associations also legitimized private rights by seeking permission to fish from the archbishops or landlords who had appropriated them. The complex arrangements detailed in the *Honorantie Civitatis Papie*, and those adumbrated in charters from Ravenna and saints' biographies from Lucca, reflect the capacity of urban markets, in special situations, to support professional free specialists even before the communal "revolution" and the attendant economic take-off.[82] The piscatory world of early medieval Italy was thus varied and fluctuating. Its life was shaped by multiple currents. Ecological changes, cultural patterns, economic motives, and social and political ambitions constantly stirred it up. In a sense it was inevitable that, like the waters upon which this world relied, it could never be wholly static.

[82] Hoffmann, "Economic Development," exaggerates the simplicity and underdevelopment of early medieval fishing, but is surely correct that "economic development" and increased population redesigned fishing and deeply changed "aquatic ecosystems" with its demands.

5   Water and milling in early medieval Italy

The Romans who farmed and grew food in Italy relied on at least three different methods to grind their grains into more palatable meal and flour. Virtuous early Republicans used hand querns, which maintained their popularity throughout Roman history on account of their simplicity for users. Larger mills also existed. Their round stones could be housed in special buildings, where they moved in circular fashion, pushed by animals (especially donkeys) or slaves and other subalterns. "Fed" grain from an opening in the center of the uppermost stone, such "sweat" mills poured meal out below. In this they differed little from hydraulic mills, whose stones, however, revolved thanks to flowing water.

None of the various grinding methods in Roman Italy superseded the others, even though they may have been chronological successors of one another. Several methods instead coexisted harmoniously, for each had much to recommend it and each had a social, economic, and ecological niche in the Roman Mediterranean.[1] While a peasant in a remote, water-less plateau might find a hand quern the best system for grinding his grain, in the foothills of the Alps, where water gushed strong and reliable, the allure of hydraulic power would be irresistible. In Rome itself, where hundreds of thousands of mouths clamored for bread, the efficiencies of mechanization were obvious. The *annona* used both "sweat" and water mills in the city, as complementary techniques for milling. Thus, in Procopius' finely told tale of a Gothic siege of Rome in 537, a flour short-age threatened the city only when the aqueducts had been cut (no water power was available) *and* there was no fodder for animals (the main source of "sweat" power). The hero of Procopius' narrative, Belisarius, responded by "inventing" yet another source of milling power, the Tiber.[2]

Thus the water mill was one among several complementary technolo-gies available to Roman grain grinders, and was no rare and eccentric

---

[1] M.-C. Amouretti, "La diffusion du moulin à eau dans l'antiquité," in A. De Reparaz (ed.), *L'eau et les hommes en Méditerranée* (Paris, 1987), pp. 14–19, lucidly and convincingly explains that several different milling technologies usually coexist in rural societies. On complementarity of mill types, see also R. Holt, *The Mills of Medieval England* (Oxford, 1988), pp. 5, 118–19.   [2] *Guerra Gotica* I, 1.19, pp. 141–5.

machine unknown to the majority of people. Local conditions determined the dynamics of its diffusion, but, by the time the fourth-century agronomist Palladius wrote his treatise on perfect agriculture, water mills were perfectly familiar to Romans everywhere. Palladius recommended their construction on the estates of his readers, confident that the utility of these machines for grinding grain would be obvious.[3] Palladius' confidence is emblematic. Sensible farmers of commercial estates in the ancient Mediterranean were familiar with this technology and understood its advantages. The machine, after all, had been around for several hundred years by the time of Palladius, who was, nevertheless, the first of the agronomists to advocate its use. In the fourth century, water mills had made their way into poetry, law codes, and, obviously, water courses in significant numbers.[4] The archeological remains from Roman Italy suggest a prevalence of technologically more difficult "vertical" water mills, but in all probability the humbler rural sites less visible to archeologists sheltered mostly "horizontal" mils (their characteristics are explained on pp. 133–6). Thus the notion that water mills suddenly exploded onto the European, or Italian, scene in the Middle Ages has wobbly foundations, though also a distinguished intellectual pedigree.[5] The wide dissemination of water mills in early medieval Italy wherever social and hydrological conditions permitted, from the Po valley to the hills of Benevento, grew from the ancient and late antique installation of these machines on many water courses in the peninsula. It was because of this prehistory that the author of Pope Leo IV's biography in the middle of the ninth century could consider water mills grinding at full capacity to be a "human need" for the new Tyrrhenian town of Centumcellae.[6]

So wide a dissemination renders the study of postclassical mills especially meaningful. For while water mills offered one of *several* solutions to the problem of grinding grains, this machine provides the historian with a microcosm within which to observe the playing out of important negotiations among people and between people and water in the early Middle Ages. In the postclassical Italian peninsula, hydraulic mills were alternatively a technology which altered the living conditions of numerous

---

[3] Palladius, *Opus Agriculturae*, ed. R. Rodgers (Leipzig, 1975), 1.41.1, p. 47.
[4] For the revisionist assessment of Roman hydrotechnologies, see K. White, *Greek and Roman Technology* (Ithaca, 1984), pp. 55–66; Ö. Wikander, *Exploitation of Water Power or Technological Stagnation?* (Lund, 1984); and his "Water Mills in Europe," *Medieval Europe* 3 (1992), pp. 9–14; D. Lohrmann, "Neues über Wasserversorgung und Wassertechnik im Mittelalter," *Deutsches Archiv für Erforschung des Mittelalters* 48 (1992), p. 186; P. Squatriti, "'Advent and Conquests' of the Water Mill in Italy," in E. Smith and M. Wolfe (eds.), *Technology and Resource Use in Medieval Europe* (Ashgate, 1997), pp. 125–38.
[5] M. Bloch, "Avènement et conquête du moulin à eau," *Annales d'histoire économique et sociale* 7 (1935), pp. 538–63, is perhaps the best and most influential exposition of this pervasive idea. See Squatriti, "'Advent and Conquests,'" for some considerations on Bloch's views.   [6] *LP* 105.99–100.

aquatic creatures and human interaction with the environment; a tool through which domination of people could be fostered; an economic resource in which to invest capital; a tool with which to redirect surplus agricultural production to new beneficiaries; and, last but not least, an effective way to reduce grain to flour. Thus water mills, deceptively flimsy wooden structures on the banks of many water courses, were a crucial human adaptation of the aquatic realm. This machine's technologies, its ramifications for various forms of wildlife, and the social repercussions for early medieval people of the presence among them of a workless grinder of grain will repay analysis.

Technologies of milling with water

As Bloch noted, techniques for grinding grain have varied considerably over time, and in the charters from the Italian peninsula this is very evident. Yet because early medieval people were most concerned with grinding, not with the techniques for doing so, they seldom wrote about the details of milling technology. Since they did not share modern historians' priorities, the redactors of early Italian charters rarely distinguished between types of water mills, and it is often arduous to determine whether a mill was driven by muscle or water power.[7] Here our concern is with hydraulic milling, but even when the location of a mill on a water course, or the presence of waterworks, or the use of the term *aquimola* gives away the source of a mill's power, it is usually not clear whether horizontal- and vertical-wheeled water mills are being described, or how a mill's gearing systems worked.[8] To the people who created the charters this was not a

---

[7] It is important, even in a discussion like this one which focuses on *water* mills, to remember that other types of mills coexisted with them. Thus, at Gaeta, where there was ample use of water power for milling in the 800s, donkeys also served (*The Chronicle of Ahimaaz*, tr. M. Salzman [New York, 1924], p. 67, tells of a sorceress who changed a youth into a donkey and relegated him to turning millstones; see also P. Skinner, *Family Power in Southern Italy* [Cambridge, 1995], p. 72); and in Rome ship-mills in 1005 shared the Tiber waters with other mills (D. Lohrmann, "Schiffsmühlen auf dem Tiber in Rom," in K. Hebers, H. Kortüm, and C. Servatius [eds.], *Ex Ipsis Rerum Documentis* [Sigmaringen, 1991], pp. 281–3). Hand querns seldom occupied the attention of the literate, but the "single mills" for which peasants refused to pay multure at Carapelle (in the central Apennines) in 779 probably were such querns (the incident would confirm Bloch, "Avènement et conquête," pp. 551, 554–6, who thought the "survival" of the hand quern a form of peasant resistance): *CDL* V, 90:293. On the postclassical northern trade in querns, see R. Hodges and D. Whitehouse, *Mohammad, Charlemagne, and the Origins of Europe* (Ithaca, 1983), p. 100.

[8] An example of the difficulties involved is *Urkunden Konrad I.*, 267:381 (964), where *molinas duas* are linked to a *tabernam*, which implies that they were not on a water course, but they *were* "in Aquapendente," a town north of Rome with a most promising name. S. Caucanas, *Moulins et irrigation en Roussillon du IXe au XVe siècle* (Paris, 1995), pp. 17–19, describes similar obscurities in southwest France.

critical technical distinction. With the exception of the Salernitan ones, which went into some detail about mills' inner mechanisms, the documents present the parts of the mills which lay *around* the mill-house as crucial, rather than those within it which fascinate historians of technology. Though they might not bother to explain how the mill's inner core had been built, early medieval Italians described mills' outlying buildings and specified whether a mill had dams, sluices, or a race (though ponds, the natural ally of all three, are never explicitly mentioned), for these waterworks were seen as the heart of the entire installation.

What can be gleaned from the recalcitrant sources suggests that any water mill was an articulated structure, comprising waterworks, a mill-house, and assorted buildings nearby.[9] The buildings were an integral part of the mill and important to its operation; sometimes they were listed as "pertaining to" the mills. Presumably they functioned as storage space for grain and for tools needed to repair the mill and keep it in working order. Some mill complexes also included a house for the miller, who could be required to reside *in situ*.[10] Rarely, mills had open yards for processing grains (*areales*), as did the Brescian abbess Ansilperga at a suburban site where a single paddle-wheel powered two mills in the 760s.[11] Some mills had fishing ponds and buildings for the preparation of fish.[12] Nor was this all that made up a mill-site, for mills were varied and complex economic units, and their structure reflected this. The assorted fields, orchards, and gardens over which many millers presided, and from which they could draw much of their sustenance in periods of low water flow or grain availability, were likewise integral to some mills.[13]

Complex sites though they could be, it is well to recall that most mills were built of wood and that not all of them were associated with grand

---

[9] For instance, *CDC* I, 103:132 (892), "cum aqueducta et andita sua"; 156:200 (934), "et cum omni ordine et pertinenciam de ipso molinum"; *CDL* II, 257:348 (771), "et omnia edifitia sua"; *CDL* III, 15:70 (742), "cum omnibus adiacentis et pertinentis suis"; *Urkunden der Karolinger* III, 29:105 (836), "cunctis adiacentis vel pertinentis seu appendiciis suis." As with houses, entryways were also prominent features in legal descriptions.

[10] Vat. Lat. 4939, 69v (724); *Il regesto di Farfa* II, ed. I. Giorgi and U. Balzani (Rome, 1879), 290:245 (853), "cum casis"; and the touched-up *CDL* III, 29:183 (c. 750), where there are "homines qui ipsas molinas regere videtur" for three mills and two houses.

[11] *CDL* III, 39:234 (767), "molinas . . . una cum areales et platea ibi posita iuxta porta et accessionem." G. Varanini, "Energia idraulica e attività economiche nella Verona comunale," in *Paesaggi urbani dell'Italia padana, secoli VIII–XIV* (Bologna, 1988), p. 343, lists another *areale* at Verona in 905; the term had other meanings too.

[12] E.g., *CDLangobardiae* 278:468 (878); 503:866 (924); or *Papsturkunde, 896–1046* II, ed. H. Zimmermann (Vienna, 1985), 424:814 (1006). Since mills had waterworks, in Spain and north Europe they doubled as fisheries: see ch. 4, n. 54.

[13] *CDL* I, 38:132 (726); *CDLangobardiae* 29:57 (765); 226:372 (863); 476:824 (918); *I diplomi di Ugo e Lotario, di Berengario II, e di Adalberto*, ed L. Schiaparelli (Rome, 1924), 79:231 (945); *M&D* V.2, 597:358 (844); 634:377 (846); 760:456–7 (862).

hydraulic and agricultural installations. In Lombardy and near Salerno some mills were tiny, flimsy structures with no land. And despite the weight of the millstones, some mills were movable. For reasons we must imagine related both to stream flow and the potential for neighborly contestation, their owners were prepared to dismantle them and even to reassemble them elsewhere. These peripatetic mills probably had minimal waterworks and none of the ramified buildings and annexes larger, more stable mills had.[14]

Regardless of the technical differences between mills' machinery and appendages, all hydraulic mills had to smooth down the inconsistencies in the erratic water supply of the streams and rivers alongside which they arose. This, perhaps, is why early medieval documents tend to focus more attention on the waterworks which did the job. Hydraulic mills shared certain basic devices for the control of water flow, in particular dams and sluices. Sluices directed naturally flowing water into artificial mill channels in the desired way.[15] Dams enabled some mills to be built where water flowed of its own accord; they also made it possible to build up water volume and to release retained water onto mill wheels. Thanks to these barrages millers had some control over rates of flow, and hence greater control over milling. Both dams and sluices could compensate for seasonal variations in water levels.[16] But though dams, like sluices and channels, could contain and mitigate excessive impetus in flow during rainy spates, their greatest utility came in dry months when they helped to build up volume and "head." Since much grinding was needed in the summer months when the grain harvests were in and the previous season's supplies had thinned out, a dam could be decisive to the efficient functioning of mills in areas with unreliable hydrology. For this reason, mills were always connected with dams in early medieval Roussillon,

---

[14] *I placiti del "Regnum Italiae"* I, ed. C. Manaresi (Rome, 1955–60), 67:245 (865), describes a mill "cum tecto seu omnes lignamen vel omnen suam ordinacionem"; see also *M&D* V.2, 855:523 (874). For movable or partially movable mills, see *CDLangobardiae* 782:1375 (978); *CDC* V, 814:175 (1029). Water rights were handy precisely to avoid such moves. Rothari's *Edict*, of course, also contemplates dismantling mills. For comparative material, see D. Lohrmann, "Le moulin à eau dans le cadre de l'économie rurale de la Neustrie (VIIe–IXe siècles)," in H. Atsma (ed.), *La Neustrie* (Paris, 1992), p. 397.

[15] A good example is *CDC* I, 328:152 (980), where a *comes palatii* Iohannes could "de predicta aqua clausurie ibidem mictere et iamdicta aqua relocare in ipso curso de arcatura nostra."

[16] N. Smith, *A History of Dams* (London, 1971), pp. 32, 149–51, writes of early medieval ineptitude at damming. Gregory of Tours, *Liber Vitae Patrum*, ed. B. Krusch (Berlin, 1885), 18.2, p. 284, on the contrary, describes a competent sixth-century dam in detail. See also Ö. Wikander, "Mill Channels, Weirs, and Ponds," *Opuscula Romana* 15 (1985), p. 151; N. Schnitter, "Barrages romains," in J.-P. Boucher (ed.), *Journée d'études sur les aqueducs romains* (Paris, 1983), pp. 333–9.

Catalonia, and al-Andalus.[17] Even in the well-watered Loire region, around 500 dams made of poles driven into the river bed, shored up with stones, determined the efficient working of water mills; so attests Gregory of Tours in one of the most detailed and famous early descriptions of these contraptions.[18]

In Italy, only at Salerno, where much milling took place on larger water courses such as the Irno, were mill dams uncommon. Elsewhere Italian millers of the early Middle Ages favored them. Indeed, Rothari, who was the first to describe their functioning in Italy, thought the destruction of dams by angry neighbors or royal officials the surest way to close down a mill.[19] Evidently, in the seventh century, people automatically built mills and dams together in the areas with which Rothari was familiar. Unfortunately, they did so blithely, without considering the consequences on flow; for, in removing some of the natural variation in water currents, barrages affected the watery environment. Upstream flow slowed and suspended sediments deposited, while downstream erosion accelerated; in both cases aquatic habitats changed for fish and people. There was no recourse for the fish, insects, and plants which were adapted to the natural rates of flow, and whose reproductive migrations, habitat temperatures, and sources of food dams disrupted.[20] For the people, instead, there were ways to react. Either the people downstream from the mill's dam who received less water after its construction, or those upstream whose land might be flooded, could take matters into their own hands and remove the offending dam forcibly. Rothari considered that where the dam imposed unwarranted hardship on the custom-

[17] Caucanas, *Moulins*, pp. 123–7; P. Bonnassie, *La Catalogne du milieu du Xe à la fin du XIe siècle* I (Toulouse, 1975), p. 461; A. Lagardère, "Moulins d'Occident musulman au moyen âge," *Al-Qantara* 12 (1991), p. 98.

[18] Gregory of Tours, *Liber Vitae Patrum* 18.2, pp. 284–5. For *clusas* near Milan, see *I placiti* 67:244 (865). On the Lambro, see *CDLangobardiae* 183:310 (852); *Museo* 24 (776); 90 (853).

[19] *Edictus Rothari*, ed. F. Bluhme (Hanover, 1869), 150, p. 34, punishes any who destroy a dam without the judge's permission. The *Leges Alamannorum* II, *Recensio Lantfridiana*, ed. K. Eckhardt (Witzenhausen, 1962), law 60, p. 62 (early 700s), regulates dams in even more detail.

[20] Dams changed conditions for algae, made water clearer (fostering the settling of suspended matter), less oxygenated (especially at the top), and deeper (less light in deeper water means less life there); and they blocked floating logs that both cleared stream beds and offered habitats to many organisms. However, R. Hoffmann, "Economic Development and Aquatic Ecosystems in Medieval Europe," *American Historical Review* 101 (1996), pp. 640–1, exaggerates water mills' ecological impact. In the United States it was not until the 1930s that damming created a truly engineered waterscape with an integrated system that completely altered the character of the waterways, and at no time in the Middle Ages were European waterways as heavily engineered as in the United States in the nineteenth century: see A. Outwater, *Water: A Natural History* (New York, 1996), pp. 103–6.

ary users of the stream, it was illicit and the *iudex* could authorize its destruction. His legislation was not ecologically motivated but tended to reestablish the ecological *status quo ante*.

Another regulating device shared by many water mills was the derivation channel. Though the nomenclature of mill races varied by region, most Italian mills relied on a conduit of some sort to lead the requisite water from its natural bed to the site considered best for milling. Mill channels and races gave mills a minimum of security from the ravages of stream spates, for they allowed mill-houses to arise at some distance from the stream banks. They also enabled the miller to direct the gushing water at the paddle in the most efficacious way, and extended his control over rates of flow and water volume. Allied with sluices, derivation canals mediated between the natural turbulence of water regimens and the delicate engineering of the mill itself.[21]

The outdoor waterworks of mills, which resolved problems common to all these machines, were similar. Also within the dark chambers of the mill-house, which concealed some differences, there were many similarities. All mills had two millstones, the top one capable of circular movement. Millstones had to be of good quality, for they worked hard and wore down fast if the stone was not hard. As local quarries did not always supply stones of the required granularity and hardness, obtaining millstones could represent a major burden for mill builders. Still, there is remarkably little evidence for any trade in millstones in early medieval Italy, even in the Po valley where stone was difficult to find and the waterways along which to move Alpine stone were tempting. Traces of the considerable movement of tufaceous millstones from Etruria, Campania, and the Vulture in Roman times vanish in early medieval records, and only later did regional economies once again came to depend on such trade.[22] Hence, most early medieval millstones were local, or at least seem to have been.

---

[21] Some examples of *aqueductus* can be found in: *Urkunden der Karolinger* IV, 5:76 (852); *I diplomi di Berengario*, ed. L. Schiaparelli (Rome, 1903), 95:252 (915); *Urkunden Konrad I* 374:514 (969). *CDLangobardiae* 482:832 (919) has an *aquario*. *Rubeas* are in *CDLangobardiae* 182:310 (852); 226:372 (863). *Serinas* is the term used by *CDLangobardiae* 482:832 (919). On the several terms used in the central Po valley, see F. Menant, *Campagnes lombardes du moyen âge* (Rome, 1993), p. 185. In the south, *arcaturia* was the preferred term: see *CDC* I, 302:117 (978); 413:276 (989); *CDC* VII, 1202:250 (1059); though *canale* also served (*CDC* V, 814:175 [1029]).

[22] J.-G. Rivolin, "Il pedaggio di Bard ed il commercio delle mole (secoli XIII–XIV)," in A. Comba (ed.), *Mulini da grano nel Piemonte medievale* (Cuneo, 1993), pp. 189–214. The Tuscan novelist of the *trecento*, F. Sacchetti, compared millstones to rubies in value (as did Boccaccio), but his imaginary audience thought this laughable (*Il trecentonovelle*, ed. A. Lanza [Florence, 1989], 67, pp. 130–1). For Roman trade, see O. Williams-Thorpe and R. Thorpe, "Millstones that Mapped the Mediterranean," *New Scientist* 1757 (1991), pp. 42–5. The postclassical tufa millstone recently found in the Sangro valley shows how archeology may transform this picture.

The difficulty of obtaining adequate stones made the miller's ability to dress the stone, to regulate its consumption, and to recut its grooves essential to his art. Even stones of great hardness could necessitate weekly recutting when they were much used. In Roman times softer tufaceous millstones were sometimes preferred because they were easier to dress and remained coarse even after much use. Poorly chiseled or smooth millstones mashed grain without pulverizing it and turned out a dark meal, almost useless in making bread, in which the oily portions of the grain kernels were unevenly distributed and formed lumps. Poorly chiseled stones also wore down more swiftly, depositing a sediment of sand in the flour. A mill's reputation and functionality could rest on the stones it housed and their proper maintenance on the part of the miller, and several Salernitan contracts of the tenth century require the millers to cut the stones owners provided properly.[23]

Despite the reticence of charters and other sources regarding the inner workings of water mills, it is clear that two main types of mill worked in the Italian peninsula before AD 1000. Documents describing the interior of mill-houses, rather than merely their outside waterworks, show that, while some mills had gearing, many others were gearless horizontal mills. This seemingly small technical distinction had wide ramifications, for the technologies involved in a horizontal mill were simpler, required less iron, and were more affordable. These circumstances help to explain the enduring popularity of the horizontal-wheeled hydraulic mill in Italy, and indeed throughout the medieval Mediterranean. They also explain why the mighty vertical-wheeled mill tended to remain the preserve of early medieval Italy's *potentes*, in a pattern familiar from early medieval Iberia.[24]

The wooden paddles of the horizontal water wheel lay, logically enough, horizontally on the water's surface or horizontal to the incoming flow at the mouth of a race, just above the outflowing water. Carving the paddles was no simple matter, for each paddle should catch as much of the water's motion as possible at the beginning of the water's impact upon it, but should not hold water after the paddle had moved beyond the optimum impact point. Thus the miller's skill as a carpenter affected his

[23] Holt, *Mills*, pp. 100–1; G. Comet, *Le paysan et son outil* (Rome, 1992), pp. 405, 416–21. For a superb twelfth-century Andalusian tale about poorly cut millstones, see Lagardère, "Moulins d'Occident," p. 84. Failure to regulate the speed of the millstones could also result in coarse, greasy, or even burned flour: Comet, *Le paysan*, p. 423; R. Berretti and E. Iacopi, "I molini ad acqua di Valleriana," in *Tecnica e società nell'Italia dei secoli XII–XVI* (Pistoia, 1987), p. 27.

[24] Gears, and hence presumably vertical water wheels, were in the following mills: *CDLangobardiae* 476:823–4 (918); *CDC* V, 819:174 (1029); *CDC* VII, 1202:250 (1054). For Iberia, see T. Glick, *From Muslim Fortress to Christian Castle* (Manchester, 1995), p. 117.

ability to use water power.[25] This skill was also handy in calibrating the axle which rose from the center of the wheel to transmit the wheel's rotations to the millstone above.

In theory, horizontal mills could arise on the banks of a water course, and indeed the charters depict some such mills lying "on" or "in" a stream or other water course.[26] In practice, however, early medieval Italians preferred to build horizontal mills next to derivation channels or races, sometimes with sluices as well. These delivered the water to the wheel in regulated amounts and accelerated flow near the paddles hugely, as Dante later noted in his image of panicked flight (*Inferno* 23.47). Horizontal water wheels could function with the natural stream of water, but they worked best when water struck their paddles in a precisely regulated way, through channels.

On account of the positioning of their paddle-wheels, horizontal mills could draw power only from the kinetic energy of the flowing waters, not from the water's weight. They worked best where water flowed swiftly, either naturally or mediated by channels. As they lacked gearing, their millstones revolved only as fast as the water wheel did, and this could be too slow a motion to grind grain. In order to increase the speed with which the water wheel spun, wheels were made smaller, which meant that horizontal wheels trapped less of the kinetic energy offered by the gushing waters.[27] In view of these technical impediments the horizontal mill has been charged with inefficiency, and has often been compared unfavorably with the vertical-wheeled mill. Bloch went so far as to call it a "technological regression."[28] But these estimations of horizontal mills demand something of this machine it was never intended for, namely efficient use of available water resources. As White observed, in most contexts water was abundant and readily available, and no one objected to its profligate use.[29] Only in hilly regions, removed from the watery wealth of mountains or plains, did inefficient use of power matter to people whose foremost concern was to obtain flour from grain, not to employ energy-efficient technology. Horizontal mills remained popular because they turned out

[25] No minute analyses of early Italian water wheels exist, but see P. Rahtz and R. Meeson, *An Anglo-Saxon Watermill at Tamworth* (London, 1992), p. 102, for a ninth-century English example.

[26] For example, *CDL* I, 38:132 (726), "intra"; *CDL* II, 257:348 (771); *Regesto di Farfa* I, 293:247, "in"; *Urkunden der Karolinger* III, 29:105 (839), "super." Similar wording in Extremadura can be found in Lagardère, "Moulins d'Occident," p. 98.

[27] Comet, *Le paysan*, pp. 428, 443, has lucid discussions.

[28] Bloch, "Avènement et conquête," p. 544. For similar evaluations, see M. Nordon, *L'eau conquise* (Paris, 1991), p. 111; J. Muendel, "The 'French' Mill in Medieval Tuscany," *Journal of Medieval History* 10 (1984), p. 229. Berretti and Iacopi, "I molini," pp. 33–4, argue instead that horizontal mills were *more* efficient than preindustrial vertical mills.

[29] White, *Greek and Roman Technology*, p. 55.

meal, as they were supposed to, in most hydrological conditions. Moreover, their initial costs of construction were lower than those of vertical-wheeled mills, and in areas where animals were scarce horizontal mills could even be cheaper to run than animal-powered "sweat" mills.[30]

In certain circumstances, however, early medieval Italians, like their ancient ancestors who seem to have preferred them, built vertical mills. These differed from horizontal mills in several respects, as their water wheels' paddles were perpendicular to the water. The vertical water wheel required gears to turn the horizontal millstone, and this gearing rendered the vertical mill more costly and complicated to build and repair than the horizontal mill. Derivation conduits enabled vertical mills to keep at a safe distance from exuberant streams, increasing their life expectancy while also optimizing the impetus of the water's current on the wheel and preventing the surges or sudden drops in flow which are natural in any water course but which affect the fineness and hence the flavor of the flour.[31]

Ansilperga's Brescian mill seems to have had water pouring onto the paddles from a conduit above the wheel. Such "overshot" wheels tapped the weight of the water as well as the motion of its current, as Dante knew. But Ansilperga's overshot mill was an anomaly; most early medieval vertical wheels rested on the channel's water and were "undershot." Regardless of their shooting and of the delicacy of their inner workings, vertical mills made more efficient use of available energy than gearless horizontal mills.[32] In situations where water was scarce, vertical wheels

---

[30] In late medieval Piedmont, horizontal water mills which required no stables or fodder for their source of power cost half what "sweat" mills did to build and run: G. Alliaud, "Molitura e ambiente in una regione povera di corsi d'acqua," in Comba, *Mulini da grano nel Piemonte medievale*, pp. 50–1.

[31] Examples of conduits with vertical mills can be found in *CDC* I, 103:132 (892); and *CDL* III, 39:234 (767). For Ansilperga's unusual synchronized Brescian mills, whose closest parallels are Spanish, see Glick, *From Muslim Fortress*, p. 118. For aqueducts and vertical, overshot mills, see R. Forbes, "Power," in C. Singer (ed.), *A History of Technology* II (Oxford, 1957), p. 596; B. Gille, "Le moulin à eau," *Techniques et civilizations* 3 (1954), p. 3. B. Blaine, "The Enigmatic Water Mill," in B. Hall and D. West (eds.), *Studies in Honor of Lynn White, Jr.* (Malibu, 1976), p. 166, explains vertical wheel location. The channeled mills in Rome (Cassiodorus, *Variarum Libri Duodecim*, ed. T. Mommsen [Berlin, 1894], 3.31, p. 95; *Guerra Gotica* I, 1.19, p. 141; *Itinerarium Einsiedelnensis*, in *Codice topografico della città di Roma* I, ed. R. Valentini and G. Zucchetti, *FSI* 88 [Rome, 1940], 88, p. 190) may have been vertical and overshot.

[32] On the efficiency and power of the vertical wheel, see T. Glick, *Islamic and Christian Spain in the Early Middle Ages* (Princeton, 1979), p. 230; Amouretti, "La diffusion," p. 14; C. Parain, "Rapports de production et développement des forces productives," *La pensée* 119 (1965), pp. 58–9, 65; and esp. Forbes, "Power," pp. 590, 598, whose figures show them to be three times more productive (without taking many important variables into account, however). On its costliness, see Amouretti, "La diffusion," p. 14; Parain, "Rapports de production," p. 60; M. Del Treppo, *Amalfi medioevale* (Naples, 1977), p. 46.

produced more revolutions per minute than their horizontal relatives, and gearing ratios accelerated the turning of the millstone. Better use of water power and gearing translated into more rapid and even grinding which produced a finer flour without sticky lumps or burnt tastes.

The toothed cog and the "lantern" of the gearing, like much of the rest of the mill, were made of wood even though they were subject to much wear and tear. Iron was also an important construction material in vertical-wheeled water mills; the Salernitan term *ferratura* found in several contracts of ninth- and tenth-century date speaks for itself. Iron reinforced those mechanical parts which absorbed much friction and tended to wear out quickly. The axles linking the water wheel and the millstone benefited from iron reinforcements, particularly on the tips. (On occasion, in later times, the axle itself could be made of iron.) For Antolinus, the Salernitan miller who negotiated to rent a mill in 918, the iron parts were vital "so that I may grind properly."[33]

The differences between vertical and horizontal mills adapted each machine to specific hydrological situations and determined great gaps between their costs of construction and especially of maintenance. In early medieval Italy vertical mills were more often present in places with strong and continuous demand for milling than in droughty regions where water flow was too feeble to turn millstones without gearing. Economic rather than strictly ecological conditions affected their feasibility. Such machines made economic sense where there were communities of people sufficient in number to constitute a center of consumption. Several of early medieval Italy's vertical mills fit neatly within the scheme suggested by Amouretti, whereby the vertical mill is associated with capital-intensive, urban centers.[34] Cities and large

[33] On the "ferramentum de molino" in general, see C. Koehne, *Das Recht der Mühlen bis zum Ende der Karolingerzeit* (Breslau, 1904), p. 17; it appears also in *Leges Alamannorum* I, *Recensio Clothariana*, ed. K. Eckhardt (Göttingen, 1958), law 20, p. 118 (early 600s). Closer to Antolinus' *ferratura* (*CDC* I, 156:200, "ut perfecte macenare possam") is a Gaetan mill of 906: *CDCajetanus* I, 19:33. On the expense of such equipment, which had to be imported, see Parain, "Rapports de production," p. 60; and Caucanas, *Moulins*, pp. 147–50.

[34] Amouretti, "La diffusion," p. 14. On distinctions between urban and rural milling, see L. Bolen, "L'eau et l'irrigation d'après les traités d'agronomie andalous du moyen âge," *Options méditerranéennes* 16 (1972), p. 67; S. Bortolani, "Acque, mulini, e folloni nella formazione del paesaggio urbano medievale (secoli XI–XIV)," in *Paesaggi urbani dell'Italia padana*, pp. 282–4; L. Chiappa-Mauri, *I mulini ad acqua nel milanese (secoli X–XV)* (Città di Castello, 1984), p. 12; T. Reynolds, *Stronger Than A Hundred Men* (Baltimore, 1983), p. 106; A. Guillerme, "Les moulins hydrauliques urbains (XIe–XIIIe s.) dans les villes du bassin parisien," *Milieux* 1 (1980), p. 45; S. Tramontana, "Mulini ad acqua nella Sicilia normanna," in *Cultura e società nell'Italia medievale* II (Rome, 1988), p. 814; J. Muendel, "Medieval Urban Renewal," *Journal of Urban History* 17 (1991), p. 368; L. Palmucci Quaglino, "Corsi d'acqua e sfruttamento dell'energia idraulica," in Comba, *Mulini da grano nel Piemonte medievale*, p. 91.

monasteries, more than manors, provided the clusters of potential beneficiaries of a vertical mill to justify the initial outlays of capital they required.[35]

However, the question of the economic rationality of vertical-wheeled water mills is far from simple. Vertical mills tended to arise close to clusters of population. This, presumably, was because their superior efficiency, which translated into swifter and finer grinding, made a difference in places where demand for milling (and perhaps for bread-worthy, finer flour, which made a lighter bread that may have enhanced its eaters' prestige) was sustained. Swifter grinding may also have enticed mill builders, interested in maximizing the number of people served by their mill and thereby the quantity of multure the mill retained. Moreover, to crowds of people whose numbers meant they had to await their turn outside a mill, but could grind by other means if they wished, smoother, swifter operations were attractive. Towns were often places of consumption of wheat, the choicest of early medieval grains and the one most suited to flour for bread rather than meal for porridges. The superior grinding which a vertical mill with adequate water supplies delivered resulted in better-ground flour, a product hand querns were incapable of producing without repeated grindings. Thus vertical mills "made sense" where there were concentrated populations.

Nevertheless, vertical-wheeled mills also existed in rural areas, far from the crowds whose hunger for flour drove builders to opt for the complexities of vertical mills. The surprising vitality of the ninth- and tenth-century countryside is sometimes associated with the imposition of more economical, rational administration of agriculture by manorial lords.[36] Thus it might be tempting to see the equally surprising presence of complex and expensive vertical mills in some parts of rural Italy as an expression of the rationalizing tendencies of manorialism. Yet many of the peasants who brought grain to these mills were not obligated by manorial custom to do so, though Carolingian capitularies certainly reveal that the

---

[35] For examples of mills whose clientele was probably urban, see: in eighth-century Modena (*CDLangobardiae* 34:66 [768]) and Rome (*Itinerarium Einsiedelnensis*, p. 190); tenth-century Rome (*Papsturkunden*, I, 134:243); tenth-century Pavia (*Urkunden Konrad I.*, 273:388) and Amalfi (Del Treppo, *Amalfi medioevale*, p. 45); and in Salerno (*CDC* I, 391:244 [987], a mill "qui edificatum est in flubio lirino non longe ab anc civitatem").

Only people of great means like the abbess of S. Salvatore–S. Giulia, Ansilperga, or her royal father, built geared, vertical mills. This was not merely because of the size of the investment necessary to build them. The people most suited to owning them were, in fact, those who had water rights and had no fear of losing an entitlement vital to the expensive machines' functioning. This meant that vertical mills were the prerogative of *potentes*.

[36] P. Toubert, "La part du grand domaine dans le décollage économique de l'Occident (VIIIe–Xe siècles)," in *La croissance agricole du haut moyen âge* (Auch, 1990), pp. 53–86, which treats mills on pp. 68–9.

Italian countryside witnessed many "informal" constrictions.[37] And even if coercion of peasants by the powerful played a role in the dissemination of mills in general, there is no particular reason for the coercers in central Lombardy and around Salerno to have opted for expensive and fragile hydraulic (especially vertical) mills. In addition, some of the mills whose vertical paddle-wheels slapped the rural waterways of Salerno and central Lombardy during the ninth and tenth centuries were not all manorial. Instead, vertical mills existed outside manors in rural Italy, just as the horizontal mills did.

In Italy the builders of the rural vertical-paddled machines evidently expected to attract enough peasant grain into the mills to justify the owners' choice of what was generally a costlier, more complex technology. In these choices non-economic, cultural factors may have played the leading role. Rustics, just like anyone else, might prefer the vertical mill to any other means of grinding because of the quality of the flour obtained from it. Owners and builders may have been drawn to vertical mills by a desire to overawe people with a grander machine. In this way water mills, even the vertical-wheeled ones which the Romans built, and which were best suited to the urban world, could also find a niche far from cities when lords sought to bolster their prestige and peasants sought finer flour.

Most of the mills with which the charters deal appear to have been horizontal water mills, a machine widely popular in the entire Mediterranean region, among Iberian merchants just as among Byzantine peasants, and a machine whose effective solution to the problems of refining grain proved valid from Roman to modern times.[38] The more sophisticated vertical-wheeled mill was not perceived as "progress" over the horizontal mill, not least since it had been common in late imperial Italy. Both types of hydraulic mill had been introduced to the Mediterranean more or less simultaneously in Hellenistic times, and both had successfully spread throughout the region.[39] In early medieval Italy each type had specific applications. For peasant communities and for people with less capital to spend, the horizontal mill was a viable machine. In areas of restricted water flow and in areas with vigorous, concentrated demand for milling, vertical mills were more useful. Some cultural expectations also shaped the dissemination of mill types. People who ate porridge did not need the

[37] See *MGH Legum Sectio II*, vol. II, ed. A. Boretius and V. Krause (Hanover, 1890), 201.7, p. 61, 211.3, p. 84, 212.2, p. 85, for a few examples.
[38] For Spain, see Lagardère, "Moulins d'Occident," p. 60; Bonnassie, *La Catalogne* I, pp. 461–4. For Byzantium, see Holt, *Mills*, p. 120; M. Kaplan, *Les hommes et la terre à Byzance du VIe au XIe siècle* (Paris, 1992), pp. 53–5, 85.
[39] J. Oleson, *Greek and Roman Mechanical Water-Lifting Devices* (Toronto, 1984), p. 375; Reynolds, *Stronger*, p. 20.

powerful smooth grinding that vertical-wheeled mills furnished, and perhaps some mills were built to impress people as much as to grind grain.[40] A preference for a specific type of grinding could determine the fortunes of milling techniques. In Italy absence of appropriate water courses and, in cases like those recorded at Carapelle in the 770s, a desire to elude lordly exactions on milling contributed to the longevity of non-hydraulic grinding methods. In sum, hydrology, the availability of muscle power, cultural predispositions and appreciation for certain cereal products, capital, and population levels varied hugely throughout Italy at different times in the early medieval centuries. Accordingly, milling techniques did too.[41] The technologies of milling existed in social contexts, responding to cultural and economic requirements there.

Water power and social power

Water, flowing steadily and swiftly, was essential to any type of water mill's work. All owners of water mills were therefore obliged to secure for their machines a steady supply of water. Such a supply had to be technically adequate to push the mills' paddles around, something which the technologies discussed above could usually arrange; but also it had to be legally beyond dispute, "free from all public contradiction" as a charter for the church of Modena from 891 puts it.[42]

Contradiction was always possible. Abbess Ansilperga's fears of a *disturbatio* or an *interdictio* over her water in Brescia were shared by other eighth-century mill-owners, as a remarkable but damaged and slightly convoluted document from the cartulary of Farfa, describing the construction of a water-driven mill near Rieti in 778, shows.[43] In an evident attempt to establish legitimate rights over a natural resource, Duke Hildeprand donated to the bishop of Rieti (and also to the monks of S. Angelo, though the document adopts the second person singular) "the water of the bed of the river Velino, where you are to build a mill." The

---

[40] For a discussion of socially differentiated grain consumption in Italy, see M. Montanari, *Alimentazione e cultura nel medioevo* (Bari, 1988), pp. 124–35; and Menant, *Campagnes*, pp. 234–44, on the central Lombard plain.

[41] Regional terminology – *arcaturia* near Salerno, and *aquimola* in the Exarchate, for instance – and variations over time in the technical vocabulary reflect this heterogeneity.

[42] *I diplomi di Guido e di Lamberto*, ed. L. Schiaparelli (Rome, 1906), 11:31: "absque ulla publica contradictione." For other examples, see *Urkunden der Karolinger* IV, 1:69 (852): "absque alicuius refregatione vel contrarietate"; 5:76 (852); *Urkunden Konrad I.*, 336:451 (967); 374:514 (969): "omnino contradictione remota."

[43] *CDL* IV, 30:84 (also in the *Regesto di Farfa* I, 104:95–6) where the duke donates "[lacuna] ... aquam de alveo fluvii Mellini, ubi molinum edificare debeas, a quo capite ipsa aqua fuerit levata ex ipsa medietate aque fluvii, et usque ubi in ipsum medium fluvium discurrerit, in tua sit potestate ad edificium ipsius molini faciendum."

actual ground on which the mill-house was to stand was added almost as an afterthought.

Similar water grants for mills, designed to secure the mills' means of production, were drawn up in several different climatic and geographic zones in the peninsula, especially in the ninth century.[44] These instances indicate that mills were theoretically separable from the water they used. They also reveal that the right to use water resources for milling was not common to all, or automatic. Owners found specific entitlements to the water, in effect private property rights, useful. They enabled mills to work smoothly, without interference from abrasive neighbors (in Latin *rivales* meant fellow river-bank folk; by implication fellow river-users were rivals). A parallel vogue existed for stream-bank rights (*riparia* and *ripas*), which were both an ancient right of access to necessary water and a newer right to use the water as one saw fit.[45] The surviving sources suggest that it was in the eighth century that a new legal conception developed, for earlier, in the *Edictum Rothari* (of 643), the stream banks, the mill on them, and the right to use the water flowing by were conceived as an indissoluble unit.[46] Separate, exclusive water rights became a special characteristic of Carolingian and later Italian contracts pertaining to mills. The new understanding accompanied the dilution of Roman, state-enforced open access to water resources.[47]

Some ninth- and tenth-century charters relating to mills, however, do leave out water rights. The omission is probably due to the nature of the temporary rent contracts by which millers let mills, rather than to freer water regimes. Rent contracts had less need to specify water entitlements than did permanent sales or gifts, and the millers assumed that the owners' water rights were established uncontestably. Only a handful of millers worried about adequate water supply in their mills, and then for ecological reasons like drought. One Salernitan miller who feared *rivales'* contestation sought the protection of the mill-owners (he probably meant

---

[44] A sampling: *CDL* II, 257:349 (784); *Chronicon Vulturnense* I, ed. V. Federici (Rome, 1925), 37:255 (817); *Urkunden der Karolinger* IV, 29:105 (836); *CDC* I, 61:76 (865); 103:132 (892); *Urkunden Konrad I.*, 374:514 (969); *CDC* II, 328:152 (980); *Papsturkunden* II, 424:814 (1006); *CDC* V, 814:174 (1029).

[45] Bank rights were important to builders of dams: *M&D* V.2, 760:456–7 (862); *Regesto di Farfa* I, 293:247; *Museo* 24 (776); 109 (863); 138 (879). In Rome they also made ship-mills accessible from land: *Papsturkunden* II, 424:814.

[46] *Edictus Rothari* 151, p. 35, treated mills built on other people's river banks. In dry places, this was contentious legal ground. An impressive corpus of *fatwas* dealing with mills and bank rights developed in Muslim Iberia: Lagardère, "Moulins d'Occident," pp. 112–13.

[47] Catalonia and Roussillon witnessed a similar process in the early Middle Ages. Peasants lost control of milling to lords and churches (Glick, *From Muslim Fortress*, pp. 117–21; Caucanas, *Moulins*, pp. 40–1).

in court, but many lords could extend their "protection" to the fields as well).[48]

One of the effects of the mounting patrimonialization of water, of its transformation into commodity, was an increased likelihood of disputes among *rivales*. Exclusive proprietary rights meant greater disregard for downstream users was possible. The Italian written record affords only glimpses of the altercations to which such disregard could give rise. These disputes were unusual in that they appear to have involved millers more than owners or farmers. In other Mediterranean societies, during the medieval period contests over water between different mill-owners or between cultivators and millers were habitual, and indeed they became common in late medieval Italy as well.[49] But before the *comuni* stepped in to disentangle the irate irrigators from the millers, water contests in Italy had been contests among millers. Millers' disputes revolved around issues of seniority, with one mill's claim to the waters prevailing over another's when it was demonstrated that it was more ancient. Seniority – proved, if possible, with documents – was the winning argument because simple access to river banks did not guarantee entitlement to use the water in much of Italy after 800 or so.[50]

More than struggles over scanty water, early medieval Italian disputes appear to have been struggles to retain the milling "monopoly" over a given area. When another mill began operating within the sphere of influence (the radius of territory within which it was convenient to carry grain to the mill) of a given mill, profits from multure might drop drastically. To avoid this inconvenience, millers and mill-owners near Salerno fiercely opposed derivations from "their" water course. However, such fierceness was quickly tamed by offering compensation to the senior mill

---

[48] For a miller requiring defense, see *CDC* II, 413:275–6, of 989.

[49] For disputes in al-Andalus, see Lagardère, "Moulins d'Occident," pp. 93, 104. The seventh-century Byzantine "Farmers' Law," tr. W. Asburner, *Journal of Hellenic Studies* 32 (1912), 83–4, p. 95, regulated the allocation of water in favor of irrigators, whose rights it presumed to be more ancient. Milan's *Statuti* 2 ("Statuti delle strade delle acque del contado di Milano fatti nel 1346," ed. G. Porro Lambertenghi, in his *Miscellanea di storia italiana* VII [Turin, 1869], pp. 375–7) privileged millers over irrigators; at Viterbo, where both milling and horticulture flourished in the *trecento*, the *comune* gave precedence to millers but gave irrigators ample weekend "turns" (A. Lanconelli, "I mulini di Viterbo (secoli XII–XIV)," in Lanconelli and R. de Palma, *Terra, acqua, e lavoro nella Viterbo medievale* [Rome, 1992], pp. 17–18, 24). City administrators feared flour dearth more than horticultural drought.

[50] In Merovingian Gaul seniority was not a decisive argument, and the older mill downstream could find itself unable to work when another mill was built upstream (until divine intervention cleared things up: Gregory of Tours, *Liber Vitae Patrum* 18.2, p. 285). The Gaulish situation in the sixth century derived from the absence of legally encoded water rights and from a culture in which access to banks guaranteed rights over waters.

and its managers. When their disputes were settled, it emerges that there was plenty of water for both mills to function. The hornets' nest had not been stirred up by competition over scarce water but by the desire to monopolize the milling of a restricted area.[51] Similarly, at the headwaters of the Aniene, the monks of Subiaco obtained a preemptive monopoly of water for milling in 967. Their charter suggests that what was at stake was not a scarce natural resource, but a lack of people willing and able to bring grain to the water mills. Subiaco obtained water "with all the water mills which are there and which might be made in the future . . . and let no one in any way dare to make other mills there."[52] Therefore water rights for mills, increasingly prominent after about 750, appear to have had economic value less because Italy was a dry "Mediterranean" country with little water than because they limited the possibility of competition from adjacent mills powered by water.

The ownership of mills

The greatest ninth-century landowners in Italy were not above owning tiny fractions of mills, recording twelfths and tenths of mills even in inventories remarkable for abbreviations and omissions of detail. At Gaeta on the Tyrrhenian coast the highest authorities exchanged fractions of water mills, calculated in "days" of income, as early as 830.[53] In one exceptional Ligurian case a monastery owned one ninety-second of a water mill.[54] Such extreme partibility arose both from inheritance customs and from the high value accorded to all mills, whether these were in rural manors or commercially oriented and near towns.

The partible control of water mills reaches back at least to 710, when it enabled several owners to derive a proportion of the benefits according to the size of their "portion" of the mill.[55] Portions of ownership were economically viable long after 710 too (consider S. Giulia's twelfths), but what the redactors of the documents meant by "portion" is not always

---

[51] Salernitan monasteries prevented water "borrowing" and undermining of rightful possession by enforcing oaths on neighbors: *CDC* I, 61:76 (861). Salerno's bishop destroyed a new mill close by, then allowed its rebuilding after receiving compensation, in 978: *CDC* II, 302:117. In tenth-century Rome, numerous mills crowded the Tiber near the island, perhaps an example of peaceful competition: Lohrmann, "Schiffsmühlen," p. 283.

[52] *Urkunden Konrad I.*, 336:451: "lacibus duobus eorumque flumine qui extenditur eius cursus per latitudinem et longitudinem usque locus qui dicitur Seminarium, cum universis aquimolis qui ibi sunt et inantea fieri possunt, cum ripis undique compositis et piscariis, in quibus aquimolis et piscariis nullo modo quilibet audeat molam facere aut piscare."   [53] *CDCajetanus* 2:3: "quadraginta et quinque die de aquimulum."

[54] S. Origone, "Mulini ad acqua in Liguria nei secoli X–XV," *Clio* 10 (1974), p. 89.

[55] E.g., *Regesto di Farfa* II, 290:245 (853); *CDL* I, 14:37 (710), is the earliest.

clear. The proprietor of a third of a mill, a common fraction in the post-classical sources, obviously did not consider that she or he owned a third of the shingles and bricks which made up the mill, and the upper millstone. Part-owners conceived of the portion as a fraction of the working time of (and hence income from) a mill. This time-income was grain, which could easily be divided. But the documents seldom specify whether the third-owner received all the income generated by a mill in four months out of a year, or all the income in one year out of three (both divisions based on time, which are normal in water-related sharing arrangements), or whether this owner received a third of all the grain exacted by the mill and stored for division until the end of the week or month (or year, as is implied by the S. Giulia polyptych).[56] Other Italian communities did not follow the example of Gaeta, where mills were sometimes divided into "days" (presumably 365 of them, even if mills lay idle for religious or hydrological reasons much of the time), though it has parallels in al-Andalus.[57] In the interests of equity, the Gaetan "days" were probably not actual calendar days, as these would deprive some part-owners of their fair share of water (during dry seasons) and available grain (when people's stocks began to thin out). The "days" therefore seem to have been fiscal subdivisions of equal value, since no one ever specified which days (shorter winter days or droughty spring ones?) were his or hers. If this is how the "days" functioned, these idiosyncratic fiscal subdivisions were effective. They allowed infinite partibility and hence flexibility for the administration of real estate; and they were concrete in a way ninety-secondths were not. However, some Gaetan contracts specified the months to which part-owners were entitled, which would have variable value and thus not be equal.[58] "Privileged," or more valuable shares in the same mill, were therefore possible.

Both when divided into slots representing time for milling and when entitled to shares of income, the portion of a mill was treated as alienable property exactly like a whole mill, everywhere in Italy. Share-owners did not consult other owners before selling or bequeathing the share, and they exercised complete dominion over it. Still, relations between portion-holders were almost mandatory. Income or time slots had to be

---

[56] Water and water benefits were often divided by time lots; for examples, see B. Shaw, "Lamasba," *Antiquités africaines* 18 (1982), p. 74, and Shaw, "Water and Society in the Ancient Maghrib," *Antiquités africaines* 20 (1984), p. 168. Amalfi's mills were divided by months (Del Treppo, *Amalfi medioevale*, p. 48). The polyptych *S. Giulia da Brescia*, in *Inventari altomedievali di terre, coloni, e redditi*, ed. A. Castagnetti et al. (Rome, 1979), pp. 64, 66, 77, 89, measured the income from mill-shares in *modia* of grain per annum.

[57] *CDCajetanus* 2:3 (830); see Skinner, *Family Power*, p. 73, who is puzzled by the system. (Cordoban judges disapproved of this potentially inequitable system of division: Lagardère, "Moulins d'Occident," p. 108.)   [58] Skinner, *Family Power*, p. 74.

allocated, millers had to be hired and if possible supervised, and the expenses of maintenance had to be confronted. Thus the mill became a socializing tool rather like the well, for the mill portion brought the owner into association with an array of people with whom she or he might otherwise have had no contact.

In origin, mill portions were created either by the necessity to pool resources facing less wealthy people who wanted to build water mills, or by the accidents of inheritance, galvanized by the equal distribution among heirs encouraged by Lombard law. But as a side effect portion-holding brought social mixing, often vertically. As share-owners sold or donated their shares to people not originally associated with the mill, mill portions unintentionally shaped social alliances. Sometimes the portion-holders were family members who had inherited their portions and among whom relations already existed, but there were also some groups of shareholders who had no evident other ties to each other. Doctors and lowly laymen entered into mill-ventures as owners of shares, alongside lesser ecclesiastical officials.[59] Through the water mill subaltern people could enter into ongoing relations with important monastic houses and other powerful people in a way which land-owning, which was not as frequently shared among socially heterogeneous people, did not encourage. As part-owners, subaltern people interacted with social superiors on unusual, theoretically equal terms, not as tenants.[60]

However, the associations of share-owners who had been the first social group created by the mills declined in Carolingian Italy. Compared to its predecessor, the ninth century saw fewer mills held in common by groups of laypeople. After 800 individual ownership by rulers, magnates, and especially ecclesiastical officials or institutions predominated in the documents. Most obviously in the Po valley, large numbers of mills passed to the Church as pious donations. Alongside this "clericalization" of water and milling, and indeed part of it, was the ability of some great lords to obtain control of many hydraulic mills, especially in the tenth century.[61]

---

[59] Examples of shared ownership can be found in: *CDC* I, 21:132 (inherited in 842 by relatives, sold to unrelated men); *CDL* I, 14:37 (unrelated men in 710); 38:132 (726; a cleric to a doctor in Pisa); 116:345 (754; a Pisan *civis*); *CDL* II, 162:101–2 (762; relatives); *Museo* 24 (776); 90 (853); *CDL* IV, 30:92 (778, whose fragmented ownership was unified by the bishop of Rieti in 31:92); *CDL* V, 15:64 (749; relatives); *S. Giulia da Brescia*, in *Inventari altomedievali di terre, coloni, e redditi*, pp. 64, 67, 77, 89; *M&D* V.2, 767:461 (864; relatives and a deacon); *Monumenti* VI, 7:12 (954; an *enfiteusis* rent to unrelated men).

[60] In practice, social inequalities among share-owners surely determined unequal access to mill income. Thus the powerful might obtain the best shares of a mill's time (with good water flow and abundant grain).

[61] These trends were attenuated in the Lucchesia and around Salerno. For examples, see: *CDC* I, 61:76 (865; doctor to a monastery); Vat. Lat. 4939, 69v (779; duke to an abbot); *CDL* I, 14:37 (710; *servi Christi* to a monastery); 116:345 (754; to a monastery); *CDL* II,

This upward mobility of water mills went hand in hand with the patrimonialization of water and water rights throughout Italy which began in the eighth century and whose first beneficiaries had been churches. Even though the documents which attest to this come from ecclesiastical archives which preserved the charters according to narrow and self-interested criteria, the rarity of later attestations to ownership of water mills by lesser individuals or groups of individuals suggests that a shift had occurred. Water mills had become the carefully regulated property of the greatest economic powers of the time, first of the churches, then also of magnates. This shift reflected both the increasing economic weight of the Church, recipient of ever larger donations of land, water, and water mills in the eighth and ninth centuries, and the new status of water as a commodity which could be patrimonialized, as it was by secular lords in the ninth and tenth centuries.[62] In 964, when Otto the Great granted "public waters" to the bishopric of Pavia to build mills with, he was working within a venerable tradition whereby rights over aqueous resources were transferred by Italian rulers for the benefit of the mighty.[63]

Mill income

In medieval Europe hydraulic mills produced different kinds of benefits for their owners, depending on the mills' location and owners' interest. Some manorial mills produced prestige, manifesting the social power of the lord. The capacity to compel peasants to use a manor's mill was a symbol of authority over people even before it was a means of extracting surplus from them. Nevertheless, the tendency to divide control of mills on manors in Italy is somewhat more perplexing. Partible manorial mills must also have been economic ventures, for a divided mill reflected no one's power clearly (to whom, among the twelve, or four, or ninety-two

162:101 (762; to two monasteries); 188:173 (765; to a monastery); 218:250 (768; to a church); 257:268 (771; cleric to a monastery); *CDLangobardiae* 29:57 (765; layman to a church); 34:66 (768; layman to a church); 183:310 (852; clergy to a hospice); 226 (863; cleric to a church); *CDL* III, 15:70 (742; king to a *fidelis*); 29:183 (c. 750; king to a monastery); 39:234 (767; king to a monastery); *Urkunden der Karolinger* IV, 29:105 (836; king to an optimate); 39:120 (839; king to a monastery); 41:129 and 58:164 (840 and 841; king to a bishop); *Regesto di Farfa* II, 293:247 (854; laymen to a monastery); *Chronicon Vulturnense* I, 35:252 (c. 815; layman to monastery); 37:254 (c. 815; layman to monastery); *CDCajetanus* 2:3 (830; bishop to a *comes*' son).
[62] Caucanas, *Moulins*, p. 101, postulates that control of milling by *potentes* (which came in the 1100s in Roussillon) was a *consequence* of the patrimonialization of water. In Italy this cause–effect link is not as strong, for the earliest lordly water mills pre-date the widespread ownership of water rights by *potentes*.
[63] *Urkunden Konrad I.*, 265:378: "molendina componeret et publicas aquas ad utilitatem ipsius ecclesie trahere."

owners was the user beholden?). Unlike power, grain-income from multure was easily divisible.[64]

Prestige and rents also accrued from commercial mills, but the dosage was different. Commercial mills' principal functions were economic. They generated respectable incomes for their owners and were designed to do so. The early medieval Italian propensity for fragmenting mill-ownership among scores of proprietors implies that people comprehended the economic benefits produced by mills. Economic rents were what most readily could be divided.

Income from water mills tended to dip and surge, for productivity reflected the agricultural cycle's uncertainty and the changeability of the weather (which determined fluctuations in stream flow). Postclassical owners excogitated several different strategies to remove or attenuate such dips in income. For example, the polyptych of S. Giulia in Brescia lists manorial mills which provided a fixed income to the nunnery. These mills were said to "render in a year so many *modia* of grain," calculated separately from the total grain expected from the manor's agrarian base.[65] This grain was the multure levied on those who ground at the mill, whether dependent peasants with no alternatives or mill-less cultivators attracted from outside the manor. The nunnery's inventory suggests that the size of the harvest, any droughts which stopped the mill-paddles, and the numbers of the outsiders drawn to the mill did not affect the nuns' income. In this system, in prosperous years the manorial peasants or the manor's supervisors (or even, if there were any, the millers) could keep any surplus produced by the fields and the mill. In lean years, on the other hand, paying the required fixed contribution would mean hunger for the peasants or even the mill's overseers. S. Giulia's mill-income collection system was rigid, and it was practical only from the point of view of a landowner with many mills and little desire to dally over the few extra *modia* of grain which good years might bring. For the nuns the knowledge that no matter what happened, short of total economic collapse, a certain amount of grain would reach their granary was an organizational boon. Their goal was stability, not maximum income. This goal characterized ecclesiastical administration of mills.

In their pursuit of regular income from mills, ecclesiastical mill-owners

---

[64] It is tempting to link the decline of partible water mills after about 850 to the advance of manorial economics, especially in the Po valley. Regardless, one should recall that manorial mills imposed obligations on their owners to grind promptly when requested to do so (e.g., in Roussillon: Caucanas, *Moulins*, pp. 110–11). Mills could be prestigious, but burdensome.

[65] Polyptych *S. Giulia di Brescia*, in *Inventari altomedievali di terre, coloni, e redditi*, pp. 54, 56, 63, 64, 66, 67, 68, 69, 73, 74, 77, 78, 85, 89, 91.

in central and northern Italy also developed other administrative mechanisms. In the tenth century the Ravennan archbishops preferred to rent manor mills to intermediaries, presumably to circumvent the difficulties of exacting revenues regularly, without sacrificing the possibility of increasing income if opportunity presented itself at the contract's end.[66] This indirect administrative style has been associated with periods of agrarian stagnation or decline in England, but there is little to suggest the region of Ravenna was struggling economically in the mid-900s.[67] Instead, the renting of Ravenna's mills fit the standard pattern whereby powerful laymen won long-term rent contracts from churches as a first step toward usurping property and rights.

From a landlord's standpoint, renting the mill was a convenient way of obtaining a fixed income from mills. Many contracts from the Lucchesia and the Exarchate of Ravenna were agreements between owners, usually major churches, and men who had no intention of milling and served only as intermediaries between the mill lord and the mill. At Lucca the status of these enterprising people was not aristocratic, though most were rich. They paid fixed rents, sometimes in money, to the owners for the privilege of running the mills as they saw fit. This involved hiring the millers, who then became responsible for exacting enough multures to cover the costs of rent.[68] Near Ravenna the renters of *fundi* with water mills were the most powerful elements in secular society. In the earlier 800s the renter-intermediaries may have sought only economic advantages from their ventures. Later, however, some mill renters may also have sought to increase their power over the cultivators of the *fundi* they rented by exercising the lordly rights associated with the farm.[69]

Lucca's tenth-century bishops, instead, administered their mills directly. They may have kept mills off their polyptychs because they did not lease them, or perhaps they recognized that mills brought widely differing revenues from one year to the next and that any attempt to define

[66] *Breviarium Ecclesiae Ravennatis (Codice Bavaro)*, ed. G. Rabotti (Rome, 1985), Appendix III, 19:230, seems to associate a mill, in ruins by 949, with signorial rights which the renters hoped to exercise. Among these may have been the obligation for peasants on the *fundo* to mill at the mill if the lord "with God helping" repaired it. But on other *fundi* near Ravenna mills did not always work in this fashion: *Monumenti* IV, 8:170 (927); VI, 4:5 (954).

[67] J. Langdon, "Water-mills and Windmills in the West Midlands, 1086–1500," *Economic History Review* 44 (1991), p. 437.

[68] *M&D* V.2, 855:523 (874; Firmo was no *potens*), is the best example; *Breviarium*, Appendix III, 19:230 (949; Ursus was a *scabinus*).

[69] For an eighth-century rent by a tribune, see *Breviarium* 22:15 (c. 820). *Breviarium*, Appendix III, 19:230, suggests more was at stake than multure, for Ursus received "omnen functionem domnicam" save justice along with the mill.

their productivity was fruitless: careful Carolingian monastic administrators like Adalhard of Corbie knew that income from mills was reliably erratic, that it depended on harvest levels, water levels, and the skill of the millers, and that simplifications like S. Giulia's were unrealistic.[70]

A modest abbey like that of Abbess Piltruda near Cividale in the 760s was interested in more frugal and flexible ways of collecting the income from the water mill (of which the convent owned half) than a rich house like S. Giulia was around 900.[71] The charter of 762 whereby Piltruda's sons donated much property to her was worded so as to guarantee that a settled proportion of the grain ground there would reach the nuns (so the *medietate* meant half the income), whether it was wheat or less noble grains. In this case the mill's owner shared with the users the risks of agricultural production and with the miller the risks created by the vagaries of water flow. Certain mill lords in ninth- and tenth-century Salerno also sought proportional rents from their millers in some cases, as did the archbishop of Ravenna on at least one occasion, and the abbey of Farfa.[72] This proportional sharing of the risks and profits of milling between miller and owner seems to have lost currency in the ninth century, save in the region of Salerno (and there, too, some monasteries exacted fixed rents from millers). Such arrangements filled owners' granaries only in situations of sustained demand for the mills' services, in densely inhabited areas, in hydrologically favorable seasons, and in years of abundant grain to grind.[73]

The prevalence of the more rigid but safer system of fixed income-extraction from mills appears related to the special needs of the great churches which had become the most numerous owners of water mills during the 800s. Profit-maximizing was not their priority; risk avoidance was. Proportional rents could fluctuate dizzily, for the mills' fortunes were, as we have seen, bound to many variables. But in the final analysis, if these ecclesiastical administrative strategies differed in detail, they all sought to transfer onto others (millers, enterprising magnates, peasants) the risks of uneven mill income and to secure for the owners steady payments of grain or money.

[70] Episcopal manors with mills at Lucca are described in *Diplomi di Ugo* 31:97; 56:168. For Adalhard, see Comet, *Le paysan*, p. 475; G. Fourquin, "Le premier moyen âge," in G. Duby (ed.), *Histoire de la France rurale* (Paris, 1975), p. 362.

[71] *CDL* II, 162:102: "nec non et molino in Palaciolo medietate . . . Ita tamen dum domina genetrix nostra advixerit ipsum frumentum in integrum in eius pertineat potestate, grano vero rustico equaliter amodo dividant [with the other owners, a monastery]."

[72] For Ravenna, a good example is "Gli archivi," 89:429 (907). For Farfa, see Lanconelli, "I mulini," p. 9.

[73] Examples of suburban mills accessible to larger communities can be found in: *CDL* III, 39:234 (presumably for a fee, in 767 the Brescians must have used Ansilperga's mill); *CDL* IV, 31:92 (778); *CDC* II, 391:244 (987); *Regesto di Farfa* II, 251:208 (821).

Income from mills took several shapes. In the Lucchesia, and occasionally in the Ravennate, money-rents existed. Money was more difficult for the payer to manipulate, and eliminated many occasions for fraud by the miller or entrepreneur, while still regularizing and stabilizing income for the owner. Still, most owners expressed the income they obtained from the water mills, directly or by renting, not in money but in measures of grain (rather than flour, which was harder to store, though it had the "value added" of milling).

The quantity of this grain was not the owners' sole preoccupation. In the transapenninic parts of the kingdom, proprietors as different as the eighth-century Friulan convent of Abbess Piltruda and the Milanese abbot of S. Ambrogio in the early tenth century also considered the quality of the grain they obtained. "Rustic" grains were unsuited to their kitchens, perhaps because they were less prestigious or perhaps because they were technically unsuitable for the types of confection these proprietors wanted to prepare. Similar concerns were expressed by Salernitan contracts of the tenth century, where only *granum* (probably wheat, the early medieval grain of choice) was exacted by owners.[74] For these owners the income of their mills was a reflection of their refinement and social status as much as an economic matter.

Mill income, in short, depended on the type of mill, its management style, its location and accessibility, and its size. Manorial water mills *could* be rented (they did not always generate income directly), but most produced an income in grain paid as a fixed amount by the manor to the owner, deriving from multure exacted on grain milled (which could include grain brought in by neighbors of the manor). Other mills were purely commercial. In the Italian southwest, and also in the Lucchesia, during the 900s their owners rented them to millers who then attempted to earn a living by charging the users for use of the mill, or to third parties who treated the mill as an investment and did not themselves mill. For the latter two types of renters, access to more effective vertical mills, to willing and numerous eaters of flour, and to vigorous, reliable water courses had a direct impact on their success. While early medieval Italian owners of mills sedulously worked to minimize the variations in income concomitant with the very nature of water power by devising contracts which guaranteed stable entries, both a wealthy and powerful class of intermediaries, and a less wealthy and powerful class of millers assumed the risks of using water to grind other people's grain.

---

[74] *CDLangobardiae* 476:824 (918) distinguished between wheat (of which the owner wanted much) and rye (of which he wanted less); *granum* was demanded by *CDC* II, 391:244 (987); 413:275 (989); 458:343 (993); *CDC* V, 814:174 (1029); *CDC* VII, 1202:251 (1059).

Watermillers

In his *Metamorphoses*, the second-century Roman novelist Apuleius had described the brutish life of the flour-dusted slaves whose lot it was to work in a "sweat" mill in northern Greece. Supervised by a simple-minded miller whose wife later had him hanged, the naked, hairless miller-slaves were branded on the forehead. The most famous medieval miller instead steps out of the pages of Chaucer's *Canterbury Tales* as a clever, rich, and determined entrepreneur in control of most aspects of his life.[75] Although these two antipodal models come from very different geographical zones, they illustrate the point that the practitioners of the art of milling, together with much else in that craft, were transformed during the medieval centuries separating Apuleius and Chaucer. Indeed, for Marc Bloch the medieval miller was a new social type, and the creation of a distinct category of free artisans involved in grinding grain was the most significant consequence of the dissemination of hydraulic milling technologies in medieval Europe.[76] By examining the case of early medieval Italy, one that Bloch overlooked, we may confirm that the professional miller's emergence in the early Middle Ages was important. Yet in the peninsula the miller was less distinctive and separate from the rest of early medieval society than Bloch and others imagined; indeed, the nature of milling with water prevented the construction of the miller as "other" in Italy. Different types of mills owned by different sorts of people worked in very diverse conditions throughout early medieval Italy. Similar variety prevailed in the class of men who physically ran the water mills.

The charters which form the basis of our knowledge of mills before AD 1000 are mostly contracts of sale or donation. Such transactions had little need to describe the millers associated with the mills, save in the event that they were property. Considering this fact, the references to the operators of mills are quite numerous. Yet early medieval millers seldom appear either as socially influential or as independent as they became in late medieval texts, and as they had been in late antique Rome. In the tenth century free but powerless agents like Antolinus, a Salernitan miller who negotiated a contract in 936, were common enough near large settlements in southern Italy.[77] Millers such as Antolinus *were* able to impose some conditions on the mill-owners when they rented mills. For example, they shared responsibility for replacing worn millstones, or required

[75] Apuleius, *Metamorphoses*, ed. D. Robertson (Paris, 1945), 9.11–14, pp. 72–4; G. Chaucer, *The Canterbury Tales*, ed. F. Robinson (Boston, 1957), General Prologue 545–66, p. 22.
[76] Bloch, "Avènement et conquête," p. 542, had northern Europe in mind but also cited the *collegium* of millers in fifth-century Rome as evidence. Forbes, "Power," p. 601, and Toubert, "La part," p. 69, followed Bloch's lead.   [77] *CDC* I, 156:200.

owners to repair structures damaged by flood, or reserved the right not to pay rents when drought prevented them from "grinding perfectly."[78] They also undertook the responsibilities and risks of the management and maintenance of mills, and expected to make some profit from the venture. These professional millers could appeal to local traditions when they drew up contracts with the mill lords, and in general avoided excessive exploitation of their special skills.[79] At Salerno, in fact, the work and skill invested by the miller gave him some minimal property rights over the mill, for he was able to remove the millstone he had cut if he decided to leave the mill at contract's end.[80] Both at Salerno and further up the Tyrrhenian coast, in Liguria, certain professional millers were well enough connected to systems of exchange to negotiate rent in coins, while others paid only in grain or labor or in combinations thereof.[81] In the southern principalities especially, but also in the Lucchesia, many millers of the 800s and 900s had more in common with Chaucer's fox-like miller than with the worn-out slaves of Roman literature.[82]

In early medieval Italy mills run by free professionals like Antolinus were only one among several solutions to the problems of running water mills. Not all millers were free to negotiate their terms or make a living from their activities. In the middle of the eighth century in central Italy some millers were subordinate men who had animalesque names (with tell-tale diminutives, like Taurulus and Ursulus) and were sold and bought together with the mill they ran, formally without control over their lives or the mill.[83]

---

[78] This was especially true near Salerno and Lucca. Lombard millers surely worried about damage to the mills too, but did not control the terms of their contracts as closely; *CDLangobardiae* 476:824 (918) makes Adalbertus responsible "in his person" for rent and controls his residency. For examples of assertive southern millers, see *CDC* II, 391:244 (987), in which Ermi the miller had Sasso, the prince's *vestiarius*, furnish the millstones, though he would dress them; 413:276 (989), in which Iohannes and Iaquintus will "conciare" the mills but pay only according to how well they have been functioning, and, while millstones are provided by the owner, "arcaturia . . . communiter nos conciemus"; *CDC* V, 814:174–5 (1029), in which Andreas will be paid for his improvements; *CDC* VII, 1202:250 (1054), "et si ipsa arcatura pro plena ruperit, pars ipsius ecclesie [the mill lord] eam faciat conciare het mundare."
[79] *CDC* II, 391:244 (987), refers to prevailing custom as the standard for rent payment. Similarly, in Friuli in 762, custom regulated the mill: *CDL* II, 162:104.
[80] *CDC* V, 814:175 (1029).
[81] Origone, "Mulini ad acqua," pp. 96–101, records money payments in the 900s. Coin payments were easier to gauge and control. They may be a sign of owners' distrust.
[82] Skinner, *Family Power*, p. 253, discusses the contradictory case of Gaeta in the tenth century, where free peasants but also slaves managed water mills.
[83] *CDL* III, 29:182–3 (c. 750); Brühl, acknowledging that this charter had a facelift in the eleventh century, still accepts its terms as authentic. In it Aistulf gave Monteamiata land "et molinas tres qui posita sunt in fluvio Vivo cum casis vel hominis qui ipsas molinas regere videtur; et fiunt rectas istas casa vel molinas per Taurulu et Ursulu cum omnia quidquid ipsas ad suas manus habere visi sunt; et due uncias de terra adauximus illorum abendi." Monteverdi had slaves in *CDL* I, 116:346 (754); see also *Regesto di Farfa* II, 251:208 (821).

These subject millers faded from the records in the first decades of the ninth century, but as late as 973 a slave (servus) toiled in a mill near Ravenna, and Petrulus the miller was a slave of the Gaetan duke in 906.[84]

Between the independent and self-conscious entrepreneurs of Salerno and Lucca in the ninth or tenth centuries and the powerless subalterns who ground S. Apollinare in Ravenna's grain in 973 was a heterogeneous class of part-time manorial millers working, as need arose, the mills on the manors which became characteristic of northern and central Italy in the Carolingian period. Numerous water-driven mills were listed in transactions involving arable land, orchards, houses, woods, and other components of the manorial unit.[85] The peasants who tilled the manors' soil, and whose versatility as a labor force was encouraged, also seem to have worked the manorial mills. A group of coloni who worked on a manor donated to Farfa in 749, and who had a written contract (as some types of serfs did, in Italy), provided labor on this manor which had a mill, but no miller.[86] The coloni's agreement with the lord must have required them to work in the mill and perhaps to use it too. Similar situations existed in the Lombard plain in the ninth century, and wherever manors prevailed. Such cases suggest that often in early medieval Italy, particularly in rural contexts, professional millers were substituted for by "unspecialized" subject laborers working at the orders of the owner of the mill and of the circumventing land. Those few notices of milling in the early medieval literary record confirm this. The rather incompetent warriors at work in a mill described by Gregory the Great in his Dialogues (composed in the 590s) were certainly amateurs. Later, so great and organized an enterprise as ninth-century Bobbio did not have a specialized miller-monk to run its mills, but rather a magister carpentarius who also had other responsibilities and probably did not himself get his dark tunic white with flour, but only directed the monastery's laborers.[87]

---

[84] Miller-slaves existed near Ravenna in the tenth century; see Monumenti I, 48:180 (973). For Gaeta, see Skinner, Family Power, p. 253.

[85] For examples, see Vat. Lat. 4939, 74r (742); CDL I, 116:345 (754); CDL II, 188:173 (765); 257:348 (771); Urkunden der Karolinger III, 29:105 (836); 39:120 (839). The inventory of S. Giulia lists many mills as part of a curte. CDL V, 90:293 (779), deals with the struggle of the Carapellans against payment of a new toll on milling to S. Vincenzo al Volturno, new (manorial?) lord of the area (CDL V, 95:308 [782] records the defeat of some of the recalcitrant peasants); C. Wickham, Studi sulla società degli Appennini nell'alto medioevo (Bologna, 1982), p. 206, analyzes these events.

[86] CDL V, 15:64 (749). On the originalities of Italian manorial labor arrangements, see B. Andreolli and M. Montanari, L'azienda curtense in Italia (Bologna, 1983), p. 158.

[87] Gregory the Great, Dialogi, ed. A. de Vogüé and P. Antin (Paris, 1978–80), 3.37, p. 412. Abbot Wala's guide to Bobbio is "Anhang 4," in L. Hartmann, Zur Wirtschaftsgeschichte Italiens im frühen Mittelalter (Gotha, 1904), p. 131. Some Germanic law, like Rothari's, did not contemplate the possibility that a separate category of people should run mills, and expected everyone to grind for themselves: Reynolds, Stronger, p. 105. But Koehne, Das Recht, pp. 39–41, showed that some codes did know "millers," a low-status group.

In early medieval Italy, therefore, it is fair to say that millers came from highly heterogeneous backgrounds and had differing degrees of specialization. Regardless of their varying status and power, they were all millers in some sense. They shared a common body of technical knowledge and performed approximately the same operations in and around the millhouse. These operations were far from simple. Controlling and maintaining the waterworks of mills was difficult and required a sound understanding of mills' hydraulics. Millers had to maintain and operate the waterworks properly: they had to clear the derivation channels of roots and leaves, fix dams and remove the silt which settled behind them, open and close sluices so as to ensure that the water reaching the millwheel had the appropriate speed and volume. All these actions affected the natural flow of the water courses upon which the mills depended, and in consequence affected the other users of the streams, human or not. The seventh-century *Edict* of Rothari indicates that on occasion the alteration of flow caused by the millers sparked wrathful reactions, including the "malevolent" destruction of dams or mills.[88]

The malevolence which the ecological (and, as we shall see, economic) alterations administered by millers awakened in the 600s seems to have intensified thereafter. Indeed, in the Middle Ages millers occupied an infamous position in literature, a result of medieval societies' bitterness toward the whole group. By the time Chaucer penned his famous satire, in transalpine Europe literary pillorying of millers was a venerable tradition whose leafy genealogical tree sank its roots in the eleventh century. Chaucer's tale suggests that indeed discord was the faithful companion of fourteenth-century English millers, and hostility directed at loutish and greedy millers may have reached its medieval apogee in the *Canterbury Tales*. But animosity developed healthily thereafter, too.[89] It was a European trait, shared by many regions until quite recently.

Why millers should be so resented has been adumbrated. They managed machines which affected the environment in which everyone lived. Though the ecological alterations they caused might be beneficial to some, like all alterations of equilibria, they left others disadvantaged and disgruntled. The *rivales*, even those impotent before the use of the waters by the mills, would form an eager public for tales about monstrous millers. And since unlike almost everyone else millers lived in millhouses, often on the outskirts of, or altogether removed from the community, they were natural outsiders. The physical distance from the space inhabited by the neighbors, made necessary by the hydrological imper-

---

[88] *Edictus Rothari* 150, p. 34, punishes any who destroy a dam without the judge's permission.

[89] G. Jones, "Chaucer and the Medieval Miller," *Modern Language Quarterly* 16 (1955), pp. 3–15. Holt, *Mills*, pp. 90–105, corrects Jones on several matters.

atives of mill construction, may have furthered suspicions about millers' activities.

But this was not all that marginalized medieval millers. An important ingredient of the medieval anti-miller literature was the miller's supposed moral impropriety. The mill-house, a place of meeting and idle waiting, came to be tied to sexual encounters and the reputation of the miller, who presided over such illicit unions, was soiled.[90] This later medieval conception of the typical activities of the mill and the miller had ancient antecedents. It was present already in Apuleius' account of a Greek "sweat" mill. For a fifth-century writer like the ecclesiastical historian Socrates Rome's mills could be depicted only as disreputable places.[91] Building on notions explicit in Apuleius, Socrates described his hero, the emperor Theodosius, rectifying the indecent situation prevailing in the mills, dens of prostitutes, pimps, and kidnappers.

The sexual transgressions over which millers were supposed to preside seem to have rendered millers odious to late antique and late medieval authors. Furthermore, in early medieval Italy millers competed with each other for grain (and maybe for water), and their contests may have tarred them with an unsavory public image. On top of these good reasons for millers' low repute, there was the more important fact that everyone lost grain to them, whether it was real or imagined grain – for millers exacted multure. Even when millers were honest they were responsible for depriving grain producers of a part of their product. Though much of the grain legitimately exacted for milling services ended up in the granaries of mill-owners as rent or manorial dues, the opprobrium felt by the grain producers clung to the millers who exacted it to begin with. They were, in the end, the physical exactors, as well as the allies of mill lords.[92]

The miller was also the most obvious culprit for other, less expected and legitimate losses of grain which users of mills imagined or actually experienced in the milling process. Baffling variations in the ratio between the volume of the grain brought to the mill and the flour taken away,

[90] Tramontana, "Mulini," p. 823, and J. Le Goff, *La civilisation de l'Occident médiéval* (Paris, 1964), p. 385, stress the miller as pimp, the mill as place of prostitution. St. Bernard, *Epistolae*, ed. J. Leclercq and H. Rochais, in *Sancti Bernardi Opera* VII (Rome, 1974), 79, p. 212, saw the mill as a dangerous place of sexual mixing.

[91] Socrates Scholasticus, *Ecclesiastical History*, ed. J. Migne (Paris, 1867), 5.18, p. 612.

[92] Le Goff ascribed the widespread hostility of cultivators for millers to the latter's association with lordly surplus-extraction, and cited famous examples of long disputes such as that which Abbot Richard of St. Albans concluded in 1331 (or so it seemed, but the Great Rising of 1381 reopened the case) by paving the monastic parlor with a grim trophy, the hand querns confiscated from unlucky peasants who had refused to allow the abbey's miller to grind their grain (Le Goff, *La civilisation*, pp. 374, 626). Caucanas, *Moulins*, pp. 210–11, agrees with Le Goff's image.

usually the outcome of the progressive dessication of the grain in the course of time after harvest, could give rise to doubts.[93] Also, millers began every transaction by measuring the grain to be paid or ground, removing the "appropriate" proportion before grinding the remainder into meal or flour. Subsequently, the millers may have weighed the flour as well. Measuring is an ambiguous and power-laden act, and those in control of the measures can easily become the object of suspicion and resentment.[94] In the act of measuring grain and flour the miller distanced himself from all those whose grain he touched. All users of the mill, even powerful lords and owners, were wary of the miller's measurements. In cases where rent owed by the miller was fixed and regular, the "full" and "just" measure employed to gauge how much grain the miller paid to the owner was in the eye of the beholder. But the miller made it himself, presumably in his own best interest.[95] Like the load to be ground, the miller's multure too, in theory fixed and regular, had to be measured, and when the miller exercised his wiles measuring the grain and flour the proportion of grain retained by the mill grew and shrank shockingly. Measurement techniques (shaking and packing down, heaping up, and so on) were the motive for the distrust of late antique millers in Rome, whose *fraudes* the urban prefect in about 488 attempted to curb by establishing a central, state-sanctioned measuring station on the Janiculum and by insisting that millers accept payment in money, whose measure was more difficult to manipulate.[96] These special skills of millers remained one of

[93] In Italy, mills were busiest between June (after the harvest) and Christmas, when grain was heavier. On seasonal variations in grain weight, see P. Camilla, "I mulini negli statuti medievali del Cuneese," in Comba, *Mulini da grano nel Piemonte medievale*, p. 162; Comet, *Le paysan*, p. 464.

[94] W. Kula, *Measures and Men* (Princeton, 1986), pp. 15–16, 149–50, has many insightful things to say on this subject. Salerno's contracts betray unease over the just measure millers used to pay rents: *CDC* II, 391:244 (987), calls for "tota [*mensura* of grain] sind culma"; 413:275 (989), "iusto tertiario"; 458:343 (9930), "granum bonum de ipsa molina culma mensurata." *CDC* VII, 1202:251 (1054), asks that the miller mill the owner's grain "sine molitura et sine detinentia (fraudulent withholding?)" and not pay with bad grain. Salernitan owners threatened heavy fines on millers who failed to pay properly.

[95] In early medieval Italy multure appears to have been levied on the grain the miller measured prior to grinding, for millers paid mill-owners in grain, not in flour. Both measuring the total grain and the multure owed were opportunities for deceit.

[96] *CIL* VI.1, ed. G. Hensen and G. de Rossi (Berlin, 1876), 1711, p. 373. The urban prefect acted "ut omnium molendinariorum fraudes amputentur." This inscription captured the interest of a northern (Reichenau-based?) visitor to Rome around 800, whose copy of it in the Einsiedeln itinerary (*Codice topografico della città di Roma* I, p. 167) is the sole surviving one. *Codex Theodosianus*, ed. T. Mommsen and P. Krueger (Berlin, 1905), 14.4.9 (417), p. 782, and 14.15.1 (364), p. 790, indicates imperial distrust of grain measurers. 14.3.16 (380), p. 777, assumes "pistores iniquos," on whom "totius criminis confertur invidia," are guilty of thefts of public grain. Koehne, *Das Recht*, p. 21, discusses Germanic law codes' fear of millers' thievery.

their famous characteristics into the early modern period. Whether actually fraudulent or not, the measuring done by millers lay at the heart of their notoriety in medieval European culture.

A miller who altered water flow, bickered with other users, exacted grain in various ways, and lived in seclusion could reasonably become alien, a pariah. In addition, the array of deceits a miller could deploy was huge at all times. By 1100 these circumstances had given rise to an intricate and fascinating European literature on the thievish miller and on the mill as haven of immorality. In the course of the twelfth and thirteenth centuries, as the Italian *comuni* developed extensive and detailed regulations for millers, provisions were introduced which scholars such as Lanconelli interpret as a sign of the widespread suspicion or distrust of the entire category.[97]

After this discussion it may come as a disappointment that overall there is little evidence that millers were especially disliked in the early medieval Italian world. It is true that in some tenth-century contracts from the Po valley, from the Lucchesia, and from around Salerno millers might be observed taking on the sinister hue from which Chaucer was to paint his memorable portrait of the wicked miller: mill-owners considered professional millers likely to cheat them in rent payments and consequently inserted clauses in contracts specifying what quality of grain they expected and how full a measure had to be for it to be considered full.[98] It is also true that no early medieval Italian information survives on the perceptions of the users of mills, who were even more hostile toward millers in contemporary Islamic Iberian societies than the mill-owners were.[99] If there is no surprise in the reticent early medieval charters revealing few strong sentiments against millers, it *is* remarkable that later medieval literary sources from the Italian peninsula never developed a strain of disgust for millers as virulent as England's or Germany's. In fact, the laws of the *comuni* which are the strongest evidence for "anti-millerism" in Italy grew more from the ruling classes' fear of rioting, a consequence of inefficient milling than from a specific animosity toward "dishonest" millers. The

---

[97] Communal laws from Rieti (Lanconelli, "I mulini," pp. 47–8), Ravenna (*Statuti* 279, in *Monumenti* IV, p. 111), and Cuneo (Camilla, "I mulini," pp. 157–62) enforce rules on weights and measures and on "fair" multures. Such regulations, according to Lanconelli, "I mulini," p. 47, are indicative of *justified* popular distrust of millers.

[98] The Cologno agreement of 918, which deprived the miller of his freedom if he failed to pay satisfactorily, is extreme: *CDLangobardiae*, 476:824. *M&D* V.2, 760:456–7 (862), implies that the miller might like to use an illegitimate measure to pay rent.

[99] The disdain for millers among Andalusian users of the tenth and eleventh centuries, evident in the *fatwas* of judges and in several amusing accounts, is treated by Lagardère, "Moulins d'Occident," pp. 60, 84–6.

millers of the region of Reggio Emilia, on the contrary, were implanted as agents of the *comune* in the difficult but vital world of grain processing.[100] The communal statutes can be placed in a long peninsular tradition of state involvement in grain provisioning and milling which reaches back to Roman antiquity. Urban authorities considered the processing of grain to feed urban populations a public service even when it was performed by private commercial mills.[101]

We may seek motives for the relatively bland hostility to Italy's early medieval millers by considering the millers' social position. Free professionals, slaves, or dependent laborers, early medieval millers were often also cultivators whose lifestyle followed much the same rhythms as everyone else's.[102] Their use of the waters did not arouse the wrath of the irrigators with whom they shared the resource to the point of engendering legal battles, possibly because their use was attuned to agriculturalists' needs, as millers too cultivated the soil, and possibly because mills were old, accepted, entitled components of local hydrologies by late antiquity. The experience of the free cultivator Merco, in Gaeta, who took over a mill in 997 for very high rents and thus became a miller in effect, may be emblematic.[103] Merco was very much enmeshed in local society, not an alien whose interests ran against the grain of Gaetan life.

In addition, since water created situations of interdependence, millowners, those who labored in mills, and those whose land or houses fronted on the stream used by the mill had much to talk about. The mill's need for water put its operators in a dependent position vis-à-vis the people upstream and downstream who were well placed to sabotage the mill or destroy it malevolently, as Rothari said. Furthermore, early medieval millers may have taken low overt multures, since many people had alternatives to their mills and had to be attracted into the mill-house

---

[100] In the *Decameron* millers do not receive the same attention Chaucer lavished on them. For references to millers in medieval Italian literature, see S. Battaglia, *Grande dizionario della lingua italiana* XI (Turin, 1981), pp. 53–4, 59; see C. Dussaix, "Les moulins à Reggio d'Emilie au XIIe et XIIIe siècles," *MEFR* 91 (1979), p. 130, on Reggio.

[101] Roman imperial involvement in supplying Rome with cereals in their finished form of bread is evident in the *Codex Theodosianus* 14.3.16 (380), p. 777; 14.3.22 (417), p. 778. On thin evidence, Lohrmann, "Schiffsmühlen," p. 285, suggests that popes maintained the publicness of the Janiculum mills until the ninth century. Dussaix, "Les moulins," p. 127, correctly places communal mill policy within the context of food-supply policy. For *comuni* that feared rioting, see Chiappa Mauri, *I mulini*, pp. 106–7. Ravenna had communal mills: *Statuti* 282, p. 112. On milling as a public service, see P. Skinner, "Mill Ownership and Social Status in Southern Italy," paper presented at the International Conference on Medieval Studies (York, 1992), p. 4.

[102] Many charters describe the gardens and fields pertaining to the mill. A sample can be found in: *M&D* V.2, 634:377–8 (846); 760:456–7 (862); 767:461–2 (864); 804:488 (867); 855:523 (874); *CDL* I, 38:132 (726).   [103] Skinner, *Family Power*, p. 253.

by at least tolerable conditions.[104] Bread was still the food of choice, but in the end the hand quern or the animal-driven mill could also produce a meal adequate for its confection. Failing that, people who did not have wheat, and even those who did, could eat gruel.

The comparative underdevelopment of the early medieval millers as a cohesive class (it was not until the twelfth and thirteenth centuries that millers formed corporations, lagging behind the fishers) certainly affected how millers were viewed. Before AD 1000, milling in the Italian peninsula, even within the same region, was done by a wide array of people, some of whom were not specifically called "millers" by their contemporaries. Without a strongly defined professional identity millers could hardly become pariahs associated with the enforcement of the *potentes'* surplus extraction, rich and alien from the rest of society.[105] The Chaucerian stereotype of the miller-scoundrel could not take root in a time when the social profile of the miller was so blurred. Instead, the various types of millers seem to have lived peacefully within the Italian communities they served.

Rather, then, than postulating the miller to have been a rapacious enemy of cohesive, homogeneous agrarian communities, a marginal figure, we should see the early medieval miller in the thick of a social world formed by his machine, its use of the waters, and his skills. The people who ate grain within the "sphere of influence" of the mill entered into a social network centered on the mill itself. Laconic early medieval documents do not reproduce the scenes of banter, gossip, and innocent or less innocent amusements which took place in twelfth-century mills and were censoriously remarked upon by St. Bernard, who advised a fellow abbot to close down his mill, where men and women mixed too freely. Yet the early medieval mill-house, where people brought the fruit of their toil for workless grinding, was surely a place of interaction too. To a large extent the social nature of this machine derived from its special relationship to the watery environment. Unlike other tools, which could be

[104] Multure levels, probably varying according to season, mill location, and user's status, were not specified in early medieval documents (they seem to have fallen under the elastic rubric "customary," as in some Salernitan contracts: *CDC* II, 391:244 [987], "ad mensuriam illam quale consuetudo est dare ipsi alii molinaturii qui tenunt ipsa alii molina," or 458:343 [993]). In Sicily about 1150 they were 7 percent (Tramontana, "Mulini," p. 812); at Ravenna in the thirteenth century they could not exceed 10 percent (*Statuti di Ravenna*, in *Monumenti* IV, 279, p. 111). Holt, *Mills*, pp. 36–52, argues for the need to draw "customers" into the mill.

[105] Fourquin, "Le premier moyen âge," p. 362, in his analysis of Adalhard of Corbie's famous provisions for the management of the monastery, determined that millers in Carolingian society were privileged people, even if serfs; see also Toubert, "La part," p. 69. This does not appear to have been the case in rural Italy, though Salerno's millers were not miserable.

managed by solitary individuals without affecting others, the water mill necessarily brought together groups of people. It was the supremely social tool.[106] Its early medieval operators enjoyed a corresponding social visibility. They were positioned at the interstice of nature and culture, where water, a natural resource, was manipulated and used to become power, economic gain, and labor-saver.

[106] Comet, *Le paysan*, p. 32, notes the special nature of mills among rural tools.

6   Conclusion: the hydrological cycle in the early Middle Ages

In a difficult passage of a difficult work by an eighth-century author who may have been a southern Italian (Ionian?) cleric with excellent Carolingian connections, and who is conventionally called Aethicus Ister, the water cycle is minutely described.[1] Using obscure, erudite language this cosmographer claimed that the winds performed an important service by lifting "a very dense haze" from the seas and transporting this vapor to the tops of mountains, giving birth to rivers when it reached the cold crags. From a modern scientific point of view, Aethicus was very close to an accurate portrayal of how the water cycle works. He offered an "atmospheric" explanation to the puzzle of why water wends endlessly downward to the sea, without ever seeming to rest or run out, and why the sea, despite this constant inflow, never (or only in extraordinary moments) brims over and spills onto the land.

But Aethicus was not content with so simplistic a model. It did not account for the existence of springs, where water burst through the surface of the earth from below. Aethicus therefore confidently described a process whereby much water flowed underground through fissures and channels which led it from the sea back to the highlands where it could surface in springs, to begin its headlong dash down to the beaches again, this time in the open air. He knew that the "bitterness" of sea water was lost during its hidden, cavernous journey by a leaching process. In a rather original image, Aethicus compared the ground to a sponge capable of absorbing sea water in its crevices and soaking up its impurities.[2] This part of Aethicus' hydrology would not win many adherents among modern scientists, who would begin by objecting that water does not, in general, flow uphill, but it had a distinguished intellectual genealogy by the middle of the eighth century, when Aethicus wrote.

[1] *Die Kosmographie des Aethicus*, ed. O. Prinz (Munich, 1993), 7, pp. 242–3. Prinz explains the Gelehrterstreit over this text in lucid and convincing terms (pp. 1–18), but H. Lowe's old opinion that Aethicus was the Irish Virgil of Salzburg still has many proponents (see *The New Cambridge Medieval History* II, ed. R. McKitterick [Cambridge, 1995], p. 686).
[2] *Die Kosmographie* 7, pp. 242–3, repeats the sponge image three times. Such use of so eminently "marine" an image might suggest something about the author's culture.

For Aethicus was hardly the first to wonder about the hydrological cycle, nor the first to contemplate two simultaneous cycles (one "atmospheric," one "subterranean") as the likeliest logic of water. Aethicus' near contemporary, the learned Bede, recorded both variants of the cycle, though he was more skeptical than others, and thought it worth prefacing the hidden underground hollows idea with a "they say." For Bede, the fact that sea water remained salty despite its constant massive dilution with fresh water posed a problem. In his mind, the best solution to this paradox was evaporation, which removed water from the sea and left salt behind. Though a dualist in his hydrology, Bede was a dualist with "atmospheric" leanings.[3]

A century before him, Isidore of Seville, the best-read of the early medieval hydrologists, had also postulated a double circuit, though one in which the underground caverns had the most prominent part.[4] The anonymous cosmographer of Ravenna, who wrote very shortly after Isidore, instead took a decidedly "subterranean" view of things.[5] To him, there was no question that the nooks and passageways under the earth's crust were the route water took as it circled back from the seas to the land. In this he accepted the orthodox Christian, and Biblical, position. For Christian writers since the fourth century had generally found most persuasive and authoritative explanations of the water cycle in certain passages in the book of Ecclesiastes (especially 1.7, "all rivers run into the sea, yet the sea is not full: unto the place from which the rivers come, thither they return again") and the Psalms which suggested, albeit a bit cryptically, that water flowed under the earth as well as over it. In the sixth century, Cosmas Indicopleustes had polemically adopted this as a specifically Christian piece of geographical knowledge, opposed to the fantasies of the unbelievers (and of some naive believers too). Actually, Plato had first elaborated this theory in detail in his *Phaedo*, earning some mordant criticisms from Aristotle for it.[6] But no early medieval student of

---

[3] *De Natura Rerum*, ed. C. Jones (Turnhout, 1975), 32–3, 38–41, pp. 221, 224–7.

[4] Isidore of Seville, *Etymologiarum sive Originum Libri XX*, ed. M. Lindsay (Oxford, 1911), 13.12 (water in the air), and 13.20 (occult passageways); and Isidore, *Liber de Rerum Natura*, ed. J. Fontaine (Bordeaux, 1960), 32–3, 41–2, pp. 287–9, 311. The latter text's hydrological sections were avidly studied in ninth-century Verona's episcopal scriptorium (pp. 82–3).

[5] *Ravennatis Anonymi Cosmographia*, ed. M. Pinder and G. Parthey (Aalen, 1962), 1.6, p. 16.

[6] The original Y. Tuan, *The Hydrological Cycle and the Wisdom of God* (Toronto, 1968), presents a wide-ranging guide to this topic. On medieval views, see also G. Sodigné-Costes and B. Ribémont, "'Aqua domestica,'" in D. Hue (ed.), *Sciences, techniques, et encyclopédies* (Caen, 1993), pp. 301–20.

Cosmas, *The Christian Topography*, trans. J. McCrindle (London, 1897), 1–3, pp. 8–20, 86, 114, compares Biblical and geographers' hydrologies. His authorities were Amos 9.6, Zechariah 10.1, and I Kings 18.41, and he made much of Noah's flood. But he also

the water cycle cited Plato as the authority for the view that the cycle functioned through subterranean recesses which replenished the "super-terranean," visible part of the ever-flowing process.

Regardless of which solution to the puzzles of the endless circulation of water they endorsed, and regardless of whether they were persuaded by astute observation of physical phenomena, or by classical texts, or Biblical authority, or by all three, to the scholars of the early Middle Ages the lessons implicit in the hydrological cycle(s) were clear. Nature was a text whose accurate interpretation uncovered religious truths.[7] Therefore, the way water flowed should tell people who understood such things something about God. In fact the hydrological cycle was so neat, so balanced, and so perfectly interconnected in its various components that it revealed the excellence of its creator. Authors as different as St. Peter Chrysologus and Hrabanus Maurus marveled at how God had ordered the circulation of waters (though the former was a "subterraneist" and the latter's *De Universo* was more preoccupied with rainfall). They admired the surprising utility of the seas to all humans, which at first sight seem a wasteland and a mistake on the part of their maker, and the unexpectedly vital role played by seemingly trivial things, like the sand on shores which held back the sea and protected human settlement. Everyone concluded that God's power and wisdom were boundless, and God's generosity also great (had God not made nature, including the water cycle, for people to enjoy?).[8]

In these conceptions there is a remarkable confidence that water everywhere, and in whatever form (in vaporous clouds, in underground caves, in briny ocean waves), is closely related to water elsewhere in other forms. Whether convinced that the hydrological cycle worked subterraneously or by means of evaporation, all postclassical commentators saw an admirable unity in water, whose endless revolutions meant that even the tiniest dribble eventually, by simple or complex routes, ended up in one great pool.[9]

This insight has informed the present study, which has woven together

observed clothes hung out to dry to make the point that evaporation could have nothing to do with the hydrological cycle.

   Phaedo, trans. R. Hackforth (Cambridge, 1955), 19–20, pp. 169–79, and Aristotle, *Metereologica*, trans. H. Lee (London, 1952), 349–51, 354–6, pp. 91–101, 133–43, took divergent positions. Pliny, Vitruvius, Seneca, and Macrobius conveyed Greek views into the Latin tradition.
[7] This was an established tradition before Christianity won hegemony: C. Glacken, *Traces on the Rhodian Shore* (Berkeley, 1967), part I, is the classic exposition.
[8] Even floods and erosion were part of the inscrutable plan: Tuan, *Hydrological Cycle*, p. 16. On sand, see Peter Chrysologus, *Collectio Sermonum*, ed. A. Olivar (Turnhout, 1975–82), 101.6–7, pp. 623–4. Tuan, *Hydrological Cycle*, pp. 8–16, and Sodigné-Costes and Ribémont, "'Aqua domestica,'" pp. 305–6, discuss moral interpretations of the water cycle.   [9] See Tuan, *Hydrological Cycle*, p. 4.

very different types of water and cultural responses to its presence or absence into a coherent tapestry. For in the end all the different waters of early medieval Italy were connected to each other. The rains on an Apennine ridge could, unnoticed, become the water which drove a mill's wheel, then give life to a monastic fishery, then stagnate and require removal from a peasant's wheat field, then end up in a channel feeding a bath complex, only to filter through layers of rock to enter a well and be hauled up, and drunk down, by a thirsty person (nor did the journey end there).

In other words, it is the nature of water to connect different places and activities, especially within a single watershed (though evaporation allows water to skip watersheds). In early medieval Italy there are many traces of people's awareness of how water usages affected each other, or of how the water cycle determined something of water's character. Millers, we have seen, worried about having access to enough water "to grind perfectly," and adjusted their manipulation of this resource so as to limit their impact on others along the waterway. Similarly, irresponsible fishers who placed their equipment without considering the nature of water courses and water's peculiar ability to bind different users together in interdependent communities risked penalties of diverse types. Even irrigators tapped into the water cycle temporarily and by turn in order to maintain equity among themselves and to limit the depletion of the main channel's water.

The linkages created by water's circulation have to do with the first main conclusion reached in these pages. Probably the most significant trend in the history of water uses in the early medieval peninsula was the patrimonialization of aqueous resources that became increasingly prominent after 700. This, too, was a reaction to the water cycle. The relentless advance of private and exclusive rights of access to and use of water was part of the effort to limit the effects of the water cycle, which naturally tended to move water from one place to another, to cause fluctuations in its availability, and to distribute access all along a watershed. Thus, both the sensitivity of millers, fishers, and peasants to other people's entitlements and access to aqueous resources and the attempt by magnates to guarantee unrestricted, unquestioned entitlement and access for themselves were results of an understanding of water cycles, and of water's unique characteristics.

The water cycle determined eminently social responses from early medieval people to the issues of use and allocation of watery resources. But water (and this has been the second theme elaborated in this study) is part of nature as well as of society. Indeed, one of the rewards of the study of the history of water is that this element facilitates environmental historical analysis. In considering early medieval Italian fishing practices the human cultural component (the demand for fish, the techniques for its capture, etc.) emerged as only one part of the story. It was accompanied by a parallel and convergent story of aquatic plant and animal life whose deeds and predispositions interacted with the fishers'. Similarly, milling with water had more than a purely technological history; it had an ecological one too, and changes in climate and hydrology launched an ongoing dialectic between agricultural practices and watery resources that made the early medieval landscape different from the Roman one.

The importance of environmental dimensions in the study of post-classical interactions with watery resources is the second main conclusion to which this study has led. A third theme, one with a much plumper historiographical tradition, is the endurance of Roman cultural patterns after the "fall" of Rome. Without pretending to end the debate between Dopschian "continuity theorists" and Pirennian "caesura theorists," this "aqueous history" has suggested that in the management of vital natural resources much was transformed, especially after the Roman state ceased to be able to enforce its will. But Roman societies also bequeathed a vast cultural patrimony to the early medieval ones which continued to inhabit many of the same places. This is very evident in the development of systems for domestic water supply after the fifth century, or in the evolution of bathing in the same period. Perhaps because water is irrepressibly cyclical and endlessly able to change the form it has taken, its history is varied and complex. In early medieval Italy the history of water, its allocation, and its control was a history of both deep changes and inexorable continuities.

Bibliography

PRIMARY SOURCES

Agnellus of Ravenna, *Liber Pontificalis Ecclesiae Ravennatis*, ed. O. Holder-Egger, *MGHSRL*, Hanover, 1878, pp. 278–391.

Ambrosius Auctpert, *Vita Paldonis, Tatonis, et Tasonis*, ed. G. Waitz, *MGHSRL*, Hanover, 1878, pp. 547–55.

Annales Beneventani, ed. O. Bertolini, in *Bullettino dell'Istituto storico italiano* 42 (1923), pp. 101–63.

Anonymus Valesianus, *Chronica*, ed. R. Cessi, Città di Castello, 1913.

Apuleius, *Metamorphoses*, ed. D. Robertson, Paris, 1945.

"Gli archivi come fonti della storia di Ravenna: regesto dei documenti," ed. B. Cavarra, G. Gardini, G.-B. Parente, and G. Vespignani, in Carile, *Storia di Ravenna* II.1, pp. 401–547.

Breviarium Ecclesiae Ravennatis (Codice Bavaro): secoli VIII–X, ed. G. Rabotti, *FSI* 110, Rome, 1985.

Capitula Domini Aregis Principis, ed. H. Pertz, *MGHLegum* IV, Hanover, 1869, pp. 207–12.

La "Carta Piscatoria" di Ravenna, ed. G. Monti, in Monti, *Le corporazioni nell'evo antico*, Bari, 1934.

Cassiodorus, *Insitutiones*, ed. R. Mynors, Oxford, 1961.

   Variarum Libri Duodecim, ed. T. Mommsen, *MGHAA* XII, Berlin, 1894.

"Catalogo delle iscrizioni e sculture paleocristiane e pre-romaniche di Pavia," ed. G. Panazza, in *Arte del primo millennio*, ed. E. Arslan, Turin, n.d., pp. 226–96.

Cato, *De Agri Cultura*, ed. A. Mazzarino, Leipzig, 1962.

Chronica Monasterii Casinensis, ed. H. Hoffmann, *MGHScriptores* XXXIV, Hanover, 1980.

The Chronicle of Ahimaaz, tr. M. Salzman, New York, 1924.

Il Chronicon Farfense di Gregorio di Catino, ed. U. Balzani, *FSI* 33, Rome, 1903.

Chronicon Monasterii Sanctae Sophiae, ed. F. Ughelli and T. Coletti, in *Italia sacra* X, Venice, 1721, pp. 415–560.

Chronicon Salernitanum, ed. U. Westerbergh, Stockholm, 1956.

Chronicon Vulturnense, ed. V. Federici, *FSI* 58, Rome, 1925.

Codex Diplomaticus Cajetanus I, ed. Monachorum Montis Casini, Montecassino, 1887.

Codex Diplomaticus Cavensis I–VII, ed. M. Morcaldi, S. Schiani, and S. de Stefano, Naples, 1873–87.

Codex Diplomaticus Langobardiae, ed. G. Porro Lambertenghi, Turin, 1878.
Codex Theodosianus, ed. T. Mommsen and P. Krueger, Berlin, 1905.
Codice diplomatico del monastero di S. Colombano di Bobbio, ed. C. Cipolla, *FSI* 52, Rome, 1918.
Codice diplomatico longobardo I–II, ed. L. Schiaparelli, *FSI* 62–3, Rome, 1929–33.
Codice diplomatico longobardo III.1–IV, ed. C.-R. Brühl, *FSI* 64–5, Rome, 1973–81.
Codice diplomatico longobardo V, ed. H. Zielinski, *FSI* 66, Rome, 1986.
Codice diplomatico longobardo, ed. C. Troya, Naples, 1852.
Codice topografico della città di Roma I, ed. R. Valentini and G. Zucchetti, *FSI* 88, Rome, 1940.
Columella, *Res Rustica*, ed. H. Boyd Ash and E. Foster, London, 1941–55.
Corpus Iuris Civilis: Codex Iustinianus, ed. P. Krueger, Berlin, 1892.
Corpus Iuris Civilis: Digesta Iustiniani Augusti, ed. T. Mommsen, Berlin, 1868–70.
De Observantia Ciborum, ed. I. Mazzini, Rome, 1984.
Diokletians Preisedikt, ed. S. Lauffer, Berlin, 1971.
I diplomi di Berengario I, ed. L. Schiaparelli, *FSI* 35, Rome, 1903.
I diplomi di Guido e di Lamberto, ed. L. Schiaparelli, *FSI* 36, Rome, 1906.
I diplomi di Ugo e Lotario, di Berengario II, e di Adalberto, ed. L. Schiaparelli, *FSI* 38, Rome, 1924.
I diplomi italiani di Lodovico III e di Rodolfo II, ed. L. Schiaparelli, *FSI* 37, Rome, 1910.
Edictus Rothari, ed. F. Bluhme, *MGHLegum* IV, Hanover, 1869, pp. 3–90.
Einhard, *Vita Karoli Magni*, ed. G. Pertz, *MGHScriptores Rerum Germanicarum i.u.s.*, Hanover, 1878.
Ennodius, *Opera*, ed. F. Vogel, *MGHAA* VII, Berlin, 1885.
Erchempert, *Historia Langobardorum Beneventanorum*, ed. G. Waitz, *MGHSRL*, Hanover, 1878, pp. 231–64.
Frontinus, *The Stratagems and Aqueducts of Ancient Rome*, ed. C. Bennet, London, 1925.
Gesta Aldrici Episcopi Cenomannensis, ed. G. Waitz, *MGHScriptores* XV.1, Hanover, 1887, pp. 308–27.
Gesta Episcoporum Neapolitanorum, ed. G. Waitz, *MGHSRL*, Hanover, 1878, pp. 402–36.
Gregory of Tours, *Liber Vitae Patrum*, ed. B. Krusch, *MGHScriptores Rerum Merovingicarum* I.2, Berlin, 1885, pp. 211–94.
Gregory the Great, *Dialogi*, ed. A. de Vogüé and P. Antin, Paris, 1978–80.
   Registrum Epistularum, ed. D. Norberg, *CCSL* 140, Turnhout, 1982.
Hippocrates, *Airs, Waters, Places*, tr. G. Lloyd, in *Hippocratic Writings*, Harmondsworth, 1978, pp. 148–69.
Die Honorantie Civitatis Papie, ed. C.-R. Brühl and C. Violante, Cologne, 1983.
Inventari altomedievali di terre, coloni, e redditi, ed. A. Castagnetti, M. Luzzati, G. Pasquali, and A. Vasina, *FSI* 104, Rome, 1979.
Le iscrizioni dei secoli VI–VII–VIII esistenti in Italia, ed. P. Rugo, Cittadella, 1975–6.
Isidore of Seville, *Etymologiarum sive Originum Libri XX*, ed. M. Lindsay, Oxford, 1911.

Liber de Rerum Natura, ed. J. Fontaine, Bordeaux, 1960.

St. Jerome, *Select Epistles*, ed. F. Wright, London, 1930.

Jordanes, *De Origine Actibusque Getarum*, ed. T. Mommsen, *MGHAA* V, Berlin, 1882.

Die Kosmographie des Aethicus, ed. O. Prinz, *MGHQuellen des Geistesgeschichte des Mittelalters* 14, Munich, 1993.

Leges Aistulfi, ed. F. Bluhme, *MGHLegum* IV, Hanover, 1869, pp. 194–204.

Leges Alamannorum I, Recensio Clothariana, ed. K. Eckhardt, Göttingen, 1958.

Leges Alamannorum II, Recensio Lantfridiana, ed. K. Eckhardt, Witzenhausen, 1962.

Leges Liutprandi, ed. F. Bluhme, *MGHLegum* IV, Hanover, 1869, pp. 96–175.

Libellus Miraculorum Sancti Agnelli (sec. X), ed. A. Vuolo, in Vuolo, *Una testimonianza agiografica napoletana*, Naples, 1987.

Le Liber Pontificalis: texte, introduction, et commentaire, vols. I and II, ed. L. Duchesne, Paris, 1886–92.

Liutprand of Cremona, *Antapodosis*, ed. J. Becker, *MGHScriptores Rerum Germanicarum i.u.s.*, Hanover, 1915, pp. 1–158.

Relatio de Legatione Constantinopolitana, ed. J. Becker, *MGHScriptores Rerum Germanicarum i.u.s.*, Hanover, 1915, pp. 175–212.

Macrobius, *Saturnalia*, ed. F. Eyssenhardt, Leipzig, 1893.

Memoratorium de Mercedibus Commacinorum, ed. F. Bluhme, *MGHSRL*, Hanover, 1878, pp. 176–80.

Memorie e documenti per servire all'istoria del ducato di Lucca IV.1–2, ed. D. Bertini, Lucca, 1818–36.

Memorie e documenti per servire all'istoria del ducato di Lucca V.2–3, ed. D. Barsocchini, Lucca, 1837–41.

MGHLegum Sectio II, vol. I, ed. A. Boretius, Hanover, 1880; vol. II.1, ed. A. Boretius and V. Krause, Hanover, 1890.

Monumenti ravennati de' secoli di mezzo I–VI, ed. M. Fantuzzi, Venice, 1801–4.

Il museo diplomatico dell'archivio di stato di Milano I, ed. A. Natale, Milan, n.d.

Die nichtliterarischen Lateinischen Papyri Italiens aus der Zeit 445–700, vols. I and II, ed. J.-O. Tjäder, Lund, 1955; Stockholm, 1982.

Palladius, *Opus Agriculturae*, ed. R. Rodgers, Leipzig, 1975.

Paul the Deacon, *Die Gedichte des Paulus Diaconus*, ed. K. Neff, Munich, 1908.

Historia Langobardorum, ed. G. Waitz, *MGHSRL*, Hanover, 1878, pp. 12–187.

Paulinus of Nola, *Carmina*, ed. G. de Hartel, *CCSL* 30, Vienna, 1894.

Epistulae, ed. W. Von Hartel, *CCSL* 29, Vienna, 1894.

Peter Chrysologus, *Collectio Sermonum*, ed. A. Olivar, *CCSL* 24, Turnhout, 1975–82.

I placiti del "Regnum Italiae" 1, 3.2, ed. C. Manaresi, *FSI* 92, Rome, 1955–60.

"Placiti del 'Regnum Italiae' (secoli IX–XI): primi contributi per un nuovo censimento," ed. R. Volpini, in P. Zerbi (ed.), *Contributi dell'istituto di storia medievale* III, Milan, 1975, pp. 245–520.

Pliny, *Naturalis Historia*, ed. L. Ian and C. Mayhoff, Stuttgart, 1967.

Procopius of Caesarea, *La Guerra Gotica di Procopio di Cesarea*, ed. D. Comparetti, *FSI* 23–5, Rome, 1895–8.

Radelgisi et Siginulfi Divisio Ducatus Beneventani, ed. F. Bluhme, *MGHLegum* IV, Hanover, 1869, pp. 221–5.

Ravennatis Anonymi Cosmographia, ed. M. Pinder and G. Parthey, Aalen, 1962.

Regesto del capitolo di Lucca 1–3, ed. P. Guidi and O. Parenti, *Regesta Chartarum Italiae* 6, 9, 18, Rome, 1910–33.

Il regesto di Farfa II, ed. I. Giorgi and U. Balzani, Rome, 1879.

Regula Benedicti, ed. A. de Vogüé, Paris, 1972.

Regula Columbani, ed. G. Walker, in *S. Columbani Opera*, Dublin, 1957, pp. 122–43.

Regula Eugippii, ed. A. de Vogüé and F. Villegas, Vienna, 1976.

Regula Magistri, ed. A. de Vogüé, Paris, 1964.

Regula S. Patris, ed. A. de Vogüé, Paris, 1982.

Regula S. Pauli et Stephani, ed. J. Migne, *PL* 66, Paris, 1866, pp. 949–58.

Rutilius Namatianus, *De Reditu Suo*, ed. E. Doblhofer, Heidelberg, 1972.

Seneca, *Lettres à Lucilius* II–III, ed. F. Préchac, Paris, 1947–57.

Naturales Quaestiones, ed. P. Oltramare, Paris, 1929.

Sicardi Principis Pactio cum Neapolitanis, ed. F. Bluhme, *MGHLegum* IV, Hanover, 1869, pp. 216–21.

Sidonius Apollinaris, *Carmina: Epistulae*, ed. W. Anderson, London, 1936–65.

Smaragdi Abbatis Expositio in Regulam S. Benedicti, ed. A. Spannagel and P. Engelbert, Siegburg, 1974.

"Statuti delle strade delle acque del contado di Milano fatti nel 1346," ed. G. Porro Lambertenghi, *Miscellanea di storia italiana* VII, Turin, 1869, pp. 311–437.

Statuti urbanistici medievali di Lucca, ed. D. Corsi, Venice, 1960.

Translatio Iuvenalis et Cassii Episcoporum Narniensium Lucam, ed. A Hofmeister, *MGHScriptores* XXX.2 (Leipzig, 1934), pp. 977–83.

Die Urkunden der Karolinger I, *Die Urkunden Pippins, Karlmanns, und Karls des Grossen*, ed. F. Mühlbacher, *MGHDiplomata Karolinorum* I, Berlin, 1956.

Die Urkunden der Karolinger III, *Die Urkunden Lothars I*, ed. T. Schieffer, *MGHDiplomata Karolinorum* III, Berlin, 1966.

Die Urkunden der Karolinger IV, *Die Urkunden Ludwigs II*, ed. K. Wanner, *MGHDiplomata Karolinorum* IV, Munich, 1994.

Die Urkunden Konrad I., Heinrich I., Otto I., ed. T. Sickel, *MGHDiplomatum Regum et Imperatorum Germaniae* I, Hanover, 1879–84.

Varro, *Rerum Rusticarum Libri*, ed. W. Davis Hooper, London, 1934.

Versus de Verona: Versum de Mediolanum Civitate, ed. G. Pighi, Bologna, 1960.

Vibius Sequester, *De Fluminibus, Fontibus, Lacubus, Nemoribus, Paludibus, Montibus, Gentibus per Litteras*, ed. C. Bursian, Tours, 1867.

Vitruvius, *De Architectura*, ed. L. Callebat, Paris, 1973.

Vita Corbiniani Episcopi Baiuvariorum, ed B. Krusch, *MGHSciptores Rerum Germanicarum i.u.s.*, Hanover, 1920, pp. 100–234.

Vita et Regula SS. P. Benedicti, Una cum Expositione Regulae ab Hildemaro Tradita, ed. R. Mittermüller (Regensburg, 1880).

Vita Rigoberti, AS January 1 (Brussels, 1863), pp. 174–80.

Vita S. Apiani, AS March 1 (Antwerp, 1668), pp. 320–6.

Vita S. Cethegi, AS June 2 (Antwerp, 1698), pp. 688–93.

La Vita S. Marini, ed. P. Aebischer, San Marino, 1974.

Vita S. Venerii, AS September 4 (Antwerp, 1763), pp. 108–20.
Vita S. Walfredi, ed. H. Mierau, in K. Schmid (ed.), *Vita Walfredi und Kloster Monteverdi*, Tübingen, 1991, pp. 38–63.
"Vita Sancti Fridiani," ed. G. Zaccagnini, in Zaccagnini, *Vita Sancti Fridiani: contributi di storia e di agiografia lucchese altomedioevale*, Lucca, 1989, pp. 151–208.

SECONDARY SOURCES

Acocella, N., "Le origini della Salerno medioevale negli scritti di Paolo Diacono," in Acocella, *Salerno medioevale e altri saggi*, Naples, 1971, pp. 49–54.
Addison, H., *Land, Water, and Food*, London, 1961.
Aebischer, P., "Les dénominations du 'moulin' dans les chartes italiennes du moyen âge," *Bulletin du change* 7 (1932), pp. 49–109.
Alessi, D., "L'uso delle terme e i frequentatori," in P. Pasquinucci (ed.), *Terme romane e vita quotidiana*, Modena, 1987, pp. 22–4.
Alexandre, P., "Histoire du climat et sources narratives du moyen âge," *Le moyen âge* 80 (1974), pp. 101–16.
Alexandre-Bidon, D., "Archéo-iconographie du puits au moyen âge (XII–XIV siècle)," *MEFR. Moyen âge* 104 (1992), pp. 519–43.
Alfieri, N., "Problemi di territorio fra Ravenna e il Po di Volano," *CCARB* 25 (1978), pp. 15–26.
Alliaud, G., "Molitura e ambiente in una regione povera di corsi d'acqua: Caluso e dintorni all'inizio del XIV secolo," in Comba, *Mulini da grano nel Piemonte medievale*, pp. 47–66.
Alpers, K., "Wasser bei Griechen und Römern: Aspekte des Wassers im Leben und Denken des griechisch–römischen Altertums," in H. Böhme (ed.), *Kulturgeschichte des Wassers*, Frankfurt, 1988, pp. 65–95.
Amarotta, A., "Gli acquedotti medievali di Salerno," *La scuola di domani* 5–6 (1979), pp. 39–40, 47–8.
  "L'ampliamento longobardo in *plaium montis* a Salerno," *Atti dell'Accademia Pontaniana* 28 (1979), pp. 297–323.
  "Dinamica urbanistica nell'età longobarda," in Leone and Vitolo, *Guida alla storia di Salerno* I, pp. 69–86.
  "L'ortomagno nelle fortificazioni longobarde di Salerno," *Atti dell'Accademia Pontaniana* 30 (1982), pp. 175–206.
  Salerno romana e medievale: dinamica di un insediamento, Salerno, 1989.
Amouretti, M.-C., "La diffusion du moulin à eau dans l'antiquité: un problème mal posé," in De Reparaz, *L'eau et les hommes en Méditerranée*, pp. 13–23.
André, J., *L'alimentation et la cuisine à Rome*, Paris, 1961.
  "La notion de *pestilentia* à Rome: du tabou religieux à l'interprétation préscientifique," *Latomus* 39 (1980), pp. 3–16.
Andreolli, B., "Contratti agrari e patti colonici nella Lucchesia dei secoli VIII e IX," *Studi medievali* 19 (1978), pp. 69–158.
  "La corvée precarolingia," in *Le prestazioni d'opera nelle campagne italiane del medioevo*, Bologna, 1987, pp. 15–33.
  "L'evoluzione dei patti colonici nella Toscana dei secoli VIII–X," *Quaderni medievali* 16 (1983), pp. 29–52.

"Formule di pertinenza e paesaggio: il castagneto nella Lucchesia alto-medievale," *Rivista di archeologia, storia, economia, e costume* 5 (1977), pp. 7–18.

"Il potere signorile tra VIII e X secolo," in Carile, *Storia di Ravenna* II, pp. 311–20.

"I prodotti alimentari nei contratti agrari toscani dell'alto medioevo," *AM* 8 (1981), pp. 117–26.

"Il ruolo dell'orticoltura e della frutticoltura nelle campagne dell'alto medioevo," *Settimane* 37 (1990), pp. 175–211.

Uomini nel medioevo: studi sulla società lucchese dei secoli VIII e IX, Bologna, 1983.

Andreolli, B., and Montanari, M., *L'azienda curtense in Italia: proprietà della terra e lavoro contadino nei secoli VIII–XI*, Bologna, 1983.

Andrews, D., "Underground Grain Storage in Central Italy," in Andrews, J. Osbourne, and D. Whitehouse (eds.), *Medieval Lazio*, Oxford, 1982, pp. 123–31.

Argoud, G., "Eau et agriculture en Grèce," in Louis, *L'homme et l'eau en Méditerranée* IV, pp. 25–43.

"Le problème de l'eau dans la Grèce antique," in De Reparaz, *L'eau et les hommes en Méditerranée*, pp. 205–19.

Ariès, P., and Duby, G. (eds.), *Histoire de la vie privée* I–II, Paris, 1985.

Arthur, P., "Naples: Notes on the Economy of a Dark Age City," in *Papers in Italian Archeology* IV, Oxford, 1985, pp. 247–59.

"Some Observations on the Economy of Bruttium Under the Later Roman Empire," *Journal of Roman Archaeology* 2 (1989), pp. 133–42.

Ashby, T., *The Aqueducts of Ancient Rome*, Oxford, 1935.

Aston, M. (ed.), *Medieval Fish, Fisheries, and Fishponds in England*, Oxford, 1988.

Aupert, P., "Les thermes comme lieux de culte," in *Actes de le table ronde organisée par l'Ecole française de Rome, nov. 1988*, Rome, 1991, pp. 185–92.

Avagliano, A., "Impianto urbano e testimonianze archeologiche," in Leone and Vitolo, *Guida alla storia di Salerno* I, pp. 33–51.

Bacchi, T., "Il bosco e l'acqua: uso dell'incolto e colonizzazione agraria del territorio ferrarese (secoli XI–XIII)," in B. Andreolli and M. Montanari (eds.), *Il bosco nel medioevo*, Bologna, 1988, pp. 187–93.

Baird Smith, R., *Italian Irrigation*, Edinburgh, 1855.

Balestracci, D., "La politica delle acque nell'Italia comunale," *MEFR. Moyen âge* 104 (1992), pp. 431–79.

Balty, J., "Problèmes de l'eau à Apamée en Syrie," in Louis, *L'homme et l'eau en Méditerranée* IV, pp. 9–23.

Barni, G., "I molini nel Milanese fino al *Liber Consuetudinum Mediolani anni MCCXVI*," *Archivio storico lombardo* 90 (1963), pp. 63–74.

Becher, H., "Das königliche Frauenkloster San Salvatore/Santa Giulia in Brescia im Spiegel seiner Memorialüberlieferung," *Frühmittelalterliche Studien* 17 (1983), pp. 299–392.

Beggio, G., "Navigazione, trasporto, mulini sul fiume: i tratti di una tipologia," in Borelli, *Una città e il suo fiume*, pp. 485–507.

Belli Barsali, I., "Problemi della topografia di Lucca nei secoli VIII–XI," *Actum Luce* 7 (1978), pp. 63–84.

"La topografia di Lucca nei secoli VIII–XI," in *Atti del 5o Congresso internazionale di studi sull'alto medioevo*, Spoleto, 1973, pp. 461–554.

Bellini, L., *Le saline dell'antico delta padano*, Ferrara, 1962.

Belting, H., "Studien zum Beneventanischen Hof im 8. Jahrhundert," *Dumbarton Oaks Papers* 16 (1962), pp. 141–93.

Benoit, P., and Wabont, M., "Mittelalterliche Wasserversorgung in Frankreich. Eine Fallstudie: Die Zisterzienser," in *Geschichte der Wasserversorgung* IV, Mainz, 1991, pp. 187–226.

Berger, A., *Das Bad in der byzantinischen Zeit*, Munich, 1982.

Bermond Montanari, G., "L'impianto urbano e i monumenti," in Susini, *Storia di Ravenna* I, pp. 223–55.

"Lineamenti di storia economica di Ravenna romana," *CCARB* 24 (1977), pp. 87–104.

"Ravenna – 1980: lo scavo della Banca Popolare," *Felix Ravenna* 127 (1985), pp. 21–36.

Ravenna e il porto di Classe, Bologna, 1983.

"Ravenna: Via Morigia," in Bermond Montanari, *Ravenna e il porto di Classe*, pp. 52–4.

"Topografia di Ravenna e di Classe," in Bermond Montanari, *Ravenna e il porto di Classe*, pp. 18–22.

"La zona archeologica di Palazzolo," *CCARB* 30 (1983), pp. 17–26.

Berretti, R., and Iacopi, E., "I molini ad acqua di Valleriana," in *Tecnica e società nell'Italia dei secoli XII–XVI*, Pistoia, 1987, pp. 23–35.

Bertolini, O., "Arechis II," *Dizionario biografico degli Italiani* IV, Rome, 1964, pp. 71–8.

"I documenti trascritti nel *Liber Praeceptorum Beneventani Monasteri S. Sophiae*," in *Studi in onore di M. Schipa*, Naples, 1926, pp. 11–47.

"Longobardi e Bizantini nell'Italia meridionale," in *Atti del 3o Congresso internazionale di studi sull'alto medioevo*, Spoleto, 1959, pp. 103–24.

"Per la storia delle *diaconiae* romane nell'alto medioevo sino alla fine del secolo VIII," *Archivio della Società romana di storia patria* 70 (1947), pp. 1–145.

Besta, E., "Fonti: legislazione e scienza giuridica dalla caduta dell'impero romano al secolo decimoquinto," in P. Del Giudice (ed.), *Storia del diritto italiano* I, Milan, 1923, pp. 3–452.

Bintliff, J., "Erosion in Mediterranean Lands: A Reconsideration of Pattern, Process, and Methodology," in M. Bell and J. Boardman (eds.), *Past and Present Soil Erosion*, Oxford, 1992, pp. 125–31.

Birebent, J., *Aquae Romanae: recherches d'hydraulique romaine dans l'est Algérien*, Algiers, 1964.

Biswas, A., *History of Hydrology*, Amsterdam, 1972.

Blackman, D., "The Volume of Water Delivered by the Four Great Aqueducts of Rome," *PBSR* 46 (1978), pp. 52–72.

Blaine, B., "The Enigmatic Water Mill," in B. Hall and D. West (eds.), *Studies in Honor of Lynn White, Jr.*, Malibu, 1976, pp. 163–76.

Blake, H., *Lancaster in Pavia (1977)*, Lancaster, 1977.

"Pavia," in *Lancaster in Italy (1979)*, Lancaster, 1979, pp. 5–12.

Bloch, M., "Avènement et conquête du moulin à eau," *Annales d'histoire économique et sociale* 7 (1935), pp. 538–63.

"Technique et évolution sociale: réflexions d'un historien," *Europe* (1938), pp. 23–32.

Bocchi, S., *La pianura padana: storia del paesaggio agrario*, Milan, 1985.

Bognetti, G.-P. "I beni comunali e l'organizzazione del villaggio nell'Italia superiore fino al mille," *Rivista storica italiana* 77 (1965), pp. 469–99.

"La Brescia dei Goti e dei Longobardi," in Treccani degli Alfieri, *Storia di Brescia* I, pp. 391–446.

"La navigazione padana e il sopravvivere della civiltà antica," in Bognetti, *L'età longobarda* IV, Milan, 1968, pp. 541–53.

"Un nuovo primato di Brescia: il banco di prova della civiltà longobarda," in Bognetti, *L'età longobarda* IV, Milan, 1968, pp. 210–20.

Bolen, L., "L'eau et l'irrigation d'après les traités d'agronomie andalous du moyen âge," *Options méditerranéennes* 16 (1972), pp. 65–77.

Les méthodes culturales au moyen âge d'après les traités d'agronomie andalous: traditions et techniques, Geneva, 1974.

Bond, C., "Mittelalterliche Wasserversorgung in England und Wales," in *Geschichte der Wasserversorgung* IV, Mainz, 1991, pp. 149–83.

"Monastic Fisheries," in Aston, *Medieval Fish, Fisheries, and Fishponds in England*, pp. 69–112.

"Water Management in the Rural Monastery," in Gilchrist and Mynum, *Archaeology of Rural Monasteries*, pp. 83–111.

Bonelli, F., "La malaria nella storia demografica ed economica d'Italia," *Studi storici* 7 (1966), pp. 659–88.

Bonfante, P., "Il diritto delle acque dal diritto romano al diritto odierno," *Archivio giuridico* 87 (1922), pp. 3–16.

Bonnassie, P., *La Catalogne du milieu du Xe à la fin du XIe siècle: croissance et mutations d'une société*, Toulouse, 1975.

"The Survival and Extinction of the Slave System in the Early Medieval West (Fourth to Eleventh Centuries)," in Bonnassie, *From Slavery to Feudalism in South-Western Europe*, Cambridge, 1991, pp. 1–59.

Borelli, G. (ed.), *Una città e il suo fiume: Verona e l'Adige*, Verona, 1977.

Bortolani, S., "Acque, mulini, e folloni nella formazione del paesaggio urbano medievale (secoli XI–XIV): l'esempio di Padova," in *Paesaggi urbani dell'Italia padana*, pp. 279–330.

Boserup, E., *The Conditions of Agricultural Growth: The Economics of Agrarian Change under Population Pressure*, New York, 1982; orig. 1965.

Braudel, F., *Civilisation matérielle et capitalisme (XVe–XVIIIe siècles)* I, Paris, 1967.

Braunstein, P., "Dal bagno pubblico alla cura corporale privata: tracce per una storia sociale dell'intimo," *Ricerche storiche* 16 (1986), pp. 523–34.

Brinkhuizen, D., "Some Notes on Recent and Pre- and Protohistoric Fishing Gear from Northwestern Europe," *Palaeohistoria* 25 (1983), pp. 8–53.

Brizzi, G., "Il sistema portuale altoadriatico e i commerci di Aquileia e Ravenna," *Antichità altoadriatiche* 13 (1977), pp. 81–105.

Brödner, E., *Die römische Thermen und das antike Badewesen*, Darmstadt, 1983.

Brogiolo, G., "La campagna dalla tarda antichità al 900 ca. D.C.," *AM* 10 (1983), pp. 73–88.

"Trasformazioni urbanistiche nella Brescia longobarda: dalle capanne in legno al monastero regio di S. Salvatore," in Stella and Brentenghi, *S. Giulia di Brescia*, pp. 179–210.

Brooks, N., "Romney Marsh in the Early Middle Ages," in Rowley, *Evolution of Marshland Landscapes*, pp. 74–94.

Brown, P., *The Body and Society: Men, Women, and Sexual Renunciation in Early Christianity*, New York, 1988.

Brown, T., "The Aristocracy of Ravenna from Justinian to Charlemagne," *CCARB* 37 (1990), pp. 393–415.

Gentlemen and Officers: Imperial Administration and Aristocratic Power in Byzantine Italy, Hertford, 1984.

Brühl, C.-R., "Das Palatium von Pavia und die *Honorantie Civitatis Papie*," *Atti del 4o Congresso internazionale di studi sull'alto medioevo*, Spoleto, 1969, pp. 189–220.

Fodrum, Gistum, Servitium Regis, Cologne, 1974.

"Königs-, Bischofs-, und Stadtpfalz in den Stadten des *Regnum Italiae* vom 9. bis zum 13. Jahrhundert," in H. Beumann (ed.), *Historische Forschungen für W. Schlesinger*, Cologne, 1974, pp. 400–19.

"Remarques sur la notion de 'capitale' et de 'résidence' pendant le haut moyen âge," *Journal des Savants* (1967), pp. 193–215.

Studien zu den langobardischen Königsurkunden, Tübingen, 1970.

Buffet, B., and Evraud, E., *L'eau potable à travers les âges*, Liege, 1950.

Bullough, D., "Social and Economic Structure and Topography in the Early Medieval City," *Settimane* 21 (1974), pp. 351–99.

"Urban Change in Early Medieval Italy: The Example of Pavia," *PBSR* 34 (1967), pp. 82–129.

Bussi, L., "Terre comuni e usi civici: dalle origini all'alto medioevo," in Galasso, *Storia del Mezzogiorno* III, pp. 213–55.

Butzer, K., "Accelerated Soil Erosion: A Problem of Man–Land Relationships," in I. Manners (ed.), *Perspectives on Environment*, Washington, DC, 1974, pp. 57–78.

"The Classical Tradition of Agronomic Science: Perspectives on Carolingian Agriculture and Agronomy," in K. Butzer and D. Lohrmann (eds.), *Science in Western and Eastern Civilization in Carolingian Times*, Basel, 1993, pp. 539–82.

Cagiano de Azevedo, M., "Aspetti urbanistici delle città altomedievali," *Settimane* 21 (1974), pp. 641–77.

"Le case descritte nel *Codex Traditionum Ecclesiae Ravennatis*," *Atti della Accademia Nazionale dei Lincei. Rendiconti. Classe di scienze morali, storiche, filologiche* 27 (1972), pp. 159–81.

"Milano da sant'Ambrogio a Desiderio," in *Casa città e campagna nel tardoantico e nell'alto medioevo*, Galatina, 1986, pp. 145–63.

Tra Bagnoregio e Ferento, Rome, 1974.

Cahn, E., *Das Recht der Binnenfischerei im deutschen Kulturgebiet von den Anfängen bis zum Ausgang des 18. Jahrhunderts*, Frankfurt, 1956.

Calò Mariani, M., "Utilità e diletto: l'acqua e le residenze regie dell'Italia meridionale fra XII e XII secolo," *MEFR. Moyen âge* 104 (1992), pp. 343–72.

Camilla, P., "I mulini negli statuti medievali del Cuneese," in Comba, *Mulini da grano nel Piemonte medievale*, pp. 153–66.

Caponera, D., "Water Laws in Hydraulic Civilizations," in G. Ulmen (ed.), *Society and History: Essays in Honor of K. Wittfogel*, The Hague, 1978, pp. 91–106.

Cardilli-Aloisi, L., "Acquedotti e mostre d'acqua dal medioevo al XIX secolo," in *Il trionfo dell'acqua*, pp. 201–2.

Carile, A. (ed.), *Storia di Ravenna* II, Venice, 1991.

Carucci, C., *La provincia di Salerno dai tempi più remoti al tramonto della fortuna normanna: economia e vita sociale*, Salerno, 1922.

Caruso, G., "Aqua Alexandriana," in *Il trionfo dell'acqua*, pp. 120–3.

Castagnetti, A., "Continuità e discontinuità nella terminologia e nella realtà organizzativa agraria: 'fundus' e 'casale' nei documenti ravennati altomedievali," in V. Fumagalli and G. Rossetti (eds.), *Medioevo rurale*, Bologna, 1980, pp. 201–19.

"La pianura veronese nel medioevo: la conquista del suolo e la regolamentazione delle acque," in Borelli, *Una città e il suo fiume*, pp. 33–138.

"Le strutture agrarie e fondiarie," in Carile, *Storia di Ravenna* II, pp. 55–72.

Castelluccio, E., *Gli acquedotti medioevali di Via Arce*, Salerno, 1955.

Cattalini, E., "Aqua Antoniniana," in *Il trionfo dell'acqua*, pp. 57–9.

Caucanas, S., *Moulins et irrigation en Roussillon du IXe au XVe siècle*, Paris, 1995.

Celli, A., *The History of Malaria in the Roman Campagna from Ancient Times*, London, 1933.

Chapelot, J., and Fossier, R., *Le village et la maison au moyen âge*, Paris, 1980.

Chevalier, R., *La romanisation de la Celtique du Pô: les données géographiques*, Paris, 1980.

Chiappa-Mauri, L., *I mulini ad acqua nel milanese (secoli X–XV)*, Città di Castello, 1984.

Chiarlone, V., "I mulini nel Piemonte bassomedievale: costruzione, funzionamento, manutenzione (secoli XIII–XIV)," in Comba, *Mulini da grano nel Piemonte medievale*, pp. 169–88.

Chroust, A., *Untersuchungen über die Langobardischen Königs- und Herzogsurkunden*, Graz, 1888.

Churchill-Semple, E., *The Geography of the Mediterranean Region: Its Relation to Ancient History*, New York, 1931.

Ciabatti, M., "Gli antichi delta del Po anteriori al 1600," in *Atti del convegno internazionale di studi sulle antichità di Classe*, Ravenna, 1968, pp. 23–33.

Ciampoltrini, G., and Notini, P., "Lucca tardoantica e altomedievale: nuovi contributi archeologici," *AM* 17 (1990), pp. 561–92.

Ciampoltrini, G., and Zecchini, M., *Capannori: archeologia nel territorio*, Lucca, 1987.

Ciampoltrini, G., et al., "Lucca tardoantica e altomedievale II: scavi 1990–1991," *AM* 21 (1994), pp. 597–627.

Cilento, N., *Italia meridionale longobarda*, Milan, 1966.

"Origine e struttura delle città in Campania," *Bollettino di storia dell'arte* 2 (1974), pp. 13–19.

Clarke, C., *The Economics of Irrigation*, Oxford, 1970.

Comba, A. (ed.), *Mulini da grano nel Piemonte medievale, secoli XII–XV*, Cuneo, 1993.

Comet, G., *Le paysan et son outil: essai d'histoire technique des céréales (France, VIIe–XVe siècle)*, Rome, 1992.

Condorelli, B., "La molitura ad acqua nella valle del torrente Farfa: VIII–XII secolo," in *Atti del 9o congresso internazionale di studi sull'alto medioevo*, Spoleto, 1983, pp. 837–41.

Corbier, M., "De Volsinii à Sestinum: cura aquae et évergétisme municipal de l'eau en Italie," *Revue des études latines* 62 (1984), pp. 236–74.

"L'évergétisme de l'eau en Afrique: Gariglianus et l'aqueduc de Cirta," *L'Africa romana* 3 (1986), pp. 275–85.

Cortesi, G., *Classe paleocristiana e paleobizantina*, Ravenna, 1980.

"Lo scavo di S. Croce e le acque del sottosuolo ravennate," *Felix Ravenna* 113 (1977), pp. 100–9.

Costa, E., *Le acque nel diritto romano*, Bologna, 1919.

Cracco Ruggini, L., "Progresso tecnico e manodopera in età imperiale romana," in *Tecnologia economia e società nel mondo romano*, Como, 1980, pp. 45–66.

Cremaschi, M., and Marchesini, A., "L'evoluzione di un tratto di pianura padana (provincie di Reggio e Parma) in rapporto agli insediamenti ed alla struttura geologica tra il XV sec. a.C. ed il XI sec. d.C.," *AM* 5 (1978), pp. 542–62.

Crosara, F., *La difesa delle acque interne: cenni storici sul territorio ravennate dall'antichità ai tempi moderni*, Rome, 1970.

Le "scole" ravennati nell'alto medioevo e la "Carta Piscatoria" del 943, Modena, 1949.

Crouch, D., *Water Management in Ancient Greek Cities*, Oxford, 1993.

Currie, C., "The Role of Fishponds in the Monastic Economy," in Gilchrist and Mynum, *Archaeology of Rural Monasteries*, pp. 147–72.

Curwen, E., "The Problem of Early Water-mills," *Antiquity* 18 (1944), pp. 130–46.

Dagron, G., "Poissons, pêcheurs, et poissonniers de Constantinople," in Mango and Dagron, *Constantinople and Its Hinterland*, pp. 57–73.

De Conno, A., "L'insediamento longobardo a Lucca," in *Pisa e la Toscana occidentale nel medioevo* I, Pisa, 1991, pp. 59–127.

De Reparaz, A. (ed.), *L'eau et les hommes en Méditerranée*, Paris, 1987.

Deichmann, F., *Ravenna: Hauptstadt des spätantiken Abendlandes* I, Wiesbaden, 1969; II.3, Stuttgart, 1989.

Del Treppo, M., *Amalfi medioevale*, Naples, 1977.

"Longobardi, Franchi, e Papato in tre secoli di storia vulturnese," *Archivio storico per le provincie napoletane* 73 (1953–4), pp. 37–59.

Delaine, J., "An Engineering Approach to Roman Building Techniques: The Baths of Caracalla," in *Papers in Italian Archaeology* IV, Oxford, 1985, pp. 195–206.

"Recent Research on Roman Baths," *Journal of Roman Archaeology* 1 (1988), pp. 11–32.

"Roman Baths and Bathing," *Journal of Roman Archaeology* 6 (1993), pp. 348–58.

Delano Smith, C., "Coastal Sedimentation, Lagoons and Ports in Italy," *Papers in Italian Archaeology* I, Oxford, 1978, pp. 25–34.

Western Mediterranean Europe: A Historical Geography of Italy, Spain, and Southern France Since the Neolithic, London, 1979.

Delatouche, R., "Le poisson d'eau douce dans l'alimentation médiévale," *Comptes rendus de l'Académie d'agriculture de France* (1966), pp. 793–98.

Dell'Acqua, M., "Morfologia urbana e tipologia edilizia," in Leone and Vitolo, *Guida alla storia di Salerno* I, pp. 55–67.

Delogu, P., "La cisterna dell'Orto del Granato," in *Caputaquis medioevale* I (Salerno, 1976), pp. 79–80.

Mito di una città meridionale: Salerno, secoli VIII–XI, Naples, 1977.

"Il principato di Salerno: la prima dinastia," in Galasso, *Storia del Mezzogiorno* II.1, pp. 239–77.

"Proposte per lo studio delle città campane nell'alto medioevo," *Bollettino di storia dell'arte* 2 (1974), pp. 53–8.

"Il regno longobardo," in P. Delogu, A. Guillou, and G. Ortalli (eds.), *Longobardi e Bizantini*, Turin, 1980, pp. 1–203.

"Storia del sito," in *Caputaquis medioevale* I, Salerno, 1976, pp. 23–32.

Di Resta, I., *Capua medioevale: la città dal IX al XIII secolo e l'architettura longobarda*, Naples, 1983.

Diehl, C., *Etudes sur l'administration byzantine dans l'Exarchat de Ravenne, 568–751*, Paris, 1888.

Dirlmeier, U., "Zu den Lebensbedingungen in der mittelalterlichen Stadt: Trinkwasserversorgung und Abfallbeseitigung," in B. Hermann (ed.), *Mensch und Umwelt im Mittelalter*, Stuttgart, 1986, pp. 150–9.

Dockès, P., "Formes et diffusion d'une innovation technique: le cas du moulin hydraulique," in *Forme ed evoluzione del lavoro in Europa, XIII–XVIII secoli*, Florence, 1991, pp. 113–54.

Dopsch, A., *Die Wirtschaftsentwicklung der Karolingerzeit*, Darmstadt, 1962.

Wirtschaftliche und Soziale Grundlagen der Europäischen Kulturentwicklung aus der Zeit von Caesar bis auf Karl der Grosse, Vienna, 1923–4.

Duby, G., *L'économie rurale et la vie des campagnes dans l'Occident médiévale*, Paris, 1962.

Guerriers et paysans, VIIe–XIIe siècle: premier essor de l'économie européenne, Paris, 1973.

Dunbabin, K., "'Baiarum grata voluptas': Pleasures and Dangers of the Baths," *PBSR* 57 (1989), pp. 6–37.

Dussaix, C., "Les moulins à Reggio d'Emilie au XIIe et XIIIe siècles," *MEFR* 91 (1979), pp. 113–47.

Dyer, C., "The Consumption of Freshwater Fish in Medieval England," in Aston, *Medieval Fish, Fisheries, and Fishponds in England*, pp. 27–38.

Dyson, S., *Community and Society in Roman Italy*, Baltimore, 1992.

Eck, W., "Organisation und Administration der Wasserversorgung Roms," in *Geschichte der Wasserversorgung* I, Munich, 1983, pp. 63–77.

"Die Wasserversorgung in römischen Reich: sozio-politische Bedingungen, Recht, und Administration," in *Geschichte der Wasserversorgung* II, Mainz, 1987, pp. 51–101.

Elmshäuser, K., "Kanalbau und technische Wasserführung im frühen Mittelalter," *Technikgeschichte* 59 (1992), pp. 1–26.

Engelhardt, B., et al., "Early Medieval Wells from Pettfach, Bavaria," in *Environment and Subsistence in Medieval Europe*, ed. G. De Boe and F. Verhaeghe (Bruges, 1997).

Evans, H., *Water Distribution in Ancient Rome*, Ann Arbor, 1994.

"Water Distribution: Quorsum et Cui Bono," in Hodge, *Future Currents in Aqueduct Studies*, pp. 21–7.

Evison, V., "Germanic Glass Drinking Horns," *Journal of Glass Studies* 17 (1975), pp. 74–87.

Fabbri, P., "Il controllo delle acque tra tecnica ed economia," in Carile, *Storia di Ravenna* II, pp. 9–25.

"L'evoluzione del quadro ambientale di Ravenna nell'antichità," *CCARB* 23 (1976), pp. 209–26.

Il Padenna: l'uomo e le acque nel ravennate dall'antichità al medioevo, Ravenna, 1975.

"Il paesaggio ravennate dell'evo antico," in Susini, *Storia di Ravenna* I, pp. 7–30.

Ravenna, geografia di un territorio, Bologna, 1974.

Fantoni, G., *L'acqua a Milano: uso e gestione nel basso medioevo*, Bologna, 1990.

Fasoli, G., "Inizio di un'indagine su gli stanziamenti longobardi intorno a Pavia," *Bollettino della Società pavese di storia patria* 5 (1953), pp. 3–12.

"Navigazione fluviale: porti e navi sul Po," *Settimane* 25 (1978), pp. 565–607.

"Il patrimonio della chiesa ravennate," in Carile, *Storia di Ravenna* II, pp. 389–400.

Feller, L., "Les patrimoines monastiques dans les Abruzzes (VIIe–Xe s.)," in M. Fixot and E. Zadora-Rio (eds.), *L'environment des églises et la topographie religieuse des campagnes médiévales*, Paris, 1994, pp. 150–5.

Fenn, P., *The Origins of the Right of Fishery in Territorial Waters*, Cambridge, MA, 1926.

Ferrari, G., *Early Roman Monasteries: Notes for the History of the Monasteries and Convents of Rome from the Vth to the Xth Century*, Vatican City, 1957.

Fevrier, P., "Permanence et héritages de l'antiquité dans la topographie des villes de l'occident durant le haut moyen âge," *Settimane* 21 (1974), pp. 41–138.

Fontanille, M.-T., "Les bains dans la médicine gréco-romaine," in A. Pelletier (ed.), *La médicine en Gaule*, Paris, 1985, pp. 15–24.

Forbes, R., "Hydraulic Engineering and Sanitation," in Singer, *History of Technology* II, pp. 663–94.

"Power," in Singer, *History of Technology* II, pp. 589–622.

Studies in Ancient Technology II, Leiden, 1965.

Fouet, M., "Exemples d'exploitation des eaux par des grands propriétaires terriens dans le sud-ouest au IVe siècle," in *Caesarodunum 10. Actes*, Tours, 1975, pp. 128–34.

Fourquin, G., "Le premier moyen âge," in G. Duby (ed.), *Histoire de la France rurale*, Paris, 1975, pp. 287–371.

Fraccaro, P., "La malaria e la storia degli antichi popoli classici," *Atene e Roma* 22 (1919), pp. 57–88.

Frayn, J., "Wild and Cultivated Plants: A Note on the Peasant Economy of Roman Italy," *Journal of Roman Studies* 65 (1975), pp. 32–9.

Freedman, P., *The Origins of Peasant Servitude in Medieval Catalonia*, Cambridge, 1991.

Frezza, A., "Resti di pesci dal monastero medievale di S. Patrizia, Napoli," *AM* 22 (1995), pp. 611–17.

Frova, A. (ed.), *Scavi di Luni* I–II, Rome, 1973–7.

Fumagalli, V., *Città e campagna nell'Italia medievale*, Bologna, 1985.

"Colonizzazione e bonifica nell'Emilia durante il medioevo," in *I 70 anni del consorzio della bonifica renana*, Bologna, 1980, pp. 27–50.

"L'evoluzione dell'economia agraria e dei patti colonici dall'alto al basso medioevo," in B. Andreolli, V. Fumagalli, and M. Montanari (eds.), *Le campagne italiane prima e dopo il mille*, Bologna, 1985, pp. 15–42.

"*Langobardia e Romania*: l'occupazione del suolo nella Pentapoli altomedievale," in Vasina, *Ricerche e studi sul Breviarium Ecclesiae Ravennatis*, pp. 95–107.

"Note per una storia agraria altomedievale," *Studi medievali* 9 (1968), pp. 359–78.

"Note sui disboscamenti nella pianura padana in epoca carolingia," *Rivista di storia dell'agricoltura* 7 (1967), pp. 139–46.

"Il paesaggio delle campagne nei primi secoli del medioevo," *Settimane* 37 (1990), pp. 21–53.

La pietra viva: città e natura nel medioevo, Bologna, 1988.

"Storia agraria e luoghi comuni," *Studi medievali* 9 (1968), pp. 949–65.

L'uomo e l'ambiente nel medioevo, Bari, 1992.

Galante, M., "Per la datazione dei documenti salernitani di epoca longobarda," *Archivio storico per le provincie napoletane* 14 (1975), pp. 367–9.

Galasso, G., *Mezzogiorno medievale e moderno*, Turin, 1975.

Il mezzogiorno nella storia d'Italia, Florence, 1977.

Galasso, G. (ed.), *Storia del Mezzogiorno* I.2, Salerno, 1991; II.1 Naples, 1988; III, Naples, 1990.

Storia d'Italia III, Turin, 1983.

Galetti, P., "Aspetti dell'insediamento nelle campagne ravennati altomedievali," in Carile, *Storia di Ravenna* II, pp. 73–83.

Una campagna e la sua città: Piacenza e territorio nei secoli VIII–X, Bologna, 1994.

"La casa contadina nell'Italia padana dei secoli VIII–X," *Quaderni medievali* 16 (1983), pp. 6–28.

"Struttura materiale e funzioni negli insediamenti urbani e rurali della Pentapoli," in Vasina, *Ricerche e studi sul Breviarium Ecclesiae Ravennatis*, pp. 109–24.

Gambi, L., "I valori storici dei quadri ambientali," in *Storia d'Italia Einaudi: Annali I*, Turin, 1972, pp. 3–60.

Ganshof, F., *Frankish Institutions Under Charlemagne*, Providence, RI, 1968.

Garbrecht, G., "Mensch und Wasser im Altertum," in *Geschichte der Wasserversorgung* III, Mainz, 1988, pp. 13–42.

"Die Wasserversorgung des antiken Pergamon," in *Geschichte der Wasserversorgung* II, Mainz, 1987, pp. 13–47.

"Wasserversorgungstechnik in römischer Zeit," in *Geschichte der Wasserversorgung* I, Munich, 1983, pp. 9–43.

Gargano, G., "La valle dei mulini e la ferriera di Amalfi," *Rassegna storica salernitana* 19 (1993), pp. 227–46.

Gasparri, S., "Il ducato e il principato di Benevento," in Galasso, *Storia del Mezzogiorno* II.1, pp. 85–146.

Gay, J., *L'Italie méridionale et l'empire byzantin depuis l'avènement de Basile I jusqu'à la prise de Bari par les Normands*, Paris, 1904.

Gazda, E., and McCann, A., "Reconstruction and Function: Port, Fishery, and Villa," in McCann, *The Roman Port and Fishery of Cosa*, pp. 137–59.

Gechter, M., "Wasserversorgung und -entsorgung in Köln vom Mittelalter bis zur frühen Neuzeit," *Kölner Jahrbuch für Vor- und Frühgeschichte* 20 (1987), pp. 219–70.

Geffcken, H., "Zur Geschichte des deutschen Wasserrechts," *Zeitschrift der Savigny-Stiftung für Rechtsgeschichte. Germanische Abtheilung* 21 (1900), pp. 173–217.

Gelichi, S., "Il paesaggio urbano tra V e X secolo," in Carile, *Storia di Ravenna* II, pp. 153–65.

Gilbertson, D., "The UNESCO Libyan Valleys Survey VIII: An Interim Classification and Functional Analysis of Ancient Wall Technology and Land Use," *Libyan Studies* 15 (1984), pp. 45–70.

Gilchrist, R. and Mynum, H. (eds.), *The Archaeology of Rural Monasteries*, Oxford, 1989.

Gille, B., "Le moulin à eau: une révolution technique médiévale," *Techniques et civilisations* 3 (1954), pp. 1–15.

Ginouvès, R., *Balaneutikè: recherches sur le bain dans l'antiquité grecque*, Paris, 1962.

Giuliani, M., "Ravenna, ricerche di geografia urbana," *Annali di ricerche e studi di geografia* 14 (1958), pp. 91–132.

Glacken, C., *Traces on the Rhodian Shore: Nature and Culture in Western Thought from Ancient Times to the End of the Eighteenth Century*, Berkeley, 1967.

Glick, T., *From Muslim Fortress to Christian Castle*, Manchester, 1995.

Irrigation and Society in Medieval Valencia, Cambridge, MA, 1970.

Islamic and Christian Spain in the Early Middle Ages, Princeton, 1979.

Gottschalk, A., *Histoire de l'alimentation et de la gastronomie depuis la préhistoire jusqu'à nos jours*, Paris, 1948.

Goubert, J.-P., *La conquête de l'eau: l'avènement de la santé à l'âge industriel*, Paris, 1988.

Grewe, K., *Planung und Trassierung römischer Wasserleitungen*, Wiesbaden, 1985.

"Römische Wasserleitungen nordlich der Alpen," in *Geschichte der Wasserversorgung* III, Mainz, 1988, pp. 45–97.

"Wasserversorgung und -entsorgung im Mittelalter: ein technikgeschichtlicher Überblick," in *Geschichte der Wasserversorgung* IV, Mainz, 1991, pp. 11–86.

Grmek, M., *Les maladies à l'aube de la civilisation occidentale*, Paris, 1983.

Guillerme, A., "La destruction des aqueducs romains des villes du nord de la France," in J.-P. Boucher (ed.), *Journées d'études sur les aqueducs romains, Lyons 26–8 mai 1977*, Paris, 1983, pp. 167–73.

"Les moulins hydrauliques urbains (XIe–XIIIe siècle) dans les villes du bassin parisien," *Milieux* 1 (1980), pp. 44–50.

"Puits, aqueducs, et fontaines: l'alimentation en eau dans les villes du nord de la France, Xe–XIIIe siècle," in *L'eau au moyen âge*, Marseille, 1985, pp. 187–200.

Le temps de l'eau: la cité, l'eau, et les techniques. Nord de la France, IIIe–XIXe siècles, Seyssel, 1983.

Guillou, A., "L'Italia bizantina dalla caduta di Ravenna all'arrivo dei Normanni," in Galasso, *Storia d'Italia* III, pp. 3–126.

Guy, M., "Changements dans les voies d'eau naturelles, variations climatiques et variations du niveau moyen des mers," in *Caesarodunum 10. Actes*, Tours, 1975, pp. 95–101.

Hanoune, M., "Thermes romains et Talmud," in R. Chevalier (ed.), *Colloque histoire et historiographie: Clio*, Paris, 1980, pp. 255–62.

Hartmann, L.-M., "Comacchio und das Po-Handel," in Hartmann, *Zur Wirtschaftsgeschichte Italiens im frühen Mittelalter*, pp. 74–90.

Zur Wirtschaftsgeschichte Italiens im frühen Mittelalter, Gotha, 1904.

Heinz, W., *Römische Thermen: Badewesen und Badeluxus im Römischen Reich*, Munich, 1983.

Herlihy, D., "L'economia della città e del distretto di Lucca secondo le carte private nell'alto medioevo," in *Atti del 5o congresso internazionale di studi sull'alto medioevo*, Spoleto, 1973, pp. 363–88.

Higounet-Nadal, A., "Hygiène, salubrité, pollutions au moyen âge: l'exemple de Périgueux," *Annales de demographie historique* (1975), pp. 81–92.

Hobart, M., "Cosa-Ansedonia (Orbetello) in età medievale," *AM* 22 (1995), pp. 569–83.

Hodge, A., *Roman Aqueducts and Water Supply*, London, 1992.

Hodge, A. (ed.), *Future Currents in Aqueduct Studies*, Leeds, 1991.

Hodges, R., and Whitehouse, D., *Mohammed, Charlemagne, and the Origins of Europe*, Ithaca, 1983.

Hoffmann, R., "Economic Development and Aquatic Ecosystems in Medieval Europe," *American Historical Review* 101 (1996), pp. 631–69.

"Fishing for Sport in Medieval Europe: New Evidence," *Speculum* 60 (1985), pp. 877–902.

"Fishponds," in J. Strayer (ed.), *Dictionary of the Middle Ages* V, New York, 1985, pp. 73–4.

Holt, R., *The Mills of Medieval England*, Oxford, 1988.

Horn, W., "Water Power and the Plan of St. Gall," *Journal of Medieval History* 1 (1975), pp. 219–57.

Hoy, S., *Chasing Dirt: The American Pursuit of Cleanliness*, Oxford, 1995.

Hubert, E., *Espace urbain et habitat à Rome du Xe siècle à la fin du XIIIe siècle*, Rome, 1990.

Hudson, P., *Archeologia urbana e programmazione della ricerca: l'esempio di Pavia*, Florence, 1981.

"Lombard Immigration and Effects on North Italian Rural and Urban Settlement," in *Papers in Italian Archaeology* IV, Oxford, 1985, pp. 225–46.

"Pavia: l'evoluzione urbanistica di una capitale altomedievale (774–1024)," in *Paesaggi urbani dell'Italia padana*, pp. 15–69.

Ingram, M., "The Use of Documentary Sources for the Study of Past Climates," in T. Wigley, et al. (ed.), *Climate and History*, Cambridge, 1981, pp. 180–204.

Jones, G., "Chaucer and the Medieval Miller," *Modern Language Quarterly* 16 (1955), pp. 3–15.

Judson, S., "Erosion and Deposition of Italian Stream Valleys During Historic Time," *Science* 140 (1963), pp. 898–99.

"Underground Waterways in Southern Etruria and Northern Latium," *PBSR* 31 (1963), pp. 74–99.

Judson, S., and Kahane, A., "The *ager veientanus* North and East of Rome," *PBSR* 36 (1968), pp. 1–218.

Kalby, L., "Per una storia urbanistica di Salerno," *Bollettino di storia dell'arte* 2 (1974), pp. 20–9.

Kaplan, M., *Les hommes et la terre à Byzance du VIe au XIe siècle: propriété et exploitation du sol*, Paris, 1992.

Kleiner, F., "The Trophy on the Bridge and Roman Triumph over Nature," *L'antiquité classique* 60 (1991), pp. 182–92.

Koehne, C., *Das Recht der Mühlen bis zum Ende der Karolingerzeit*, Breslau, 1904.

Kosch, C., "Wasserbaueinrichtungen in hochmittelalterliche Konventanlagen Mitteleuropas," in *Geschichte der Wasserversorgung* IV, Mainz, 1991, pp. 89–146.

Kotel'nikova, L., *Mondo contadino e città in Italia dal XI al XIV secolo*, Bologna, 1975.

Krahwinkler, H., *Friaul im Frühmittelalter*, Vienna, 1992.

Krautheimer, R., *Rome: Profile of a City, 312–1308*, Princeton, 1980.

Kreutz, B., *Before the Normans: Southern Italy in the Ninth and Tenth Centuries*, Philadelphia, 1991.

Kula, W., *Measures and Men*, Princeton, 1986.

Lagardère, V., "Moulins d'Occident musulman au moyen âge (IX au XV siècles): al-Andalus," *Al-Qantara* 12 (1991), pp. 59–118.

Lagazzi, L., *Segni sulla terra: determinazione dei confini e percezione dello spazio nell'alto medioevo*, Bologna, 1991.

Lamb, H., "The Early Medieval Warm Epoch and Its Sequel," *Palaeogeography. Palaeoclimatology. Palaeoecology* 1 (1965), pp. 13–37.

Lanciani, R., *I commentari di Frontino intorno le acque e gli acquedotti*, Rome, 1880.

Lanconelli, A., "I mulini di Viterbo (secoli XII–XIV)," in Lanconelli and de Palma, *Terra, acque, e lavoro nella Viterbo medievale*, pp. 3–71.

Lanconelli, A., and de Palma, R., *Terra, acque, e lavoro nella Viterbo medievale*, Rome, 1992.

Langdon, J., "Water-mills and Windmills in the West Midlands, 1086–1500," *Economic History Review* 44 (1991), pp. 424–44.

Le Gall, J., *Le Tibre, fleuve de Rome dans l'antiquité*, Paris, 1953.

Leclercq, J., and Chabrol, F., "Bains," in *Dictionnaire d'archéologie chrétienne et de liturgie* II, Paris, 1925.

Leighton, A., *Transport and Communication in Early Medieval Europe, AD 500–1100*, New York, 1972.

Leone, A., and Vitolo, E. (eds.), *Guida alla storia di Salerno e della sua provincia*, Salerno, 1982.

Lestcocquoy, J., "Administration de Rome et diaconies du VII au IX siècle," *Rivista di archeologia cristiana* 6 (1929), pp. 261–98.

Leveau, P., "Mentalité économique et grands travaux hydrauliques: le drainage du lac Fucin. Aux origines d'un modèle," *Annales ESC* 48 (1993), pp. 3–16.

Levy, E., *West Roman Vulgar Law: The Law of Property*, Philadelphia, 1951.

Lieciejwicz, L. (ed.), *Torcello: scavi 1961–1962*, Rome, 1977.

Lipparini, T., "Geomorfologia del territorio di Ravenna e di Classe," in *Atti del convegno internazionale di studi sulle antichità di Classe*, Ravenna, 1968, pp. 63–9.

Lizier, A., *L'economia rurale dell'età prenormanna nell'Italia meridionale, secoli IX–XI*, Palermo, 1907.

Lloyd, J., and Lewis, P., "Water Supply and Urban Population in Roman Cyrenaica," *Annual Report: The Society for Libyan Studies* 8 (1976–7), pp. 35–40.

Lohrmann, D., "Le moulin à eau dans le cadre de l'économie rurale de la Neustrie (VIIe–IXe siècles)," in H. Atsma (ed.), *La Neustrie*, Paris, 1992, pp. 367–406.

"Neues über Wasserversorgung und Wassertechnik im Mittelalter," *Deutsches Archiv für Erforschung des Mittelalters* 48 (1992), pp. 179–88.

"Schiffsmühlen auf dem Tiber in Rom nach Papsturkunden des 10.–11. Jahrhunderts," in K. Hebers, H. Kortüm, and C. Servatius (eds.), *Ex Ipsis Rerum Documentis: Festschrift für H. Zimmermann*, Sigmaringen, 1991, pp. 277–86.

"Travail manuel et machines hydrauliques," in J. Hamesse and C. Muraille-Samaran (eds.), *Le travail au moyen âge*, Louvain-la-neuve, 1990, pp. 35–47.

Longo, G., "Il regime delle concessioni e delle derivazioni di acque pubbliche nel diritto romano classico e giustinianeo," in *Studi alla memoria di G. Zanobini* V, Milan, 1965, pp. 361–84.

Lorcin, M.-T., "Humeurs, bains, et tisanes: l'eau dans la médicine médiévale," in *L'eau au moyen âge*, Marseille, 1985, pp. 261–73.

Louis, P. (ed.), *L'homme et l'eau en Méditerranée*, Lyons, 1984–7.

Luzzatto, G., *Breve storia economica dell'Italia medievale*, Turin, 1982.

McCann, A., "The History and Topography," in McCann, *The Roman Port and Fishery of Cosa*, pp. 15–43.

McCann, A. (ed.), *The Roman Port and Fishery of Cosa*, Princeton, 1987.

McClendon, C., *The Imperial Abbey of Farfa: Architectural Currents of the Early Middle Ages*, New Haven, 1987.

MacDonald, W., *The Architecture of the Roman Empire* II, New Haven, 1986.

McKay, A., *Houses, Villas, and Palaces in the Roman World*, Ithaca, 1975.

Magdalino, P., "Church, Bath, and Diakonia in Medieval Constantinople," in R. Morris (ed.), *Byzantine Church and Society*, Birmingham, 1990, pp. 165–88.

Maioli, M., "Aggiornamento sulla situazione conoscitiva delle ville rustiche di epoca romana a Ravenna e in Romagna," *CCARB* 37 (1990), pp. 249–79.

"Appunti sulla tipologia delle case di Ravenna in epoca imperiale," *CCARB* 33 (1986), pp. 195–220.

"Classe, podere Chiavichetta," in Bermond Montanari, *Ravenna e il porto di Classe*, pp. 65–84.

"Ravenna, Piazza Arcivescovado: domus romana," in Bermond Montanari, *Ravenna e il porto di Classe*, pp. 55–9.

"I ritrovamenti della zona di Classe," in Bermond-Montanari, *Ravenna e il porto di Classe*, pp. 60–4.

"Strutture economico-commerciali e impianti produttivi nella Ravenna bizantina," in Carile, *Storia di Ravenna* II, pp. 223–47.

Maioli, M., and Prati, L., "Le memorie: l'acquedotto," in Prati, *Flumen Aqueductus*, pp. 27–50.

"I siti lungo il tracciato," in Prati, *Flumen Aqueductus*, pp. 51–90.

Malissard, A., *Les Romains et l'eau*, Paris, 1994.

Manderscheid, H., *Bibliographie zum römischen Badewesen unter besonderer Berücksichtigung der öffentlichen Thermen*, Munich, 1988.

"Römische Thermen: Aspekte von Architektur, Technik, und Ausstattung," in *Geschichte der Wasserversorgung* III, Mainz, 1988, pp. 101–25.

Mango, C., "The Water Supply of Constantinople," in Mango and Dagron, *Constantinople and Its Hinterland*, pp. 9–18.

Mango, C., and Dagron, G. (eds.), *Constantinople and Its Hinterland*, Aldershot, 1995.

Manselli, G., "Elementi organici e razionali nell'urbanistica ravennate," *Felix Ravenna* 101 (1970), pp. 27–37.

Martin, J.-M., "Città e campagna: economia e società (sec. VII–XIII)," in Galasso, *Storia del Mezzogiorno* III, pp. 259–382.

La Pouille du VIe au XIe siècle, Rome, 1993.

Mazzarino, S., "Note sulla tradizione culturale di Ravenna e sull'anonimo ravennate," *Rivista di studi bizantini e neoellenici* 12–13 (1965), pp. 99–117.

Mazzi, M.-S., *Salute e società nel medioevo*, Florence, 1978.

Mazzucato, O., "Relazione sui pozzi medievali rinvenuti sotto il Teatro Argentina," *Bullettino della commissione archeologica comunale di Roma* 81 (1968–9), pp. 102–13.

Menant, F., *Campagnes lombardes au moyen âge*, Rome, 1993.

" 'Fossata cavere, portas erigere': le rôle des fossés dans les fortifications médiévales de la Plaine Padane," *Aevum* 56 (1982), pp. 205–16.

Merten, E., *Bäder und Badegepflogenheiten in der Darstellung der Historia Augusta*, Bonn, 1983.

Michael, A., *Irrigation: Theory and Practice*, New Delhi, 1978.

Mira, G., *La pesca nel medioevo nelle acque interne italiane*, Milan, 1937.

Mirabella Roberti, M., "Archeologia e arte di Brescia romana," in Treccani degli Alfieri, *Storia di Brescia* I, pp. 233–320.

Montanari, M., *L'alimentazione contadina nell'alto medioevo*, Naples, 1979.

Alimentazione e cultura nel medioevo, Bari, 1988.

"Il paesaggio rurale della Pentapoli nell'alto medioevo," in Vasina, *Ricerche e studi sul Breviarium Ecclesiae Ravennatis*, pp. 145–62.

"I prodotti e l'alimentazione," in Carile, *Storia di Ravenna* II, pp. 85–100.

Montanari Pesando, M., "Carenza idrica e attività molitorie nella Chieri medievale (secoli XII–XV)," in Comba, *Mulini da grano nel Piemonte medievale*, pp. 11–46.

Mor, C., "Il *Digesto* nell'età preirneriana e la formazione della *vulgata*," in Mor, *Scritti di storia giuridica altomedievale*, Pisa, 1977, pp. 83–234.

"Il diritto romano nel sistema giuridico longobardo del secolo VIII," in Mor, *Scritti di storia giuridica altomedievale*, Pisa, 1977, pp. 681–98.

"Pavia capitale," in *Atti del 4o Congresso internazionale di studi sull'alto medioevo*, Spoleto, 1969, pp. 19–31.

"Per la storia dei libri giustinianei nell'età preirneriana," in Mor, *Scritti di storia giuridica altomedievale*, Pisa, 1977, pp. 11–23.

Moreschini, D., "Dal bagno ai *balnea*," in M. Pasquinucci (ed.), *Terme romane e vita quotidiana*, Modena, 1987, pp. 11–14.

Morris, R., "Dispute Settlement in the Byzantine Provinces in the Tenth Century," in W. Davies and P. Fouracre (eds.), *The Settlement of Disputes in Early Medieval Europe*, Cambridge, 1986, pp. 125–47.

Motta, R., "La decadenza degli acquedotti antichi e la conduzione dell'acqua mariana," in *Il trionfo dell'acqua*, pp. 203–5.

Muendel, J., "The 'French' Mill in Medieval Tuscany," *Journal of Medieval History* 10 (1984), pp. 215–47.

"The Horizontal Mills of Medieval Pistoia," *Technology and Culture* 15 (1974), pp. 194–225.

"Medieval Urban Renewal: The Communal Mills of the City of Florence, 1351–1382," *Journal of Urban History* 17 (1991), pp. 363–89.

"The Millers of Pistoia, 1200–1430," *Journal of European Economic History* 6 (1977), pp. 393–412.

Natella, P., "Il *castellum caputaquis* fra documentazione e storia," in *Caputaquis medioevale* II, Naples, 1984, pp. 9–53.

"Il territorio di Capaccio dall'antichità all'alto medioevo," in *Caputaquis medioevale* I, Salerno, 1976, pp. 9–22.

Nielsen, I., *Thermae et Balnea: The Architecture and Cultural History of Roman Public Baths*, Aarhus, 1990.

Nordon, M., *L'eau conquise: les origines et le monde antique*, Paris, 1991.

Oleson, J., *Greek and Roman Mechanical Water-Lifting Devices*, Toronto, 1984.

"The Spring House Complex," in McCann, *The Roman Port and Fishery of Cosa*, pp. 98–128.

Onori, A., *L'abbazia di S. Salvatore a Sesto e il lago di Bientina: una signoria ecclesiastica, 1250–1300*, Florence, 1984.

Origone, S., "Mulini ad acqua in Liguria nei secoli X–XV," *Clio* 10 (1974), pp. 89–120.

Ortalli, J., "L'edilizia abitativa," in Carile, *Storia di Ravenna* II, pp. 167–92.

"Edilizia residenziale e crisi urbanistica nella tarda antichità: fonti archeologiche per la Cispadana," *CCARB* 39 (1992), pp. 557–604.

Osheim, D., *An Italian Lordship: The Bishopric of Lucca in the Late Middle Ages*, Berkeley, 1977.

Outwater, A., *Water: A Natural History*, New York, 1996.

Pace, P., *Gli acquedotti di Roma*, Rome, 1983.

Paesaggi urbani dell'Italia padana nei secoli VIII–XIV, Bologna, 1988.

Palmucci Quaglino, L., "Corsi d'acqua e sfruttamento dell'energia idraulica: il Cuneese nei secoli XII–XVI," in Comba, *Mulini da grano nel Piemonte medievale*, pp. 91–106.

Panazza, G., "Brescia e il suo territorio da Teodorico a Carlomagno," in *I Longobardi e la Lombardia: Saggi*, Milan, 1978, pp. 12–42.

Panessa, G., "Le risorse idriche dei santuari greci nei loro aspetti giuridici ed economici," *Annali della Scuola normale superiore di Pisa* 13 (1983), pp. 359–87.

Pani Ermini, L., "'Renovatio murorum' tra programma urbanistico e restauro conservativo: Roma e il ducato romano," *Settimane* 39 (1992), pp. 485–530.

Parain, C., "Rapports de production et développement des forces productives: l'exemple du moulin à eau," *La pensée* 119 (1965), pp. 55–70.

Parsons Lillich, M., "Cleanliness with Godliness: A Discussion of Medieval Monastic Plumbing," in B. Chauvin (ed.), *Mélanges à la mémoire du père A. Dimier* III, Aubois, 1982, pp. 123–49.

Pasquali, G., "Economia e paesaggio rurale dei 'deserta' alle porte di Ravenna:

l'isola litoranea di Palazzolo dal VI al XIV secolo," in Pasquali, *Agricoltura e società rurale in Romagna nel medioevo*, Bologna, 1984, pp. 33–60.

"Gestione economica e controllo sociale di S. Salvatore–S. Giulia dall'epoca longobarda all'età comunale," in Stella and Brentenghi, *S. Giulia di Brescia*, pp. 131–45.

Patitucci Uggeri, S., "Aspetti dell'insediamento nell'area lagunare a nord di Ravenna tra tardoantico e altomedievo," *CCARB* 30 (1983), pp. 391–432.

"Il delta padano nell'età dei Goti," *CCARB* 36 (1989), pp. 113–38.

"L'insediamento bizantino e altomedievale nel delta del Po (secoli VI–XI)," in *Atti della tavola rotonda tenuta a Bologna il 26 giugno 1979 su il delta del Po*, Bologna, 1985, pp. 63–112.

Pavis d'Escurac, H., "Irrigation et vie paysanne dans l'Afrique du Nord antique," *Ktema* 5 (1980), pp. 177–91.

Peduto, P., "Insediamenti altomedievali e ricerca archeologica," in Leone and Vitolo, *Guida alla storia di Salerno* II, pp. 441–73.

"Nel mondo dei Longobardi," *Archeo* 57 (1989), pp. 116–19.

Peduto, P., Romito, M., Galante, M., Mauro, D., and Pastore, I., "Un accesso alla storia di Salerno: stratigrafie e materiali dell'area palaziale longobarda," *Rassegna storica salernitana* 10 (1988), pp. 9–63.

Peroni, A., "Pavia 'capitale longobarda': testimonianze archeologiche e manufatti artistici," in *I Longobardi e la Lombardia: Saggi*, Milan, 1978, pp. 103–20.

Pertile, A., *Storia del diritto italiano dalla caduta dell'impero romano alla codificazione* IV, Roma, 1893.

Petracco-Sicardi, G., "La casa rurale nell'alto medioevo come insediamento e come costruzione," *AM* 7 (1980), pp. 363–5.

Pini, A., "Energia e industria tra Sàvena e Reno: i mulini idraulici bolognesi tra XI e XV secolo," in *Tecnica e società nell'Italia dei secoli XII–XVI*, Pistoia, 1987, pp. 1–22.

Pinna, M., "Il clima nell'alto medioevo: conoscenze attuali e prospettive di ricerca," *Settimane* 37 (1990), pp. 431–51.

Pisani-Sartorio, G., "Gli antichi acquedotti di Roma: dai pozzi ai condotti," in *Il trionfo dell'acqua*, pp. 27–30.

de Planhol, X., *L'eau de neige: le tiède et le frais*, Paris, 1995.

Potter, T., *The Changing Landscape of South Etruria*, New York, 1979.

"Marshland Drainage in the Classical World," in Rowley, *Evolution of Marshland Landscapes*, pp. 1–19.

Roman Italy, Berkeley, 1986.

Poupardin, R., *Etudes sur l'histoire des principautés lombardes de l'Italie méridionale*, Paris, 1907.

Les institutions politiques et administratives des principautés lombardes de l'Italie méridionale, Paris, 1907.

Pratesi, F., "Gli ambienti naturali e l'equilibrio ecologico," *Storia d'Italia Einaudi: Annali* VIII, Turin, 1985, pp. 51–109.

Prati, L. (ed.), *Flumen Aqueductus: nuove scoperte archeologiche dagli scavi per l'acquedotto di Romagna*, Bologna, 1988.

Purcell, N., "Rome and the Management of Water: Environment, Culture, and Power," in G. Shipley and J. Salmon (eds.), *Human Landscapes in Classical Antiquity*, London, 1996, pp. 180–212.

Racine, P., "Poteri medievali e percorsi fluviali nell'Italia padana," *Quaderni storici* 61 (1986), pp. 9–32.

Radcliffe, W., *Fishing from Earliest Times*, New York, 1921.

Rahtz, P., "Medieval Milling," in D. Crossley (ed.), *Medieval Industry*, London, 1981, pp. 1–15.

Rahtz, P., and Bullough, D., "The Parts of an Anglo-Saxon Mill," *Anglo-Saxon England* 6 (1977), pp. 15–37.

Rahtz, P., and Meeson, R., *An Anglo-Saxon Watermill at Tamworth*, London, 1992.

Randsborg, K., *The First Millennium AD in Europe and the Mediterranean*, Cambridge, 1991.

Raspi Serra, J., and Laganara Fabriano, C., *Economia e territorio: il Patrimonium Beati Petri nella Tuscia*, Naples, 1987.

Rattue, J., *The Living Stream: Holy Wells in Historical Context*, Woodbridge, Suffolk, 1995.

Rebuffat, R., "Vocabulaire thermal," in *Les thermes romains: actes de la table ronde organisée par l'Ecole française de Rome, nov. 1988*, Rome, 1991, pp. 1–34.

Reynolds, T., *Stronger Than a Hundred Men: A History of the Vertical Water Wheel*, Baltimore, 1983.

Ricci, C., "Il vivaio dell'arcivescovado di Ravenna," *Bollettino d'arte del ministero della pubblica istruzione* 13 (1919), pp. 32–6.

Riché, P., *Daily Life in the World of Charlemagne*, Philadelphia, 1978.

Righini, V., "Materiali e tecniche da costruzione in età tardoantica e alto-medievale," in Carile, *Storia di Ravenna* II, pp. 193–221.

Rivolin, J.-G., "Il pedaggio di Bard ed il commercio delle mole (secoli XIII–XIV)," in Comba, *Mulini da grano nel Piemonte medievale*, pp. 189–214.

Roberts, B., "The Rediscovery of Fishponds," in Aston, *Medieval Fish, Fisheries, and Fishponds in England*, pp. 9–16.

Robins, F., *The Story of Water Supply*, Oxford, 1946.

Robinson, O., "Baths, an Aspect of Roman Local Government Law," *Sodalitas: scritti in onore di A. Guarino*, Naples, 1984, pp. 1065–82.

Roncuzzi, A., "Topografia di Ravenna antica: le mura," *CCARB* 39 (1992), pp. 691–742.

Roncuzzi, A., and Veggi, L., "Contributi allo studio dell'evoluzione topografica ed idrografica nel territorio ravennate," in *Atti del convegno internazionale di studi sulle antichità di Classe*, Ravenna, 1968, pp. 91–114.

Rossini, E., "Longobardi e Franchi in Lombardia. Problemi di navigazione interna," in *Atti del 6o Congresso internazionale di studi sull'alto medioevo*, Spoleto, 1980, pp. 593–8.

"Verona nell'alto medioevo: problemi di navigazione interna," in *Verona in età gotica e longobarda. Atti*, Verona, 1982, pp. 209–33.

Rotili, M., *Benevento romana e longobarda*, Ercolano, 1986.

Rouge, J., "La legislation justinienne de l'eau," in F. Metral and J. Metral (eds.), *L'homme et l'eau en Méditerranée* II, Lyons, 1982, pp. 111–15.

Rousselle, A., "Abstinence et continence dans les monastères de Gaule méridionale à la fin de l'antiquité et au début du moyen âge," in *Homage à André Dupont*, Montpellier, 1974, pp. 239–54.

Porneia: de la maitrise du corps à la privation sensorielle (IIe–IVe siècle de l'ère chrétienne), Paris, 1983.

Rowley, R. (ed.), *The Evolution of Marshland Landscapes*, Oxford, 1981.

Ruf, F., "Die Suppe in der Geschichte der Ernährung," in I. Bitsch (ed.), *Essen und Trinken im Mittelalter und Neuzeit*, Sigmaringen, 1987, pp. 165–81.

Ruggiu Zaccaria, A., "Indagini sull'insediamento longobardo a Brescia," in *Contributi dell'Istituto di archeologia dell'Università del sacro Cuore* 2 (1969), pp. 110–50.

Russo Mailler, C., "L'acqua dall'antichità al medioevo: le terme flegree," *Quaderni medievali* 26 (1988), pp. 79–98.

Saguì, L., "'Balnea' medievali: trasformazione e continuità della tradizione classica," in Saguì, *L'esedra della Crypta Balbi*, pp. 98–116.

"Crypta Balbi (Roma): conclusione delle indagini archeologiche nell'esedra del monumento romano. Relazione preliminare," *AM* 20 (1993), pp. 409–18.

"L'esedra e il complesso dei bagni nel medioevo: un problema topografico," in Saguì, *L'esedra della Crypta Balbi*, pp. 95–7.

Saguì, L. (ed.), *L'esedra della Crypta Balbi nel medioevo (XI–XV secolo)*, Florence, 1990.

Scagliarini, D., *Ravenna e le ville romane in Romagna*, Ravenna, 1968.

Scagliarini Corlaita, D., "L'edilizia residenziale nelle città romane dell'Emilia-Romagna," *Studia archaeologica* 27 (1983), pp. 283–334.

Scheid, J., "Sanctuaires et thermes sous l'empire," in *Actes de la table ronde organisée par l'Ecole française de Rome, nov. 1988*, Rome, 1991, pp. 205–14.

Schiavo, A., *Acquedotti romani e medioevali*, Naples, 1935.

Schipa, M., "Storia del principato longobardo di Salerno," *Archivio storico per le provincie napoletane* 12 (1887), pp. 79–127, 209–64, 513–88, 740–77.

Schmid, K., "Merkwürdigkeiten um einen langobardischen Heiligen aus Tuszien," in K. Schmid (ed.), *Vita Walfredi und Kloster Monteverdi*, Tübingen, 1991, pp. 1–18.

Schmiedt, G., *Il livello antico del mar Tirreno: testimonianze dei resti archeologici*, Florence, 1972.

Schretz, J., *Untersuchungen über die Quellen der Kosmographie des anonymen Geographen von Ravenna*, Munich, 1942.

Schwartz, H., "Patterns of Public and Private Water Supply in North Africa," in J. Humphrey (ed.), *Excavations at Carthage 1977* VI, Ann Arbor, 1981, pp. 50–4.

Schwarzmaier, H., *Lucca und das Reich bis zum Ende des 11. Jahrhundert*, Tübingen, 1972.

Sereni, E., *Storia del paesaggio agrario italiano*, Bari, 1984.

Shaw, B., "Lamasba: An Ancient Irrigation Community," *Antiquités africaines* 18 (1982), pp. 61–103.

"The Noblest Monuments and the Smallest Things: Wells, Walls, and Aqueducts in the Making of North Africa," in Hodge, *Future Currents in Aqueduct Studies*, pp. 63–91.

"Water and Society in the Ancient Maghrib: Technology, Property, and Development," *Antiquités africaines* 20 (1984), pp. 121–73.

Singer, C. (ed.), *A History of Technology* II, Oxford, 1957.

Skinner, P., *Family Power in Southern Italy: The Duchy of Gaeta and Its Neighbours, 850–1139*, Cambridge, 1995.

"Noble Families in the Duchy of Gaeta in the Tenth Century," *PBSR* 60 (1992), pp. 353–77.

Slicher Van Bath, B., *The Agrarian History of Western Europe, AD 500–1850,* London, 1963.

Smedema, L., and Rycroft, D., *Land Drainage: Planning and Design of Agricultural Drainage Systems,* Ithaca, 1983.

Smidt, W., *Das Chronicon Beneventanum Monasterii S. Sophiae: eine quellenkritische Untersuchung,* Berlin, 1910.

Smith, N., *A History of Dams,* London, 1971.

Man and Water: A History of Hydrotechnology, London, 1975.

Sodigné-Costes, G., and Ribémont, B., "'Aqua domestica': l'eau et les techniques de l'eau dans les encyclopédies médiévales," in D. Hue (ed.), *Sciences, techniques, et encyclopédies,* Caen, 1993, pp. 301–20.

Sokolov, R., "Through a Mill, Coarsely," *Natural History* 103 (1994), pp. 72–4.

Spadea, R., "Lo scavo della stazione 'Lido' (Reggio Calabria)," *MEFR. Moyen âge* 103 (1991), pp. 689–707.

Spurr, M., *Arable Cultivation in Roman Italy, c. 200 BC–c. AD 100,* London, 1986.

Squatriti, P., "Marshes and Mentalities in Early Medieval Ravenna," *Viator* 23 (1992), pp. 1–16.

"Water, Nature, and Culture in Early Medieval Lucca," *Early Medieval Europe* 4 (1995), pp. 21–40.

Starace, F., "L'ambiente ed il paesaggio dai Latini a Ruggero d'Altavilla (1130–1154)," in Galasso, *Storia del Mezzogiorno* I.2, pp. 211–76.

Steane, J., "The Royal Fishponds of Medieval England," in Aston, *Medieval Fish, Fisheries, and Fishponds in England,* pp. 39–68.

Steane, J., and Foreman, M., "Medieval Fishing Tackle," in Aston, *Medieval Fish, Fisheries, and Fishponds in England,* pp. 137–86.

Stella, C., and Brentenghi, G. (eds.), *S. Giulia di Brescia: archeologia, arte, storia di un monastero regio dai Longobardi al Barbarossa,* Brescia, 1992.

Steward, J., "Irrigation Without Agriculture," *Papers of the Michigan Academy of Sciences* 12 (1930), pp. 149–56.

Susini, G. (ed.), *Storia di Ravenna* I, Venice, 1990.

Taviani-Carozzi, H., *La principauté lombarde de Salerne, IXe–XIe siècle,* Rome, 1991.

TeBrake, W., *The Medieval Frontier,* College Station, TX, 1986.

Thomas, R., and Wilson, A., "Water Supply for Roman Farms in Latium and South Etruria," *PBSR* 64 (1994), pp. 139–96.

Thornton, M., and Thornton, R., "The Draining of the Fucine Lake: A Quantitative Analysis," *The Ancient World* 12 (1985), pp. 105–20.

Tölle-Kastenbein, R., *Antike Wasserkultur,* Munich, 1990.

Tomassetti, G., *La campagna romana antica medioevale e moderna* V, Florence, 1979.

Toubert, P., "La part du grand domaine dans le décollage économique de l'Occident (VIIIe–Xe siècles)," in *La croissance agricole du haut moyen âge,* Auch, 1990, pp. 53–86.

Les structures du Latium médiévale, Rome, 1973.

Tozzi, P., and Harari, M., *Eraclea Veneta: immagine di una città sepolta,* Parma, 1984.

Traina, G., "Paesaggio e 'decadenza': la palude nella trasformazione del mondo antico," in A. Giardina (ed.), *Società romana e impero tardoantico* III, Bari, 1986, pp. 711–30.

Paludi e bonifiche nel mondo antico: saggio di archeologia geografica, Rome, 1988.

Tramontana, S., "Mulini ad acqua nella Sicilia normanna," in *Cultura e società nell'Italia medievale* II, Rome, 1988, pp. 811–24.

Treccani degli Alfieri, G. (ed.), *Storia di Brescia* I, Brescia, 1961.

Il trionfo dell'acqua: acque e aquedotti a Roma, IV–XX s., Rome, 1986.

Tuan, Y., *The Hydrological Cycle and the Wisdom of God: A Theme in Geotheology*, Toronto, 1968.

Turcan, M., "L'eau dans l'alimentation et la cuisine a l'époque romaine," in Louis, *L'homme et l'eau en Mediterranée* III, pp. 21–8.

Uggeri, G., *L'insediamento antico e altomedievale del delta del Po*, Bologna, 1984.

Le origini del popolamento nel territorio ferrarese, Cento, 1987.

La romanizzazione dell'antico delta padano, Ferrara, 1975.

Ugolini, P., "La formazione del sistema territoriale e urbano della Valle Padana," *Storia d'Italia Einaudi. Annali* VIII, Turin, 1985, pp. 161–240.

Varanini, G., "Energia idraulica e attività economiche nella Verona comunale: l'Adige, il Fiumicello, il Fibbio (secoli XII–XIII)," in *Paesaggi urbani dell'Italia padana*, pp. 333–72.

Vasina, A., "Il *Breviarium* nella storia della chiesa ravennate," in Vasina, *Ricerche e studi sul Breviarium Ecclesiae Ravennatis*, pp. 9–32.

"Possessi ecclesiastici ravennati durante il medioevo," *Studi romagnoli* 18 (1967), pp. 333–67.

Vasina, A. (ed.), *Ricerche e studi sul Breviarium Ecclesiae Ravennatis*, Rome, 1985.

Veggiani, A., "Considerazioni geologiche sulla captazione e sul tracciato dell'acquedotto romano di Ravenna," *Studi romagnoli* 31 (1980), pp. 3–19.

"Il delta del Po e l'evoluzione della rete idrografica padana in epoca storica," in *Atti della tavola rotonda tenuta a Bologna il 24 novembre 1982 su il delta del Po*, Bologna, 1982, pp. 39–68.

"Le vicende idrografiche del Rubicone e della Rigossa tra Gambettola e Montiano nei tempi storici," *Studi romagnoli* 39 (1985), pp. 305–13.

Venditelli, M., "Diritti e impianti di pesca degli enti ecclesiastici romani tra X e XIII secolo," *MEFR. Moyen âge* 102 (1992), pp. 387–430.

Verdon, J., "Recherches sur la pêche et la pisciculture en Occident pendant le haut moyen âge," in *Actes du 102e congrès national des sociétés savantes: section d'archéologie et d'histoire de l'art*, Paris, 1979, pp. 337–49.

Vielliard, R., *Recherches sur les origines de la Rome chrétienne: essai d'urbanisme chrétien*, Mâcon, 1941.

Vigarello, G., *Le propre et le sale: l'hygiène du corps depuis le moyen âge*, Paris, 1985.

Violante, C., "La signoria rurale del secolo X," *Settimane* 38 (1991), pp. 329–85.

Vita-Finzi, C., *The Mediterranean Valleys: Geological Changes in Historical Times*, Cambridge, 1969.

Voigt, K., *Beitrage zur Diplomatik der langobardischen Fürsten von Benevent, Capua, und Salerno (seit 774)*, Göttingen, 1902.

Von Falkenhausen, V., "La Longobardia meridionale," in Galasso, *Storia d'Italia* III, pp. 251–364.

Ward-Perkins, B., "La città nell'alto medioevo," *AM* 10 (1983), pp. 111–24.

From Classical Antiquity to the Middle Ages: Urban Public Building in Northern and Central Italy, AD 300–850, Oxford, 1984.
"Luni: The Decline and Abandonment of the Roman Town," in *Papers in Italian Archaeology* I, Oxford, 1978, pp. 313–22.
"Luni: The Prosperity of the Town and Its Territory," in G. Barker and R. Hodges (eds.), *Archeology and Italian Society*, Oxford, 1981, pp. 179–90.
"Sepolture e pozzi d'acqua," in Frova, *Scavi di Luni* II, pp. 664–71.
"The Towns of Northern Italy: Rebirth or Renewal?" in R. Hodges and B. Hobley (eds.), *The Rebirth of Towns in the West, AD 700–1050*, London, 1988, pp. 16–27.
"Two Byzantine Houses at Luni," *PBSR* 49 (1981), pp. 91–8.
Ward-Perkins, J., *Landscape and History in Central Italy*, Oxford, 1964.
White, K., *Greek and Roman Technology*, Ithaca, 1984.
Whitehouse, D., "Raiders and Invaders: The Roman Campagna in the First Millennium," in *Papers in Italian Archaeology* IV, Oxford, 1985, pp. 207–13.
Wickham, C., "La città altomedievale: una nota sul dibattito in corso," *AM* 15 (1988), pp. 649–51.
Early Medieval Italy: Central Power and Local Society, 400–1000, London, 1983.
"Economia e società rurale nel territorio lucchese durante la seconda metà del secolo XI: inquadramenti aristocratici e strutture signorili," in *Sant'Anselmo vescovo di Lucca*, Rome, 1992, pp. 391–422.
"European Forests in the Early Middle Ages," *Settimane* 37 (1990), pp. 479–545.
The Mountains and the City: The Tuscan Appennines in the Early Middle Ages, Oxford, 1988.
"Settlement Problems in Early Medieval Italy: Lucca Territory," *AM* 5 (1978), pp. 495–503.
Studi sulla società degli Appennini nell'alto medioevo: contadini, signori, e insediamento nel territorio di Valva (Sulmona), Bologna, 1982.
Wijntjes, W., "The Water Supply of a Medieval Town," *Rotterdam Papers* IV, Rotterdam, 1982, pp. 189–203.
Wikander, Ö., *Exploitation of Water Power or Technological Stagnation? A Reappraisal of the Productive Forces of the Roman Empire*, Lund, 1984.
"Mill Channels, Weirs, and Ponds: The Environment of Ancient Water Mills," *Opuscula Romana* 15 (1985), pp. 143–54.
"The Use of Water Power in Classical Antiquity," *Opuscula Romana* 13 (1981), pp. 91–104.
"Water Mills and Aqueducts," in Hodge, *Future Currents in Aqueduct Studies*, pp. 141–8.
"Water Mills in Ancient Rome," *Opuscula Romana* 12 (1979), pp. 13–36.
"Water Mills in Europe: Their Early Frequency and Diffusion," *Medieval Europe* 3 (1992), pp. 9–14.
Williams-Thorpe, O., and Thorpe, R., "Millstones that Mapped the Mediterranean," *New Scientist* 1757 (1991), pp. 42–5.
Winkelmann, O., "Hygienische Aspekte der Wasserversorgung antiker Städte," in *Geschichte der Wasserversorgung* III, Mainz, 1988, pp. 159–70.
Wittfogel, K., *Oriental Despotism: A Comparative Study of Total Power*, New Haven, 1957.

Yegül, F., *Baths and Bathing in Classical Antiquity*, New York, 1992.
"The Small City Bath in Classical Antiquity and a Reconstruction Study of Lucian's 'Baths of Hippias,'" *Archaeologia classica* 31 (1979), pp. 108–31.
Zaccagnini, G., *Vita Sancti Fridiani: contributi di storia e di agiografia lucchese alto-medioevale*, Lucca, 1989.
Zaffagnini, L., "Il *portus Augusti* e la viabilità terrestre della fascia costiera romagnola dall'epoca romana a quella bizantina," *Felix Ravenna* 101 (1970), pp. 39–94.
Zeepvat, R., "Fishponds in Roman Britain," in Aston, *Medieval Fish, Fisheries, and Fishponds in England*, pp. 17–25.
Zellinger, J., *Bad und Bäder in der altchristlichen Kirche*, Munich, 1928.
Zielinski, H., "Il documento principesco nel Mezzogiorno longobardo tra diploma imperiale e documento privato," *Rassegna storica salernitana* 15 (1991), pp. 7–23.
Zug Tucci, H., "Il mondo medievale dei pesci tra realtà e immaginazione," *Settimane* 31 (1985), pp. 291–360.

Index

Printed in the United States
17281LVS00006B/83

9 780521 522069